BEHAVIOR SCIENCE:

Philosophical, Methodological, and Empirical Advances

Edited by

HAYNE W. REESE
West Virginia University

LINDA J. PARROTT
Saint Mary's University

LEA LAWRENCE ERLBAUM ASSOCIATES, PUBLISHERS

1986   Hillsdale, New Jersey   London

Lawrence Erlbaum Associates, Inc., Publishers
365 Broadway
Hillsdale, New Jersey 07642

Library of Congress Cataloging-in-Publication Data
Main entry under title:

Behavior science.

  Bibliography: p.
  Includes indexes.
  1. Behavioral assessment.   2. Behavior modification.
I. Reese, Hayne Waring, 1931–   . II. Parrott,
Linda J.
BF176.5.B44 1986   150.19′43   85-29261
ISBN 0-89859-766-8

Printed in the United States of America
10 9 8 7 6 5 4 3 2 1

Contents

Contributors

Daniel J. Bernstein
Department of Psychology
209 Burnett Hall
University of Nebraska, Lincoln
Lincoln, NB 68588-0308
••
Joseph V. Brady
Department of Psychiatry and
  Behavioral Sciences
The Johns Hopkins University School
  of Medicine
720 Rutland Avenue
Baltimore, MD 21205
••
Rosalind Burns[1]
Department of Psychology
West Virginia University
Box 6040
Morgantown, WV 26506-6040
••
Dennis J. Delprato
Department of Psychology
Eastern Michigan University
Ypsilanti, MI 48197
••
Lyle Grant
Athabasca University

Box 10000
Athabasca, Alberta
Canada T0G 2R0
••
Cloyd Hyten
Department of Psychology
West Virginia University
Box 6040
Morgantown, WV 26506-6040
••
Richard W. Malott
Psychology Department
Western Michigan University
Kalamazoo, MI 49008
••
Linda J. Parrott
Department of Psychology
Saint Mary's University
Halifax, Nova Scotia
Canada B3H 3C3
••
Hayne W. Reese
Department of Psychology
West Virginia University
Box 6040
Morgantown, WV 26506-6040

••
Emilio Ribes
Escuela Nacional De Estudios
   Profesionales Iztacala
Coordinacion General De
   Investigacion
Universidad Nacional Autonoma
Apartado Postal 314
Tlalnepantla
Mexico 54000

••
Phyllis N. Williamson
Program Director
Geropsychiatric Unit
New Mexico State Hospital
P.O. Box 1388
Las Vegas, NM 87701

---

[1]Now at: Department of Psychology, University of Massachusetts, Amherst, MA 01002

Preface

The senior editor of the present volume is also editor of the series *Advances in Child Development and Behavior*. Perhaps such a position makes one overly sensitive to competing "advances" books, but they seem to abound in developmental psychology. In fact, they seem to abound in all fields of psychology except behavior analysis, in which they are very rare. The dearth of "advances" books in behavior analysis does not reflect an absence of advances in this field. On the contrary, we spent uncountable hours conversing about the status and future of behavior science, based on published articles and oral presentations, and we became convinced that the field is healthy and is advancing in appropriate ways. Indeed, when we decided to develop the present volume our major problem was to decide which advances we should include and which person on the forefront we should ask to cover each one. We do not, however, represent this volume as a compendium of all the advances in behavior science, nor even of the most important ones. Rather, it is a compendium of advances that we found most interesting—and we immodestly included some of our own work in that category. We hope the reader will agree with our assessment, for the most part at the least.

The following summary of the contents of the volume is intended as a guide to selective reading. The chapters can be grouped to reflect three kinds of advances that are represented: theoretical or philosophical, empirical, and methodological. The chapters are summarized in the order of their appearance in the volume.

1. Reese analyzes the role of theory in the behavior analysis of private events and other behaviors that are unavailable to third-party observation, and concludes that theoretical analysis is essential to this kind of behavior analysis.

2. Parrott continues this line of argument and uses J. R. Kantor's postulates to provide a concrete demonstration of the role of theoretical analysis in dealing with "inapparent psychological events," as she says.

3. A further demonstration of the power of Kantor's approach is found in Delprato's paper: Delprato points out that the assumption of response independence has dominated behavioral research and theory and has made identification of response patterning difficult; but he shows that with recent developments in multiple-response analytic methods, behavior science can advance to the higher stage of integrated-field theory.

4. Ribes uses the concept of *contingency mediation* to analyze language as behavior, and shows that this essentially Kantorian approach generates fruitful research issues and reduces the gap between the behavioral and structural approaches to language.

5. Grant addresses a basic problem in cognitive psychology—categorization—and demonstrates that the use of behavior analytic concepts and methods to attack this problem is not only possible but is indeed fruitful.

6. In the same vein, Hyten and Burns address social behavior; but because they emphasize the importance of focusing on both the "source" organism and the "reactor" organism involved in a given social relation, and the importance of demonstrating *social control* of social behavior, they also call for the use of interactive methodologies.

7. Williamson describes contributions that are—or can be—made by behavior analysis to the field of gerontology, not only for application and intervention but also for basic work. She notes a number of obstacles they encounter; not the least of the obstacles is the prevalence of mentalistic and medical terms such as *dementia, memory disorder,* and *sensory deficit,* which need to be redefined behaviorally before they can be dealt with effectively.

8. Malott deals with self-management and other kinds of rule-governance, not only as processes to be studied but, perhaps more importantly, as behaviors to be practiced. He says of his chapter: "It is a report from the front lines of what I call 'thorough-going behaviorism,' that is, an attempt to be a behavior analyst 24 hours a day, in all features of life, not just on the job working with special populations."

9. Bernstein and Brady describe the use of residential laboratories with programmed environments for the study of a variety of behaviors, such as prosocial and antisocial behaviors and verbal and nonverbal assessments of values.

Reese and Parrott note theoretical advances in behavior science; Parrott, Delprato, and Ribes argue specifically for the use of Kantor's theory to advance behavior science. The advances offered by Grant, Hyten and Burns, and Williamson are in the application of more traditional behavior analytic concepts and methods to nontraditional problems; they address problems traditionally assigned, respectively, to cognitive psychology, social psychology, and gerontology. Malott's advance is in the use of a freer, less experimental technology, specifically for the study of self-management and other rule-governed behaviors. The advance covered by Bernstein and Brady is the use of residential laboratories with programmed environments for continuous observation of behavior; this methodological advance yields an enormous increase in the precision of the experimental analysis of behavior.

We are indebted to our home institutions, West Virginia University and Saint Mary's University, for supporting the production of this volume by defraying expenses and providing facilities. We are especially grateful for the expert secretarial assistance of Mrs. Ann Davis.

Hayne W. Reese
Linda J. Parrott

1

On the Theory and Practice of Behavior Analysis

Hayne W. Reese
West Virginia University

INTRODUCTION

The topic of this chapter is the relation between theory and practice in the behavior analysis of phenomena that are conceptualized as "complex interactions" by some behavior analysts and as "mental operations" by some other kinds of psychologists. The phenomena are also conceptualized as "cognitive processes" by another group, but many in this group seem to be disguised mentalists, as Skinner (1974, p. 77) noted and as seen, for example, in their use of "in the head" as a vaguely physiological euphemism for "in the mind." My conclusion in this chapter is that among those who deal with these complex phenomena, behavior analysts differ from methodological behaviorists and the harder-headed—or less tender-minded—cognitivists more in what they say they do, than in what they do. Farkas (1980) reached a similar conclusion about behavior modification, which is an applied branch of behavior analysis: it differs from other kinds of psychotherapy more in what the practitioners say they do than in what they actually do.

An essential preliminary point is that the difference between group and single-subject designs is irrelevant to the issue. Although in fact "No one goes to the circus to see the average dog jump through the hoop significantly oftener than untrained dogs raised under the same circumstances" (Skinner, 1956, p. 228), neither does anyone go to the circus to see how this behavior can be developed and maintained in the individual dog. As Skinner added, "or to see an elephant demonstrate a principle of behavior." Group and single-subject designs are methods for the collection and, traditionally, the analysis of data. Methods and data or knowledge are intimately related and both are "fuzzy" concepts in the

1

sense that they refer to domains that are not sharply differentiated. Nevertheless, methods and knowledge can be distinguished from one another. Research methods are not knowledge; they are ways to obtain or to apply knowledge. Neither kind of design—group and single-subject—can be guaranteed to yield useful knowledge; both can be used wisely and both can be used foolishly. However, their relative merits are not at issue in this chapter; rather, the issue here is why certain complex phenomena are studied and how the data obtained—by whatever method—are interpreted.

INDIRECT BEHAVIOR ANALYSIS

According to Skinner (1980), in the early years of behavior analysis seldom a week went by without some new and startling discovery, but in recent years the rate of such discoveries has fallen drastically and people often seem to pick up threads that do not lead anywhere. One possible explanation of these trends is that the limits of usefulness of the direct analysis of behavior are being approached and therefore direct analyses have been yielding smaller and smaller increments in knowledge. At the same time, however, the methods of direct analysis have become so well understood that they are highly effective not only for behavior modification and other practical applications but also for *indirect* analyses of problems that are important for theoretical reasons. Being theoretical, indirect analyses may or may not lead anywhere. (The rationale for designating indirect analyses and the reasons for doing them as "theoretical" is developed in the section on *Analysis of Behavior Analysis.*)

An analysis of behavior is indirect if it involves inferences about the behavior of interest instead of direct observation of this behavior, or if it involves an analogue of the behavior of interest instead of the behavior itself. The inferential and analogical methods are used when changes in the behavior of interest are not directly observable or not directly manipulable. Examples are behaviors that change too rapidly for direct observation, behaviors that cannot be manipulated ethically, and, usually, behaviors that are covert.

The Inferential Method

Role in Studying Private Events.   If all words had existential reference, then speech referring to private events and complex interactions would demonstrate the existence of these events and interactions (as substance or as essence, depending on whether their existence were conceptualized as real or ideal). However, some words have metaphorical reference, as when *agony* (from Greek *agōn*, contest) refers to pain and when *volume* (from Latin *volumen*, scroll) refers to a quality of sounds; some words, like *demon* and *unicorn*, have imaginary reference; and as Kantor (1942) said, some words have only "autistic" reference. Thus, the existence of private events and complex interactions is not a conclusion, required and proved by the evidence; rather, it is either (a) an *assumption*, that is, a supposed fact that is taken for granted without proof, at least tentatively, or (b) an *inference*, that is, a probable conclusion, which the evidence supports but does not prove.

If private events and complex interactions are *assumed* to exist, their labels are "primitive terms" definable denotatively (i.e., by pointing) and not linguistically. In methodological behaviorism "all *primitive* terms . . . that refer to the private (mental) experience of subjects are taboo" (Spiker, 1977, p. 95). If they are admitted in behavior analysis to refer to private events and complex interactions, behavior analysis would have no principled reason to reject the assumption of mental activities and other covert organismic processes. However, if private events and complex interactions are *inferred* to "exist," their labels are "defined terms," "introduced by means of a definition that specifies which observations must be made in order to confirm or disconfirm any statement in which the [words occur]" (Spiker, 1977, p. 95). The "existence" of private events and complex interactions, as defined terms, thus has an empirical basis in observed phenomena. ("Existence" is in quotation marks because a defined term does not refer to an object that can be said to exist; it refers to a pattern of observations. The point having been made, the quotation marks are omitted hereafter.) In Skinner's approach, the existence of private events is clearly an inference.

The major problem in the study of private events is that they are not susceptible to third-party observation. The assumption has been made (e.g., Ledoux, 1981) that the person who experiences a private event can function as a third party—"the private event is public to the person in whom it occurs." If so, the person's verbal report of the occurrence of the private event is interpretable as a factual report and not merely as verbal behavior. The contention is supported when the pattern of the reports is similar across subjects, on the argument that one must otherwise assume a "grand conspiracy" among the subjects (Ledoux, 1981). An argument against this kind of support is that the subjects could be lying or attitudinizing for socially sanctioned reasons without entering into a conspiracy among themselves. However, this counterargument is empty unless the social sanctions involved are explicitly identified and empirically demonstrated. The existence of such social sanctions has been questioned. Social sanctions, according to Place (1978), "are aimed, not only at discouraging deliberate misrepresentation or lying, they are also aimed at discouraging any kind of loosening in the consistency and rationality of the connection between what is said and what is done on which our common sense mentalistic predictions and explanations of behaviour depend" (p. 617). Nevertheless, a stronger counterargument is possible: The social sanctions that result in suppression, repression, or distortion of private events are powerful and pervasive, as Freud concluded, and could lead to similarity of distortions or errors of self-observation without any deliberate conspiracy on the part of the subjects.

In spite of the dubitability of the content of verbal reports about purported private events (which Ledoux appeared to recognize in referring to the "questionable description of the topography" of private events), objective evidence about private events can be obtained. Specifically, the analysis could deal with the rate of occurrence of verbal reports (as Ledoux recommended) rather than their content, and nonverbal "reports" could be used instead of verbal. For example, G. Baron (1981) instructed subjects to manipulate the quality and quantity of imagined consequences of key-pressing, and obtained variations in the rate of key-pressing consistent with effects of manipulating objective consequences. However, what Baron observed was that instructions had certain effects that would be expected if subjects followed the instructions and if imagined consequences functioned like objective consequences. She did not directly observe any contingent covert stimuli, and therefore conclusions about covert reinforcers are inferences. Inference is the only way to go from observed phenomena to unobserved phenomena.

Usefulness of Inference.   The examples cited in the preceding subsection provide precedents for the acceptance of inference as a useful research tool. Given these precedents, and given the demonstrated usefulness of inference in other natural sciences—such as the inference of subatomic particles from the evidence of tracks in cloud chambers—the reluctance of behavior analysts to accept inferences about covert behavior is difficult to understand. For example, Parsons (1976) implied that making inferences about covert problem-solving behavior is inconsistent with a "natural science approach to behavior" (p. 193). Such inferences are unnecessary when direct analysis is possible (Parsons, personal communication, December 1, 1980). However, when direct analysis is not possible, inference can be used without violating the canons of natural science.

The reluctance of behavior analysts to use inference is the more surprising because of the demonstrated usefulness of inference in psychology, including experimental psychology. For example, Zeaman and House (1963) theorized that discriminative learning involves two processes. One is attentional learning, that is, learning to attend to the stimulus dimension, such as color or size, that differentiates the positive stimulus from the negative stimulus (in a two-stimulus problem); the other is instrumental learning, that is, learning which value on this dimension, such as red or small, is associated with reward. In behavior analysis terms, the first process is learning a "precurrent behavior" (e.g., Parsons, 1976; Skinner, 1968) that generates functional stimuli; overt examples are looking at, listening to, sniffing, savoring, and feeling of (Skinner, 1974, p. 104).[1] The

---

[1]J. R. Kantor used the adjective *precurrent* in the same sense: "Thought as a precurrent reaction system precedes the occurrence of the final or end reaction which it indeed conditions" (1922, p. 282). "Substitute reactions operate as precurrent or anticipatory responses to some other final reaction, and this is exactly why they are meaning-reactions. . . . The entire significance of a

second process is learning which of the functional stimuli is discriminative for reinforcement and which for nonreinforcement.

Relevant data were collected by Zeaman and House (1963) in a study of two-stimulus discriminative learning in mentally retarded children. Zeaman and House presented the data in the form of backward learning curves plotted separately for subgroups that were relatively homogeneous in speed of acquisition. Plotting the data separately for homogeneous subgroups reduces the distorting effects of using group means as data points for the learning curve (e.g., Spence, 1956, pp. 59–61; see also Hayes, 1953; Hayes & Pereboom, 1959; Hilgard & Campbell, 1937; Sidman, 1952). Plotting curves "backward" from the criterion run instead of "forward" from Trial 1 reduces distortion when learning is initially slow and subsequently rapid (Hayes & Pereboom, 1959). The curves obtained by Zeaman and House exhibited two phases, the first with little or no improvement in performance and the second with fairly rapid rise to the criterion level. Zeaman and House interpreted the first phase to reflect primarily attentional learning and the second to reflect primarily instrumental learning. They found that the curves of the subgroups differed almost entirely in the duration of the first phase, with little difference in the second phase. They inferred that some children learn attending, which is a precurrent behavior, more slowly than others but that children are more nearly equal in the speed of instrumental learning.

Another example is extensive research by Belmont and Butterfield on memory development. In their usual task, the duration of each stimulus presentation was controlled by the subject, and the durations were recorded and later examined to determine where long pauses occurred within the list of items. The locations of long pauses, together with task analyses, were used as a basis for inferences about the cognitive processes (mental operations) subjects used to remember the list (for an excellent history and summary of this research, see Butterfield, Siladi, & Belmont, 1980).

Task analysis is no novelty in behavior analysis; it is an essential feature of, for example, shaping, programmed instruction, and the training of precurrent behaviors (research examples are, respectively, Weisberg & Simmons, 1966; Cohen, 1962; and Parsons, 1973). However, it is also no novelty in other approaches; it is an essential feature of computer simulation approaches (e.g., Klahr & Siegler, 1978) and Belmont and Butterfield's so-called instructional approach (e.g., Belmont & Butterfield, 1977; Butterfield et al., 1980). The difference is that in the latter approaches the task is analyzed not on the basis of the behaviors that are required but on the basis of cognitive operations, or covert behaviors, that are required. I do not see any *principled* difference, except with

---

meaning-reaction lies in the fact of its operation as a determiner of a succeeding final response to a given stimulating object or condition" (1921, p. 242). Incidentally, John B. Watson used the phrase "substitute stimulus," referring to responses, in essentially the same sense as Kantor's "substitute reaction" (Watson, 1930, chap. 11; see especially Fig. 20, p. 258).

respect to the necessity to use inference in the test of the task analysis in the latter cases.

The Analogical Method

The analogical method may be more readily accepted by behavior analysts than the inferential method, because of the emphasis in behavior analysis on observable behavior (cf. Farkas, 1980) and because of the wish of most behavior analysts to avoid making inferences about covert behavior (e.g., Parsons, 1976). An example that shows great promise is the analogical analysis of "complex interactions," which are usually covert but have been studied analogically through analysis of overt behaviors that are presumed to have the same functions. Examples are Bowe and Dinsmoor's (1981) study of observing in pigeons as key-pecking and Parsons and Ferraro's (1977) study of mediation in children as key-pressing.

Parsons and Ferraro (1977) commented that in the functional analysis of behavior, "the function of a response is considered independently of its form" (p. 239), and therefore studying overt behavior is a means for understanding behavior that presumably has the same function as the overt behavior but is not easily observed or is not externally observable at all. On this argument, analysis of the overt behavior is not an indirect, analogical analysis of the covert behavior; rather, it is a direct analysis of the behavior of interest. A problem is that the argument seems to involve a verbal bridge, apparently going from "the function of a response is considered independently of its form" to something like "the function of a response is independent of its form." Both of these statements are empirical, but the first refers to a procedure and the second refers to a behavioral "law" that is not testable in the functional analysis of behavior because the covert form of behavior cannot be studied directly. Not being testable in this approach, it becomes a mere assumption if it is admitted at all. Consequently, analysis of the functions of overt behavior is analysis of a model—a simulation or analogue—whenever the behavior of primary interest is covert. When the analogical method is used, the behavior of primary interest is inferred, as argued in the subsection on *The Inferential Method*. The primary interest is not in the overt behaviors as such, but rather in these behaviors as analogues of covert behaviors that are *inferred* on the basis of observed outcomes, as in problem solving, for example. However, inference is necessarily based on theory, as I have argued in detail elsewhere (Reese, 1971). Briefly, the argument is that inference takes the form of a syllogism: *If A occurs, then B occurs; B occurred; therefore, A occurred.* The major premise (*If A, then B*) functions as a theory (however miniature or low-level such a theory may be). Thus, theory is involved in both the inferential method and the analogical method. (The point is further developed in the section on *Analysis of Behavior Analysis*. The fact that the form of the syllogism is logically invalid is well known and irrelevant to the point that theory is necessarily involved in inference.)

A RESEARCH EXAMPLE

Background

The Training of Precurrent Behaviors.   According to Skinner (1968), the standard method of instruction about precurrent behavior is indirect, dealing with outcomes rather than with how they were obtained:

> [The teacher] sets problems to be solved and reinforces the student when he solves them or punishes him when he does not. . . . [The] student may learn to think when the teacher simply poses problems and reinforces solutions, but he will almost always think inefficiently rather than with the good form which others have discovered before him. (p. 118)

A direct approach is possible, however:

> Special reinforcers must be made contingent on the topography of the behavior rather than its outcome. Only under rare circumstances will the ultimate advantages of thinking teach a student to think. The teacher must arrange effective contingencies which respect the topography of thinking. (p. 119)

The distinction between the methods seems to need clarification in two ways, regarding what is reinforced and whether the use of shaping is necessary.

What is Reinforced?   Although Skinner (1953, p. 247) has explicitly defined the solution to a problem as behavior, in the context of the previous quotations it refers to the solved problem, not to problem solving. That is, *solutions* in this context are the outcomes of behaviors, or stimulus products of behaviors, rather than the behaviors themselves. However, solutions in this sense cannot be reinforced or punished, only behaviors can be. (The phrase "reinforces the student . . . or punishes him" in the first quotation above is imprecise, of course; although such phrases may not mislead a behaviorist, they "can easily lead to ineffective procedures, for one can refer to a reinforcement procedure without specifying behavior" [Hineline, 1980, p. 73].) Therefore, the first quotation above refers to a method of instruction in which the teacher reinforces effective—or successful, or correct—problem solving or punishes ineffective—unsuccessful, incorrect—problem solving. (To avoid the imprecise language in "the teacher reinforces" problem solving, one could say "the teacher implements a procedure that results in reinforcement of" problem solving.) In short, solutions in the sense of behavior are reinforced, and the reinforcement is contingent on solutions in the sense of outcomes of this behavior.

In the method recommended in the second quotation above, the teacher also reinforces or punishes behavior. The difference between the methods is therefore not in reinforcement or punishment of outcomes versus topographies, but in reinforcement or punishment of behaviors at the end of the problem-solving chain versus behaviors that occur earlier in the chain and alter the situation so that the end behaviors can be emitted (Parrott, personal communication, November 19, 1980; Skinner, 1953, p. 247). The distinction, in other words, refers to reinforcement or punishment of solutions (in the sense of behavior) versus precurrent behaviors (Parsons, personal communication, December 1, 1980). However, although Skinner (1974) has noted that the skin is an artificial boundary for applicability of the principles of behavior, it is not an artificial boundary for *application* of the principles of behavior. Consequently, direct instruction of precurrent behaviors requires that they be overt (Skinner, 1968, pp. 124–125).

Is Shaping Necessary?   The second question is whether shaping is required in the recommended method, as implied in the second quotation previously mentioned (cf. Skinner, 1968, pp. 65–66, in which topography is mentioned and shaping is discussed). Except in shaping, reinforcement in operant conditioning is usually contingent on outcomes rather than topographies. (To avoid possible misunderstanding, perhaps the preceding sentence should have been written: "Except in shaping, the presentation or withdrawal of stimuli following occurrences of behaviors is usually contingent on the stimulus products of the behaviors rather than the topographies of the behaviors." The assertion, in other words, is not that outcomes are reinforced but that reinforcement of behaviors is usually contingent on their outcomes rather than their topographies.) For example, the delivery of a food pellet in an operant conditioning chamber is more likely to be contingent on the occurrence of a criterion excursion of the lever than on the topography of the lever-pressing (except when the research question demands otherwise, as in research on the effects of effortfulness of lever-pressing—e.g., Mowrer & Jones, 1943). However, although shaping is often a useful procedure, it is usually necessary only when the desired behavior has a zero base rate and cannot be prompted. But precurrent behaviors seem often to have nonzero base rates, and in any case can often be prompted by verbal instructions (cf. Butterfield et al., 1980). Therefore, the emphasis on shaping—and on the topography of the behavior—is misplaced.

In addition, Skinner said: "It is rarely possible to define an operant topographically . . . without the sharper delineation of properties that is given by the act of conditioning" (1938, p. 22). "We construct an operant by making a reinforcer contingent on a response, but the important fact about the resulting unit is not its topography but its probability of occurrence" (1969, p. 7). And according to Keller, operant behavior "takes in all those movements of an organism that may at some time be said to have an effect upon or do something to his outside world. Operant behavior *operates* on this world" (Keller, 1954, p. 2, 1969, p. 5; see also Catania, 1979, pp. 32, 356–358).

Keller's reference to "movements" may need clarification. Guthrie distinguished between *movements* and *acts,* the former defined by topographies of muscular contractions and the latter by outcomes. He noted that Skinner assumed that learning involves acts, such as bar-pressing, and pointed out that "Bar pressing is an act, in the sense that it names the outcome of movements which are not specified" (1960, p. 27). The occurrence of particular operant behavior, then, is defined by the occurrence of particular outcomes, and therefore in this sense reinforcement is always contingent on outcomes. The final point is that making reinforcement contingent on outcomes has been demonstrated to be effective for teaching certain complex interactions. Examples are the work of Goetz and Baer (1973) demonstrating the development of creative block-building; the work of Holman, Goetz, and Baer (1977) demonstrating the development of creative painting; and the work of Paniagua and Baer (1982) analyzing correspondence between verbal and nonverbal behavior. In this research, reinforcement was contingent on the appearance of new arrangements of blocks, new painted forms, or conceptual agreement between saying and doing, that is, on products or outcomes rather than on behavioral topographies. The success of the procedure is consistent with the general success of education in teaching reading and arithmetic, for example, by dealing with outcomes. After all, most of us seem to have learned the ultimate advantages of thinking without having had reinforcement contingent on the topography of thinking.

Summary. The argument is that no special techniques, such as shaping, are necessarily required for the teaching of precurrent behaviors. Nevertheless, according to Parsons and Ferraro (1977), precurrent behaviors have a special status in behavior analysis.

Complex behaviors, such as attending, mediating, problem solving, and self control, are analyzed in terms of the independent variables affecting their probability of occurrence. In a functional view, these behaviors are of special interest because they do not have any apparent direct effect on external contingencies of reinforcement, but instead affect subsequent behavior. Behavior having this function is termed precurrent. Skinner (1968) has suggested that precurrent behaviors are conditioned and maintained by their ultimate effect on subsequent behaviors. . . . So-described, precurrent interactions take on the defining characteristics of operant chains. A chain consists of a response sequence in which one response produces the conditions that make the subsequent response more probable. Precurrent responses may be considered as early links in a chain, and the subsequent behaviors they alter as the terminal links that lead to reinforcement. (p. 238)

The Parsons and Ferraro Study

Parsons and Ferraro studied an overt form of mediation, conceptualized as an operant chain. Although they saw their study as a direct analysis of overt precurrent behavior, it can be interpreted as an indirect analysis of covert precurrent behavior. So interpreted, the study is an excellent example of analogical behavior analysis, and therefore I analyze it here in detail.

Procedure.   Parsons and Ferraro (1977) used a delayed matching-to-sample task, with an apparatus containing

> a token dispenser and 5 stimulus-response keys arranged in a Greek cross pattern. The center key was the sample-stimulus key, and the left and right keys were the comparison-stimulus keys. These 3 keys could be illuminated independently with either red or green light. The top and bottom keys served as mediating keys and could be illuminated with white light. (p. 240)

In two experiments, with boys $4\frac{1}{2}$ to 5 years old, the sample-stimulus key was lighted red or green, and response to it turned off the color and illuminated the mediating keys. In Experiment 1, responses to the two mediating keys were differentially reinforced on the basis of the color of the sample stimulus. After the subjects learned this discrimination, differential reinforcement of responses to the mediating keys was discontinued, but appropriate responses were followed immediately by illumination of the comparison-stimulus keys and responses to the comparison-stimulus key that matched the previously presented sample stimulus were reinforced. After subjects achieved a criterion of 90% correct responses to the comparison-stimulus keys, delayed matching to sample was tested by introducing a variable delay between mediating-key responses and illumination of the comparison-stimulus keys. The procedure in Experiment 2 was the same except that responses to the mediating keys were differentially reinforced on the basis of their position—either the top key or the bottom key was always appropriate—rather than on the basis of the color of the sample stimulus. Six test sessions were given. In the first two and last two, a response to a mediating key was required; in the middle two, responses to mediating keys were prohibited and illumination of the comparison-stimulus keys followed responses to the sample-stimulus key after the variable delay[2]

---

[2]In this paragraph I have consistently referred to behaviors as "responses"; everywhere else in the chapter I have used the term *response* only in quotations and in references to stimulus-response interpretations of behavior. The use of *response* to refer to operant behavior is not necessary for clarity (e.g., "pressing a key" is no harder to comprehend than "responding to a key") and its use is probably a holdover from methodological behaviorism. By derivation from the Latin, a *response* is a reply or an answer, which requires an antecedent-consequent relation. The term is therefore apt in the stimulus-response model of methodological behaviorism and in references to respondent behavior in behavior analysis. However, it is inappropriate and can be misleading in references to operant behavior, because it implies an eliciting stimulus.

Results and Interpretations. In Experiment 1, the accuracy of the comparison-key presses was found to be essentially perfect regardless of delay when mediating-key presses were permitted, and declined with increasing delay when mediating-key presses were prohibited. The mediating-key presses were made repeatedly during the delays, at a rate of roughly once a second. In Experiment 2, the accuracy of matching declined with increasing delay whether or not mediating-key presses were permitted. In both experiments, the mediating-key press produced the comparison stimuli, which were discriminative for the availability of reinforcement, thus fitting the definition of an operant chain. However, the mediating-key presses were followed by greater accuracy of delayed matching only when they had been discriminated on the basis of color. Thus, the chain was effective only when the mediating-key presses were differential with respect to the sample stimulus to be matched.

An analogue with verbal mediators is provided by other research, in which young children were found to perform more poorly on a discriminative-learning task when the stimuli were different colors than when they were different forms (Calvin, Clancy, & Fuller, 1956; Calvin & Clifford, 1956). Apparently, the children used the same label for both color stimuli, naming them "color," for example, or "colored card." The use of an undifferentiated name is analogous to the mediating-key presses in Parsons and Ferraro's Experiment 2, in which these key-presses were differentiated on position; and the use of differential color names, such as "blue" and "green" in the Calvin and Clifford study, is analogous to the mediating-key presses in Parsons and Ferraro's Experiment 1, in which these key-presses were differentiated on color. According to stimulus-response learning theory, the use of an undifferentiated name should interfere with discriminative performance through the "acquired equivalence of cues" and the use of differential names should facilitate discriminative performance through the "acquired distinctiveness of cues" (Dollard & Miller, 1950). Equivalence and distinctiveness are not produced by altering the initial stimulus, in this theory, but by adding a stimulus produced by a mediating response. A delay between the initial stimulus and the terminal response can be bridged by mediation only if the mediating response (naming, key-pressing, or whatever) occurs repetitively during the delay; and preventing emission of the mediating response will eliminate its function. Clearly, then, the method used by Parsons and Ferraro is useful for methodological behaviorists interested in studying mediation as well as for behavior analysts interested in studying precurrent behaviors— whether overt and studied directly or covert and studied analogically.

Another important finding of the Parsons and Ferraro study was that when the mediating-key presses were prohibited, in Test Sessions 3 and 4, accuracy of matching declined with increasing delay. This finding can be interpreted to indicate that the mediating function did not generalize from the trained form— key-pressing—to another form that was probably in the subjects' repertoire— naming the colors—and that is usually an effective delay-bridging mediator (e.g., Constantine & Sidman, 1975; Spiker, 1956). This interpretation is tentative, however, because as Constantine and Sidman (1975) noted, the mediating function is confounded with behaving differentially per se: Constantine and Sidman found that naming pictures facilitated pictorial matching to sample, but they noted that the effect of naming was not necessarily attributable to mediation because naming is also "a differential response to each sample picture, and this feature of naming, rather than its potential mediating function, may account for [its] effectiveness" (Constantine & Sidman, 1975, p. 688; Kendler, 1964, made a similar point about verbalization and reversal-shift performance). The same possibility is tenable for the Parsons and Ferraro study and other "mediation" studies, and therefore although this research demonstrated that certain precurrent behaviors are functional, the nature of their function was not established. (As discussed later, however, other research shows that the function is indeed mediational.)

ANALYSIS OF BEHAVIOR ANALYSIS

Several points about indirect behavior analysis are illustrated by the Parsons and Ferraro study. These points are discussed in the present section as a framework for analyzing behavior analysis in general.

Nature of Mediation

Definition of Mediation. As interpreted in this chapter, the Parsons and Ferraro study dealt with an analogue of mediation, not as it is conceptualized in cognitive theory (e.g., Flavell, 1970, 1977; Reese, 1979) or Soviet theory.(Cole & Scribner, 1978), but more as it is conceptualized in stimulus-response learning theories (e.g., Dollard & Miller, 1950; Goss, 1961; Hull, 1939; Reese, 1962, 1963; Spence, 1956, Fig. 5, p. 50). Mediation is defined in cognitive theory and Soviet theory as the effect of "operations," "processes," or "activities" that are generally covert but that in any case determine the organism's perception, understanding, or assimilation of environmental input (e.g., Cole & Scribner, 1978). That is, this type of mediation involves a transformation of sensory input to produce an effective stimulus. For example, selective attention to the color of a large red square transforms this stimulus into a red patch of indeterminate size and shape. In stimulus-response learning theory, in contrast, mediation involves substitution of an effective stimulus for the input stimulus (Reese, 1971). In the usual stimulus-response formulation (Goss, 1961), which is shown in Fig. 1.1, the effective stimulus for the final response is not the initial stimulus but rather

FIG. 1.1.   The stimulus-response conception of mediation (Goss, 1961). The initial stimulus (S) elicits (straight arrow) a mediating response (r_m), which produces (wavy arrow) a mediating stimulus (s_m) that elicits the final response (R). The mediating response and stimulus are symbolized with lower case letters when they are covert.

the stimulus produced by the mediating response that is elicited by the initial stimulus. For example, if a large red square is verbally labeled "green," it can function like a green stimulus with respect to the final response. Mediation of this type affects the *function* of a stimulus, in contrast to the cognitive type of mediation, which affects the *nature* of the stimulus—the large red square becomes an amorphous red patch.

The mediating behavior in the Parsons and Ferraro study is not readily interpretable within cognitive or Soviet theory but is easily interpreted within stimulus-response theory. A plausible stimulus-response interpretation is shown in Fig. 1.2. In this interpretation, the function of the "mediating" responses was not to transform the sample stimulus but to produce a stimulus that was differentially discriminable for reinforcement of subsequent responses. Nevertheless, although the behavior analytic and stimulus-response conceptions of mediation are similar, they are not identical.

Mediation is defined in stimulus-response learning theory as a kind of relational term. As Goss (1961) specified, a mediating response must be preceded by a stimulus and followed by a change in a subsequent response. Because this definition includes an outcome—an effect on subsequent behavior—a mediator is not identifiable as such until its effect has been observed. In this respect, a mediator is like operant behavior as customarily defined, not by form or topography, but by function or effect on the environment. Thus, for example, a behavior is precurrent only if it affects subsequent behavior. However, in stimulus-response learning theory, the principles of mediation are the same as for any other stimulus-response associations: A stimulus elicits a mediating response, which produces a stimulus that elicits a terminal, instrumental response, and these associations are learned and maintained by reinforcement. In behavior analysis, in contrast, precurrent behaviors are not elicited and they are said to be maintained not by reinforcement but by "their ultimate effect on subsequent behaviors." That is, precurrent behaviors are not themselves directly reinforced; rather, they are maintained because the subsequent behaviors they affect are reinforced.

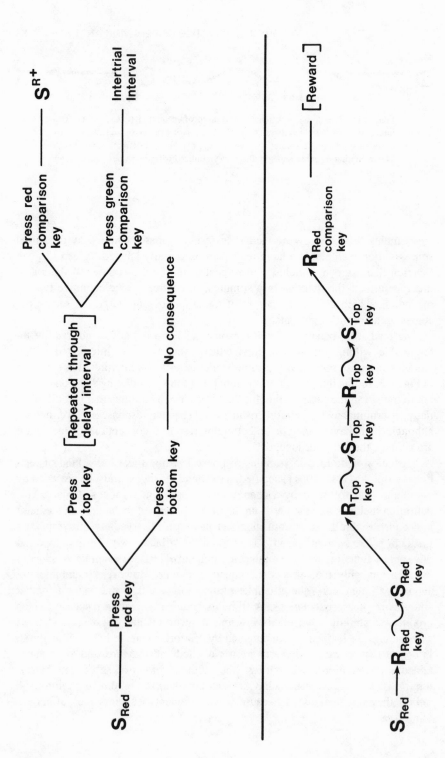

14

Mediational Deficiency. The Parsons and Ferraro study demonstrated that boys $4\frac{1}{2}$ to 5 years old can learn precurrent behavior or, as other psychologists have said, can use a mediator. This result is important because children of this age often do not spontaneously use mediators. They are said to be in a stage of mediational deficiency, and a question of theoretical and practical importance is whether the deficiency results from (a) absence of the mediator from the children's behavioral repertoire, (b) failure to emit mediating behavior that is in their repertoire, or (c) failure of emitted behavior to alter subsequent behavior. The last two of these possible sources are called, respectively, production deficiency (Flavell, Beach, & Chinsky, 1966) and mediation deficiency (Flavell et al., 1966) or control deficiency (Kendler, 1972).

Extensive research on mediational deficiency has been conducted in the United States, by T. S. Kendler among others (e.g., Flavell), and in the Soviet Union. For example, Kendler (1964) used a reversal-learning task in which young children were instructed to verbalize the reinforcement contingencies, such as "The square is the winner and the circle is the loser" (Exp. 1 format) or "Black wins and white loses" (Exp. 2 format). She found that some of the children transferred the verbalization intact to the reversal task and continued to recite it while choosing the correct stimulus—saying "Black wins and white loses," for example, while choosing the white stimulus.

Luria (1961) summarized Soviet research demonstrating a very similar phenomenon. In several of the studies young children were instructed to squeeze a rubber bulb when a positive signal was presented and not to squeeze it when an inhibitory signal was presented. Their performance was fair, except when they were required to say "Press!" or "Don't press!" depending on which signal was presented and then to squeeze or not squeeze in accordance with the self-instruction. Although the children verbalized appropriately, both self-instructions were most often followed by squeezing the bulb. Thus, young children's own speech (before about age 5 years in this research) had a nonspecific, impelling or triggering effect on their motor behavior instead of a selectively regulative effect.

FIG. 1.2. Mediation in the Parsons and Ferraro study. *Top panel:* Example of sequences of events in Test Sessions 1, 2, 5, and 6. Sample-stimulus key (S) is illuminated red; pressing it permits pressing top or bottom mediating key; pressing bottom mediating key has no consequence (and is eventually followed by pressing top mediating key); pressing top mediating key illuminates the comparison-stimulus keys after a variable delay; pressing green comparison-stimulus key initiates the intertrial interval; pressing red comparison-stimulus key is reinforced. *Bottom panel:* Interpretation of the uppermost sequence in the top panel as stimulus-response mediation. The red sample-stimulus, or, as shown, the stimulus produced by response to it, is a stimulus for a chain of responses to the top mediating key, each response in the chain producing a stimulus that elicits a repetition of the response until the comparison-stimulus keys become available for responding, when this change in the stimulus complex permits the stimulus produced by the mediating response to elicit response to the red comparison-stimulus key.

European research outside the Soviet Union has confirmed these results (for references, see Bronckart & Ventouras-Spycher, 1979). In behavior analysis terms, saying "Press!" and "Don't press!" produced functionally the same stimuli, that is, stimuli in a single class discriminative for squeezing.

American attempts to replicate the Soviet findings were generally unsuccessful (Fuson, 1979; Miller, Shelton, & Flavell, 1970; Wozniak, 1972); but most of the failures seem to be attributable to methodological problems (Wozniak, 1972). Apparently, the children tended to verbalize not before the motor behavior, as in much of the research summarized by Luria, but simultaneously with the motor bheavior, after the motor behavior, or not at all (Meacham, 1979). If the verbalization were the mediator, then the test of the Soviet findings would not be valid unless the verbalization preceded the motor behavior. However, if the verbalization were itself mediated, then the relative timing of the verbalization would not be critical with respect to whether or not mediation occurred (Reese, 1971, 1979). That is, overt speech (and other behavior) may be mediated rather than mediating. This possibility is consistent with the assumed relation between "primary" speech and autoclitic speech in Skinner's theory of verbal behavior. Primary speech can be said to mediate autoclitic speech: Primary speech is precurrent and is tacted by autoclitic speech (Skinner, 1957, e.g., pp. 315, 327). Or, put another way, the stimulus products of primary speech become part of the situation in which autoclitic speech occurs.

Causes of Mediational Deficiency

Although the reality of mediational deficiency is well established (for reviews see Flavell, 1970, 1977; Kendler, 1979; Reese, 1962, 1963, 1976), its causes are not well established even after more than two decades of research since the phenomenon was first named (Reese, 1962).

A characteristic of children—and even severely retarded individuals—who exhibit mediational deficiency is that they can be induced to use mediators by training or instructions, as shown by the Parsons and Ferraro study and other, previous research (for reviews, see Belmont & Butterfield, 1977; Hagen, Jongeward, & Kail, 1975). However, their use of mediators often stops when the instructions or other prompts are discontinued. For example, Constantine and Sidman found, as have other investigators (e.g., see Hagen et al., 1975), that instructions can induce young or retarded subjects to use a strategy, or emit a behavior, that they do not spontaneously use, or emit; but when the instructions are dropped the strategy, or behavior, often drops out. In behavior analysis terminology—which the Parsons and Ferraro study demonstrates is applicable— developmentally young individuals who emit certain behaviors in certain circumstances do not emit behaviors precurrently unless given appropriate training (Parsons & Ferraro) or instructions (Constantine & Sidman). However, the precurrent behaviors are controlled by stimuli other than "their ultimate effect on subsequent behaviors,'' and are not maintained when the controlling stimuli are removed.

A Possible Cause.   One possible cause of mediational deficiency is that the mediator is not controlled by appropriate stimuli. Constantine and Sidman suggested that gradually fading out the instructions instead of discontinuing them abruptly—as had been done in the relevant research—might result in maintenance of the precurrent behavior. Presumably, fading out the instructions would shift control to the subsequent behaviors in the operant chain. The suggestion has been confirmed; Parsons (1976), for example, found that instructions could be faded out without disrupting precurrent behaviors. The same effect has been obtained when the precurrent behaviors were trained through reinforcement rather than prompted by instructions: Grimm, Bijou, and Parsons (1973) used instructional praise (e.g., "That's good counting," "That's a good circle") to train precurrent behaviors, and found that these behaviors persisted after the instructional praise was faded out. Thus, mediational deficiency may reflect a lack of control of precurrent behaviors by their ultimate effect on subsequent behaviors.

Other Possible Causes.   Other conditions are probably also involved, however. Parsons reported that in research conducted in his laboratory after the Parsons and Ferraro (1977) study, he has not found the decrements observed by other investigators when the task does not explicitly require mediating, and he suggested that the difference in findings may reflect differences in the nature of the reinforcement contingencies used (personal communication, December 1, 1980). If the payoff for correct choices is great enough, the decrement may not appear. The suggestion is testable, and confirmation would resolve one of the current puzzles about mediational deficiency.

Parsons (1976) listed five other conditions that might lead to mediational deficiency or, as he said, conditions "under which precurrent interactions may fail to materialize" (p. 192). They are:

1. Setting events "may preclude a problem solving episode if deprivation of the reinforcer is insufficient" (p. 192). The result would be that the problem-solving chain is not initiated, which is "production deficiency." With respect to setting events, incidentally, Skinner has not emphasized their role, as Morris (1978) noted, but their having a role is entirely consistent with his approach, as Morris also noted. Some behavior analysts, furthermore, emphasize the role of setting events (Gewirtz, 1971b) or, as Kantor called them, "setting factors" (Kantor, 1970, p. 106; see also Bijou & Baer, 1978). Setting events or factors can be conceptualized as changing the three-term contingency into a four-term contingency (Morris, 1978), but they seem to be "more equal" than the other elements in the contingency, determining, for example, whether or not a con-

tingent stimulus will function as a reinforcer (Gewirtz, 1971b, Footnote 2, p. 281).

2. The subject's repertoire may lack one or more of the required behaviors. This cause has also been suggested by stimulus-response theorists.

3. "A given stimulus may control responses which compete with problem solving, or precurrent behaviors may be evoked by aspects of the problem irrelevant to its solution" (p. 192). This condition involves the discriminative function of the stimuli within a sequence; it is very similar to another of the causes assumed in stimulus-response learning theory, but goes somewhat beyond it.

4. Similarly, "In cases where discriminative stimuli are response-produced, if the responses are covert, they may produce stimuli too weak to function effectively in controlling subsequent responses in the sequence" (p. 192). Parsons cited Skinner's *Verbal Behavior* (1957) as documentation, but the concept of the strength of an unobservable stimulus sounds like a free invention within behavior analysis. My argument is not that the concept has no empirical referent but that its theoretical basis is not clear in behavior analysis. An anecdotal example is shifting from subvocal to vocal counting during a long tally when the setting becomes noisy (Parrott, personal communication, November 19, 1980). Presumably, subvocal counting produces stimuli that are too weak to function effectively in a noisy setting, and counting aloud produces stimuli that are sufficiently strong. (The concept of stimulus strength is not problematic in stimulus-response learning theory. An example is Hull's concept of the stimulus trace, which by definition declines in intensity as a function of time. Such a concept is acceptable in stimulus-response learning theory because, as Spence [1941] noted, it is an intervening variable defined in terms of observables and no physiological referent is implied. In other words, reduction to a physiological process that might be directly observable is not involved; rather, the concept is a shorthand symbol for the relata and the relations specified in the definition. In this sense, whenever the relata and the relations are observed, the concept is observed.)

5. "Failure to maintain the response flow" may result from "the absence of conditioned reinforcers within the sequence" (p. 192). This possible role of conditioned reinforcers is discussed in the next subsection.

Concept of Reinforcement

The Descriptive Concept. Behavior modification is an applied branch of behavior analysis, as mentioned in the introductory remarks, but a widening gap has been developing between the theory and practice of the application. Applied behavior analysis has come to deal with procedures rather than with principles, and is technological rather than conceptual (Birnbrauer, 1979; Deitz, 1978; Hayes, Rincover, & Solnick, 1980). Birnbrauer (1979) noted the scarcity of principles for determining which procedures should be effective in behavior modification. He illustrated his point by describing the results of a study of two children who exhibited undesired behavior. For one child an adult's imitating the undesired behavior reduced the frequency of the behavior, but for the other child an adult's imitating the undesired behavior increased its frequency. For a strict, thoroughgoing radical behaviorist, these contradictory results are neither surprising nor bothersome. Morse and Kelleher (1977) emphasized that no concept "predicts reliably when events will be reinforcers or punishers; the defining characteristics of reinforcers and punishers are how they change behavior" (p. 176). They are facts, and they are not explainable by reference to anything outside the conditions of their observation (Bijou & Baer, 1978, p. 46; Catania, 1979, pp. 75–76).

In asking for research on underlying principles, Birnbrauer was implicitly rejecting the mere fact-finding approach to behavior. Behavior is lawful and as Kantor (1970) and others (e.g., Catania, 1978; Hineline, 1980; Wood, 1978) have noted, "Reinforcement works" is not the only law. Kantor criticized behavior analysis for reliance on reinforcement as the only behavioral change process. It was the only process used by Hineline (1980) in his analysis of the language of behavior analysis. It was also the only process Skinner (1957) specified for strengthening verbal behavior, according to MacCorquodale (1970). However, MacCorquodale argued that "the possibility of some acquisition process other than reinforcement is not itself overwhelming to Skinner's system" (p. 93). Skinner (1974, chap. 3) has discussed the role of natural selection in behavioral change; and although natural selection is a product rather than a process, some kind of biogenetic change process is implicated. However, acquisition processes other than reinforcement are arguably relevant only to respondent behavior and even then only to its unconditioned form.

With respect to operant behavior, reinforcement is defined, in part, by acquisition and therefore all processes of acquisition of operant behavior by an individual organism would be reinforcement, by definition. One might argue that an acquisition process other than reinforcement would be implicated if the process involved no contingent presentation or withdrawal of a stimulus, which complete the definitions of positive and negative reinforcement, respectively; but as Parrott (personal communication, November 19, 1980) noted, all behaviors represent change and consequently one can always find a contingent stimulus. Thus, in practice, acquisition would always be attributable to reinforcement even if no contingent stimuli were observed. An example is Skinner's use of the concept of "automatic reinforcement" (e.g., Skinner, 1968) in the absence of empirical demonstration either that a stimulus was presented or withdrawn upon the occurrence of the behavior in question, or given such a demonstration, that the stimulus presentation or withdrawal produced by the behavior affected occurrences of the behavior. (Incidentally, given the definition of reinforcement such phrases as "noncontingent reinforcement" and "response-independent reinforcement" are meaningless technically, although little real misunderstanding seems to have resulted from use of such phrases to refer to time-dependent and other "response-independent" schedules of stimulus presentation. These, however, should be called behavior-independent schedules; see Footnote 2.)

Theoretical Conceptions. Gewirtz (1971a, 1971b) has criticized what he (1971b) called "hyphenated-reinforcement" conceptions such as "intrinsic-reinforcement," "self-reinforcement," and "vicarious-reinforcement." According to Gewirtz, these conceptions are reducible to extrinsic reinforcement. I would extend the list to include "automatic reinforcement" and certain "hyphenated-reinforcer" concepts found in behavior analysis: "conditioned reinforcers," "generalized reinforcers," and "ecological reinforcers." These concepts have perfectly acceptable definitions as descriptive concepts, but the definitions are widely ignored in that the concepts are almost invariably used as theoretical concepts (Reese, 1980).

For example, the concept of conditioned reinforcers is often used in a theoretical way. Baer, Peterson, and Sherman (1967) suggested that "The development of imitative repertoires . . . could be accounted for by the effects of conditioned reinforcement," and the conditioned reinforcer could be "the stimulus class of behavioral similarity," which is "a correspondence of some sort between the stimulus output of the child's behavior and the stimulus output of the model's" (p. 415). Similarly, Sherman and Thomas (1968) invoked conditioned reinforcement to explain the effect of delay on switching between fixed-ratio and variable-ratio schedules of reinforcement:

> Since the delay interval was imposed only preceding a one-response ratio in the variable schedule, it is possible that the stimulus conditions which accompanied the delay interval acquired conditioned reinforcing properties which served to reinforce immediately those switching responses which produced the delay. This would serve to reduce the effect of the delay intervals in general. (p. 702)

This kind of usage is theoretical—or "hypothetical," which means the same thing in this context (see the subsection on *Role of Theory*)—because the association of the supposed conditioned reinforcer with a known reinforcer was not systematically manipulated and because the supposed conditioned reinforcer was not presented or withdrawn contingently with the occurrence of any specified behavior. But even if a stimulus had the required history, it would not be a reinforcer unless it had the required effect, so why the concern about its history? The definition of reinforcers includes nothing about why a stimulus has the reinforcing function (Morse & Kelleher, 1977).

Clearly, then, the concept of conditioned reinforcers and the other hyphenated-reinforcer concepts are useful more for explanation than for description. Their use in explanations is not necessarily reprehensible in behavior analysis, because as shown in the next subsection theory has an established role in behavior analysis. However, their use in explanations should be interpreted as a prediction, because explanation in behavior analysis is in fact description: To behavior analysts, "the description of functional relationships relating manipulable or controllable environmental events to observable behavioral outcomes does constitute explanation" (Wood, 1978, p. 82). Or as Skinner (1938) said, "No property is a valid defining property of a [response] class until its experimental reality has been demonstrated" (p. 41); this criterion is used to identify "experimentally real concepts" (p. 42) by demonstrating that they are "validly descriptive—that they lead to consistent and reproducible experimentation" (p. 42). Thus, if the use of hyphenated-reinforcement concepts is interpreted as prediction, the analysis has not been done until experimenters test and confirm the predictions.

Role of Theory

Nature of Theory.   Honig and Staddon (1977) suggested that "Skinner's strictures against theorizing and 'botonizing' have discouraged both systematic exploration of non-schedule variables, such as species differences and types of reinforcer, and persistent attempts to make theoretical inferences" (p. 2). However, Honig and Staddon called attention to the extensive theorizing in many of the contributions to their *Handbook of Operant Behavior,* and Skinner in fact has noted that "A theory is essential to the scientific understanding of behavior as a subject matter" (1972, p. 302).

I personally do not find theory intrinsically objectionable, but many behavior analysts make suspicion of theory an article of faith. Admittedly, they express less suspicion of the inductive type of theory, in which the axioms are empirical laws, inference and deduction are minimized, and the constructs are descriptive (Marx, 1976); but in practice, behavior analytic theories often contain unverified assumptions as axioms, many inferences and deductions, and constructs without observable referents, including dispositional constructs (as defined by Bergmann, 1957, pp. 59–67) and theoretical constructs (as defined by Kaplan, 1964, chap. 2; see also MacCorquodale & Meehl, 1948, and Spence, 1948, on hypothetical constructs and intervening variables). Such theories have the characteristics of "functional" theories and some of the characteristics of "deductive" theories (as these types were defined by Marx, 1976: The axioms include "theoretical" assumptions, inference and deduction are emphasized, and "theoretical" constructs are included). An example is Bijou and Baer's (1978) analysis of child development. They explicitly attempted to avoid theory except in the inductive sense, but I believe that their theory often became at least "functional" (in Marx's sense), especially in their analysis (chaps. 10, 11) of the types of phenomena under consideration in the present chapter. Apparently, then, as in the difference between behavior modifiers and other kinds of psychotherapists, the objection of behavior analysts to theory is usually found more in what they say than in what they do.

Three cases in point are Skinner's (1957) analysis of verbal behavior, which is almost entirely theoretical (MacCorquodale, 1970); the development of several theories of how conditioned reinforcement works (for review, see Fantino, 1977); and Skinner's use of the concept of reinforcement in explaining, for example, why one reads a novel, looks at a painting, and listens to music. One does such things "because one is reinforced when one does so" (Skinner, 1974, p. 187). This explanation is based on the proposition that behavior occurs only if reinforced (at least intermittently), but as implied earlier, the concept of automatic reinforcement is theoretical in the absence of empirical demonstration that the contingent presentation or withdrawal of a stimulus maintains the behavior in question. These three cases are instructive because they illustrate three important characteristics of theory, regarding the content of a theory, the scope of a theory, and the distinction between theory and hypothesis.

1. A theory need not contain "abstract" or "highly defined" terms; a theory is a group of laws, which can be highly conjectural as in theories of the "deductive" type but which can also be strictly empirical as in theories of the "inductive" type. In either case, if the theory is the "hierarchical" type (Kaplan, 1964, p. 298) some of the laws it contains serve as axioms (major premises) from which others can be deduced (Bergmann, 1957, pp. 31–37; Kaplan, 1964, p. 298); and if the theory is the "concatenated" type (Kaplan, 1964, p. 298) the laws are interrelated in a network constructed rationally rather than deductively.

2. The *scope* of a theory is determined by the diversity of the laws it contains and the range of phenomena covered by these laws (Bergmann, 1957, p. 32). If the scope is narrow, the theory is low-level (cf. Feigl, 1953), but it is nonetheless a theory. The three illustrative cases cited previously reflect theories varying in scope: (a) Skinner's theory of verbal behavior is relatively wide in both diversity of laws and range of phenomena covered, and therefore is a relatively high-level theory. (b) The theories of conditioned reinforcement are lower in both diversity of laws and range of phenomena covered, and therefore are lower-level. (c) The theory of automatic reinforcement seems to be very limited in diversity of laws and therefore even though it is fairly wide in range of phenomena purportedly covered, it seems to be a fairly low-level theory.

Two problems here are that, first, scope is not a precise concept, as Bergmann (1957, p. 32) noted, and therefore the relative level of a theory cannot be determined precisely; and second, the adjective "low-level" has a pejorative connotation that is unintended but is hard to ignore. The point is that theories vary in scope, and are still identifiable as "theories" even if they are empirical and narrow.

3. A theory that is strictly empirical and very narrow may be identified as a hypothesis rather than as a theory. Technically, a hypothesis is a conjecture about a fact that is not yet well established, or not yet established at all

(Bergmann, 1957, p. 34). The conjecture can be said to be theoretical as well as hypothetical if it is derived from a theory or, more relevant to the present discussion, if it is proposed as an explanation of an already established fact or law, that is, if it is used as an additional axiom in a hierarchical theory or as an additional nexus in a concatenated theory. Thus, for example, the suggestions of Baer et al. (1967) about the role of conditioned reinforcement in the development of imitation and about the nature of the conditioned reinforcer can be interpreted as hypotheses to be tested, but even if the research is never done, they constitute a tentative theory explaining the development of imitation. If the research is done and the suggestions are confirmed, the tentative theory loses its tentativeness, or some of it, but it remains a theory—a group of interrelated laws—explaining the development of imitation.

Invented Processes.   Behavior analysis is said to be characterized by a refusal to invoke "events, processes, or mechanisms which are hypothesized or invented for the purpose of mediating between behavior and its empirical determinants" (MacCorquodale, 1970, p. 91). However, in spite of this avowed refusal, some behavior analysts (as I have already mentioned) have invented reinforcers to explain relations between observed behavior and its observed antecedents. In this respect they are consistent with Skinner, who has invoked evolutionary selection as the basis for reinforceability and has assumed that the product of learning is change in the nervous system (Skinner, 1971, p. 114; 1974, pp. 213–215). Additional examples are the frequent references in behavior analysis to the "existence" of behavior in a behavioral repertoire, particularly when the reference is to "existence in some strength." These notions seem to be fully compatible with Hull's (1943) concept of "habit strength," but without some explicit theoretical framework, such as Hull had developed, they are free inventions.

Skinner (1953) also invented an evolutionary and cultural history that avoids the infinite regress of value judgments and that also, according to Zuriff (1980), avoids the infinite regress of the pragmatic truth criterion adopted in behavior analysis. As Zuriff documented, Skinner's criterion for determining that verbal behavior is "true" is that "it leads to behavior that is 'effective,' 'successful,' 'useful,' 'efficient,' productive of practical consequences, 'expedient,' 'workable,' or 'productive' " (Zuriff, 1980, pp. 344–345, parenthetical material deleted). However, determining the consequences of the generated behavior requires further behavior, which "is accepted as true only if it meets the pragmatic criterion of generating effective behavior" (p. 345), and so forth. According to Zuriff, Skinner's solution to the problem of ethical criteria also solves this problem of the truth criterion: "Because of a specific phylogenetic and cultural history, humans have evolved so that they are affected in certain ways by verbal behavior; that is, they believe certain verbal behavior to be true. For the most part, they do so without applying any explicit criteria of truth but rather because of human nature" (Zuriff, 1980, p. 348). Worded differently, this assumption is that humans instinctively believe that certain kinds of assertion are true. This assumption is clearly an example of the kind of "explanatory fiction" Skinner has persistently warned against, and clearly demonstrates that behavior analysts have not persistently eschewed theory.

Incidentally, this particular instance of theorizing was unnecessary because in pragmatism the basic principle is that nothing is real unless it makes a difference, or, better, nothing is worth considering real unless it makes a difference (James, 1907). Therefore, although the infinite regress in the workability criterion of truth is a logical possibility, it makes no pragmatic difference and therefore can be ignored. Failure to appreciate this point may reflect a deep-seated problem with the philosophy of behavior analysis—its pragmatism is incomplete and, apparently, incompletely understood by many of its proponents. Why else would a behavior analyst worry about the infinite regress of the workability criterion of truth? Within the ground rules of pragmatism the logical possibility of infinite regress makes no difference in any actual application of the criterion and therefore makes no difference in the philosophy, except to note that absolute truth is nonexistent. The felt need to postulate an innate stopping place in the regress is reminiscent of the mechanists' conception of truth, which is absolute. (Skinner [1974, p. 136] explicitly rejected the possibility of empirical absolute truth; but mechanistic overtones are also detectable in the conception of the three-term contingency, as Kantor [1970] noted.) Finally, behavior analysts seem often to take practicality as the whole of pragmatism—or contextualism, as Pepper (1942) called it. Contextualism involves much more than practicality, and in many of these other respects behavior analysis is inconsistent with contextualism (Reese, 1982, 1984).

Invented Behaviors.   J. R. Kantor has suggested that "it is partially because TEAB [the experimental analysis of behavior] halts before complex human behavior which cannot be treated by customary TEAB methods, that so much more or less legitimate opposition to it has been developed" (Kantor, 1970. p. 105). Kantor proposed that behavior analysts "should attempt to disclose the salient components of feeling and emotional behavior, volitional and voluntary actions, the creative processes of imagination as well as the behavior called inventing, thinking, problem solving, and reasoning in whatever situations they are performed" (p. 105). He was calling, in other words, for experimental analysis of private events, including the complex interactions discussed in the present chapter. Actually, such analyses had already begun before Kantor's article was published (examples include analyses of imitation and of language development: Baer et al., 1967; Brigham & Sherman, 1968; Guess, Sailor, Rutherford, & Baer, 1968; Hart & Risley, 1968). The relevant point here, however, is what the experimental analysis of these phenomena involves.

Stoddard (1968) demonstrated that subjects who attain the same outcome—solution of a problem—may not have attained it in the same way. This finding poses a problem for behavior analysis, because behaviors are defined by outcomes, that is, a specific behavior is defined not by its topography but by its effect on the environment. For example, a bar-press is defined not by a specified sequence of muscular contractions but by a criterion excursion of the bar. Analogously, then, the solution of a problem should define a specific behavior, "problem solving" (for problems of a specified kind). So defined, however, "problem solving" is not actually a "behavior." It is an abstraction, just as, for example, "oddity" is an abstraction (Stoddard, 1968). For that matter, any operant is an abstraction: Skinner (1969) said, "An operant is a class, of which a response is an instance or member. . . . It is always a response upon which a given reinforcement is contingent, but it is contingent upon properties which define membership in an operant. Thus a set of contingencies defines an operant" (p. 131). That is, an operant is an abstraction and as such cannot be directly reinforced; only instances can be reinforced, even though the instances are consequated precisely because they are instances (i.e., they have the properties that define membership in the operant).

Even though an operant is an abstraction, it is a descriptive concept. It does not refer to any isolable entity, but it is nevertheless descriptive in that it refers to concrete behaviors that have some property in common. Put another way, to say that certain behaviors are in a class is to say that these behaviors have a property in common, not to say why they have this property in common. Therefore, behavior classes can be identified, modified, or formed, but they cannot be used as explanations.[3] An example is imitation, which can be *described* as a behavior class but cannot be *explained* by its being a behavior class. Incidentally, if imitating is an operant, it is even more abstract than other operants in that the property that defines membership is a specified kind of similarity between any behavior emitted by the subject and a preceding behavior emitted by a model. The defining properties therefore include any behavior by the model and any behavior by the subject that is similar in a criterial way to that behavior. (For further discussion, see A. Baron & Galizio, 1982; Reese, 1980.)

Because an operant is abstract, it cannot be analyzed by direct manipulation. Direct analysis must deal with instances of an operant, that is, with specific behaviors. Consequently, Kantor's call for experimental analysis of private events can be answered only by use of inferential or analogical methods.

Finding an appropriate basis for inference or an appropriate analogue can be difficult, obviously, and one source of difficulty may be the terminology behavior analysts use. Behavior analysts seem to favor the use of present participles

---

[3]I refer here to "behavior classes" for consistency with Footnote 2, even though "response classes" admittedly sounds better because of long tradition.

instead of gerunds—*eating behavior* and *smoking behavior,* for example, instead of *eating* and *smoking.* Often, as in these examples, the practice is harmless because the verbs clearly refer to behaviors. Sometimes, however, the practice is dangerous because the verb does not clearly refer to any specific behavior or set of behaviors, as in such phrases as *attending behavior, matching behavior, mediating behavior,* and *problem-solving behavior.* The danger is exacerbated when the modifier is derived from a noun instead of a verb, because the referent is even less likely to be a behavior (i.e., an action). Examples are *attentional behavior, choice behavior, cognitive behavior, emotional behavior, oddity behavior, self-instructional behavior,* and, when it refers to language rather than speech, *verbal behavior.*[4]

The point is that using the phenomenon of interest as a modifier of the word *behavior* does not necessarily make the phenomenon a behavior, and conceptualizing it as a behavior analogous to an overt behavior can be misleading. The usefulness of the overt analogue depends on the assumption that the covert processes function like the overt behaviors. This assumption is theoretical because it cannot be directly tested by third-person consequation of the presumed covert behaviors. It might be testable by third-person consequation of overt signs of covert behaviors, but the relation between the overt signs and the covert behaviors is inferred, as in the task analyses done by cognitivists, again implicating theory.

Given the precedents of the use of theory in behavior analysis, and given the precedent of the definition of operant behavior by outcomes, I see no reason not to define covert precurrent behavior by outcomes, as is done with mediation in methodological behaviorism. Theory is required for such a definition, because inference is involved:

If the mediator occurs, then the terminal behavior will be $X;$

if the mediator does not occur, then the terminal behavior will be $Y.$

The terminal behavior is observed to be $X.$

Therefore, the mediator occurred.

Theory is implicated in the specification of the alternative terminal behaviors, which also requires specification of the nature and role of the mediator. "Precurrent behavior" can be substituted for "mediator" in the above syllogism. The advantage of this approach over the use of an overt analogue is that no assumption need be made about the similarity of functioning of the overt and covert behavior, and yet the effects of fading instructions, training with intermittent reinforcement, and so on, can be investigated. The disadvantage is that the

---

[4]The distinction between language and speech is a structure-function distinction—between language as a grammatical and semantic system and speech as the actual vocal output (Deese, 1970, pp. 3–4) or speech as vocal *or* nonvocal behavior such as writing (Skinner, 1957, p. 2). As Skinner has noted, "What the logician or linguist calls a sentence is not necessarily verbal behavior in any sense which calls for a behavioral analysis" (1974, pp. 98–99).

underlying theory may be wrong—a thread that does not lead anywhere—but if it is, the overt analogue may also lead nowhere. Anyway, as Kantor (1947) said, "many scientific discoveries have been made on the basis of false beliefs" (p. 110).

CONCLUSIONS

In the discussion following the oral presentation of the present chapter, someone asked how behavior analysts should deal with the problems raised. I answered, with less than full seriousness, that they should become methodological behaviorists. A fully serious answer is that they should recognize, with methodological behaviorists, the potential usefulness of theory. A study by Parsons (1976) yields a further example. In this study, a period of extinction was followed by a return to baseline conditions, with reinforcement for correct solutions but no direct reinforcement for precurrent behaviors. Two subjects exhibited a decline in performance during extinction, but in the return to baseline conditions they immediately recovered the high level of accuracy they had attained before extinction. An earlier comment by Weiner (1970) is relevant:

> Organisms who have been extinguished are not necessarily organisms who have been returned to their pre-conditioning state. Said another way, you don't necessarily make organisms naive by extinguishing their behavior. (pp. 449–450)

Weiner was being idiomatic when he referred to "organisms who have been extinguished," because he obviously meant to refer to behaviors that have been extinguished. However, the intended comment is surprising:

> Behavior that has been extinguished is not necessarily behavior that has been returned to its preconditioning state. Said another way, you don't necessarily eliminate behavior by extinguishing it.

One might wonder where behavior goes when it is extinguished—or learned, for that matter—and what it is like there. An empirical behavior analysis cannot provide answers, but theoretical answers are possible. To explain the phenomenon in question, one might postulate that behavior that has been extinguished continues to "exist in some strength," but as already noted this postulate is a free invention unless it has a theoretical rationale. The theoretical rationale would entail specific meanings of "existence" and "strength," perhaps by specifying what continues to exist and where it continues to exist, as in Hull's (1934) theory of the habit-family hierarchy. In short, some empirical phenomena raise questions that seem to require theoretical answers. Such answers should be formulated if they would make a difference. If they would make no difference, they would give only the illusion of understanding; but unless they are formulated, we cannot know whether they make a difference.

Schnaitter (1978) made essentially the same point in discussing the role of interpretation in the analysis of private events: "interpretations should not be viewed as defective, inferior, or second rate attempts at analysis" (p. 10). They can be used as sources of predictions and of controlling efforts and they are useful if the predictions are confirmed and the controlling efforts are effective, even without direct analysis of the phenomena that are interpreted.

Covert precurrent behaviors are by definition private events, but they can be studied through overt analogues. The overt analogues—that is, overt precurrent behaviors—are attributed a causal status that Skinner (1974, pp. 104–106, 209) seemed to deny to private events. Actually, however, Skinner denied that including them in an analysis of behavior contributes to the prediction and control of behavior—his pragmatic criterion for the truth of an analysis. But this assertion has a theoretical basis, the assumption that knowing an individual's reinforcement history (and, of course, the current setting conditions) is functionally the same as knowing the individual's current private events. This assumption is testable if a theory if formulated to permit inferences about private events and hence analysis of overt analogues.

The use of private events and covert precurrent behaviors in explanations has the same problems as the use of hyphenated-reinforcer concepts in explanations. These uses can be viewed as proposals for research; but in practice the research seems often not to be done because the explanations give a false sense of complete understanding. When the research is actually done, it sometimes turns out to be fruitless, following up threads that lead nowhere. Herein lies the major problem with the theorizing in the behavior analysis of complex interactions: Behavior analysts who do not recognize the theorizing as such are likely to be incautious about the pitfalls. Many behavior analysts seem not to recognize their theorizing as such and to do their work more on the basis of "implicit theory" (Skinner, 1972, p. 305) than on the basis of explicit theory.

In conclusion, the behavior analysis of complex interactions has been no less theoretical (or inventive) than the analysis in methodological behaviorism and some cognitive analyses. The major differences are that the terms used in behavior analysis usually *sound* less theoretical.

ACKNOWLEDGMENTS

An earlier (and shorter) version of this chapter was presented at the meeting of the Association for Behavior Analysis, Dearborn, Mich., May 1980. I am indebted to Linda J. Parrott and Joseph A. Parsons for extensive commentaries on drafts of the present version.

REFERENCES

Baer, D. M., Peterson, R. F., & Sherman, J. A. (1967). The development of imitation by reinforcing behavioral similarity to a model. *Journal of the Experimental Analysis of Behavior, 10,* 405–416.

Baron, A., & Galizio, M. (1982, February). *Instructional control of human operant behavior.* Paper presented at the First International Symposium on the Science of Behavior: Language and Behavior, P. Harzem & E. Ribes (Chairs), Universidad Nacional Autónoma de México, Mexico City.

Baron, G. (1981, May). *Parameters of covert (imagined) reinforcement: A preliminary investigation.* Paper presented at the meeting of the Association for Behavior Analysis, Milwaukee, WI.

Belmont, J. M., & Butterfield, E. C. (1977). The instructional approach to developmental cognitive research. In R. V. Kail, Jr., & J. W. Hagen (Eds.), *Perspectives on the development of memory and cognition* (pp. 437–481). Hillsdale, NJ: Lawrence Erlbaum Associates.

Bergmann, G. (1957). *Philosophy of science.* Madison: University of Wisconsin Press.

Bijou, S. W., & Baer, D. M. (1978). *Behavior analysis of child development.* Englewood Cliffs, NJ: Prentice-Hall.

Birnbrauer, J. S. (1979). Applied behavior analysis, service and the acquisition of knowledge. *Behavior Analyst, 2*(1), 15–21.

Bowe, C. A., & Dinsmoor, J. A. (1981). Temporal vs. spatial information as a reinforcer of observing. *Bulletin of the Psychonomic Society, 17,* 33–36.

Brigham, T. A., & Sherman, J. A. (1968). An experimental analysis of verbal imitation in preschool children. *Journal of Applied Behavior Analysis, 1,* 151–158.

Bronckart, J. P., & Ventouras-Spycher, M. (1979). The Piagetian concept of representation and the Soviet-inspired view of self-regulation. In G. Zivin (Ed.), *The development of self-regulation through private speech* (pp. 99–131). New York: Wiley.

Butterfield, E. C., Siladi, D., & Belmont, J. M. (1980). Validating theories of intelligence. In H. W. Reese & L. P. Lipsitt (Eds.), *Advances in child development and behavior* (Vol. 15, pp. 95–162). New York: Academic Press.

Calvin, A. D., Clancy, J. J., & Fuller, J. B. (1956). A further investigation of various stimulus-objects in discriminative learning by children. *American Journal of Psychology, 69,* 647–649.

Calvin, A. D., & Clifford, L. T. (1956). The relative efficacy of various types of stimulus-objects in discriminative learning by children. *American Journal of Psychology, 69,* 103–106.

Catania, A. C. (1978). What constitutes explanation in psychology. *Behavioral and Brain Sciences, 1,* 55–56.

Catania, A. C. (1979). *Learning.* Englewood Cliffs, NJ: Prentice-Hall.

Cohen, I. S. (1962). Programmed learning and the Socratic dialogue. *American Psychologist, 17,* 772–775.

Cole, M., & Scribner, S. (1978). Introduction. In L. S. Vygotsky, *Mind in society: The development of higher psychological processes* (M. Cole, V. John-Steiner, S. Scribner, & E. Souberman, Eds.; pp. 1–14). Cambridge, MA: Harvard University Press.

Constantine, B., & Sidman, M. (1975). Role of naming in delayed matching-to-sample. *American Journal of Mental Deficiency, 79,* 680–689.

Deese, J. (1970). *Psycholinguistics.* Boston: Allyn & Bacon.

Deitz, S. M. (1978). Current status of applied behavior analysis: Science versus technology. *American Psychologist, 33,* 805–814.

Dollard, J., & Miller, N. E. (1950). *Personality and psychotherapy: An analysis in terms of learning, thinking, and culture.* New York: McGraw-Hill.

Fantino, E. (1977). Conditioned reinforcement: Choice and information. In W. K. Honig & J. E. R. Staddon (Eds.), *Handbook of operant behavior* (pp. 313–339). Englewood Cliffs, NJ: Prentice-Hall.

Farkas, G. M. (1980). An ontological analysis of behavior therapy. *American Psychologist, 35*, 364–374.

Feigl, H. (1953). Unity of science and unitary science. In H. Feigl & M. Brodbeck (Eds.), *Readings in the philosophy of science* (pp. 382–384). New York: Appleton-Century-Crofts.

Flavell, J. H. (1970). Developmental studies of mediated memory. In H. W. Reese & L. P. Lipsitt (Eds.), *Advances in child development and behavior* (Vol. 5, pp. 181–211). New York: Academic Press.

Flavell, J. H. (1977). *Cognitive development*. Englewood Cliffs, NJ: Prentice-Hall.

Flavell, J. H., Beach, D. R., & Chinsky, J. M. (1966). Spontaneous verbal rehearsal in a memory task as a function of age. *Child Development, 37*, 283–299.

Fuson, K. C. (1979). The development of self-regulating aspects of speech: A review. In G. Zivin (Ed.), *The development of self-regulation through private speech* (pp. 135–217). New York: Wiley.

Gewirtz, J. L. (1971a). Conditional responding as a paradigm for observational, imitative learning and vicarious-reinforcement. In H. W. Reese (Ed.), *Advances in child development and behavior* (Vol. 6, pp. 273–304). New York: Academic Press.

Gewirtz, J. L. (1971b). The roles of overt responding and extrinsic reinforcement in "self-" and "vicarious-reinforcement" phenomena and in "observational learning" and imitation. In R. Glaser (Ed.), *The nature of reinforcement* (pp. 279–309). New York: Academic Press.

Goetz, E. M., & Baer, D. M. (1973). Social control of form diversity and the emergence of new forms in children's blockbuilding. *Journal of Applied Behavior Analysis, 6*, 209–217.

Goss, A. E. (1961). Verbal mediating responses and concept formation. *Psychological Review, 68*, 248–274.

Grimm, J. A., Bijou, S. W., & Parsons, J. A. (1973). A problem-solving model for teaching remedial arithmetic to handicapped young children. *Journal of Abnormal Child Psychology, 1*, 26–39.

Guess, D., Sailor, W., Rutherford, G., & Baer, D. M. (1968). An experimental analysis of linguistic development: The productive use of the plural morpheme. *Journal of Applied Behavior Analysis, 1*, 297–306.

Guthrie, E. R. (1960). *The psychology of learning* (rev. ed.). Gloucester, MA: Peter Smith.

Hagen, J. W., Jongeward, R. H., Jr., & Kail, R. V., Jr. (1975). Cognitive perspectives on the development of memory. In H. W. Reese (Ed.), *Advances in child development and behavior* (Vol. 10, pp. 57–101). New York: Academic Press.

Hart, B. M., & Risley, T. R. (1968). Establishing use of descriptive adjectives in the spontaneous speech of disadvantaged preschool children. *Journal of Applied Behavior Analysis, 1*, 109–120.

Hayes, K. J. (1953). The backward curve: A method for the study of learning. *Psychological Review, 60*, 269–275.

Hayes, K. J., & Pereboom, A. C. (1959). Artifacts in criterion-reference learning curves. *Psychological Review, 66*, 23–26.

Hayes, S. C., Rincover, A., & Solnick, J. V. (1980). The technical drift of applied behavior analysis. *Journal of Applied Behavior Analysis, 13*, 275–285.

Hilgard, E. R., & Campbell, A. A. (1937). Vincent curves of conditioning. *Journal of Experimental Psychology, 21*, 310–319.

Hineline, P. N. (1980). The language of behavior analysis: Its community, its functions, and its limitations. *Behaviorism, 8*, 67–86.

Holman, J., Goetz, E. M., & Baer, D. M. (1977). The training of creativity as an operant and an examination of its generalization characteristics. In B. C. Etzel, J. M. LeBlanc, & D. M. Baer (Eds.), *New developments in behavioral research: Theory, method, and application. In honor of Sidney W. Bijou* (pp. 441–471). Hillsdale, NJ: Lawrence Erlbaum Associates.

Honig, W. K., & Staddon, J. E. R. (1977). Introduction. In W. K. Honig & J. E. R. Staddon (Eds.), *Handbook of operant behavior* (pp. 1–6). Englewood Cliffs, NJ: Prentice-Hall.

Hull, C. L. (1934). The concept of the habit-family hierarchy and maze learning: Part I [and] Part II. *Psychological Review, 41*, 33–54, 134–152.

Hull, C. L. (1939). The problem of stimulus equivalence in behavior theory. *Psychological Review, 46*, 9–30.

Hull, C. L. (1943). *Principles of behavior.* New York: Appleton-Century-Crofts.

James, W. (1907). *Pragmatism: A new name for some old ways of thinking.* New York: Longmans, Green.

Kantor, J. R. (1921). An objective interpretation of meanings. *American Journal of Psychology, 32*, 231–248.

Kantor, J. R. (1922). An analysis of psychological language data. *Psychological Review, 29*, 267–309.

Kantor, J. R. (1942). Toward a scientific analysis of motivation. *Psychological Record, 5*, 225–275.

Kantor, J. R. (1947). *Problems of physiological psychology.* Granville, OH: Principia Press.

Kantor, J. R. (1970). An analysis of the experimental analysis of behavior (TEAB). *Journal of the Experimental Analysis of Behavior, 13*, 101–108.

Kaplan, A. (1964). *The conduct of inquiry.* San Francisco: Chandler.

Keller, F. S. (1954, 1969). *Learning: Reinforcement theory.* New York: Random House. (2nd ed. 1969)

Kendler, T. S. (1964). Verbalization and optional reversal shifts among kindergarten children. *Journal of Verbal Learning and Verbal Behavior, 3*, 428–436.

Kendler, T. S. (1972). An ontogeny of mediational deficiency. *Child Development, 43*, 1–17.

Kendler, T. S. (1979). The development of discrimination learning: A levels-of-functioning explanation. In H. W. Reese & L. P. Lipsitt (Eds.), *Advances in child development and behavior* (Vol. 13, pp. 83–117). New York: Academic Press.

Klahr, D., & Siegler, R. S. (1978). The representation of children's knowledge. In H. W. Reese & L. P. Lipsitt (Eds.), *Advances in child development and behavior* (Vol. 12, pp. 61–116). New York: Academic Press.

Ledoux, S. (1981, May). *Private events, experiment and theory.* Paper presented at the meeting of the Association for Behavior Analysis, Milwaukee, WI.

Luria, A. R. (1961). *The role of speech in the regulation of normal and abnormal behavior.* New York: Liveright.

MacCorquodale, K. (1970). On Chomsky's review of Skinner's *Verbal Behavior. Journal of the Experimental Analysis of Behavior, 13*, 83–99.

MacCorquodale, K., & Meehl, P. E. (1948). On a distinction between hypothetical constructs and intervening variables. *Psychological Review, 55*, 95–107.

Marx, M. H. (1976). Formal theory. In M. H. Marx & F. E. Goodson (Eds). *Theories in contemporary psychology* (2nd ed., pp. 234–260). New York: Macmillan.

Meacham, J. A. (1979). The role of verbal activity in remembering the goals of actions. In G. Zivin (Ed.), *The development of self-regulation through private speech* (pp. 237–263). New York: Wiley.

Miller, S. A., Shelton, J., & Flavell, J. H. (1970). A test of Luria's hypothesis concerning the development of verbal self-regulation. *Child Development, 41*, 651–665.

Morris, E. K. (1978). Some relationships between the psychologies of Kantor and Skinner. *Interbehaviorist, 8*(4), 3–12.

Morse, W. H., & Kelleher, R. T. (1977). Determinants of reinforcement and punishment. In W. K. Honig & J. E. R. Staddon (Eds.), *Handbook of operant behavior* (pp. 174–200). Englewood Cliffs, NJ: Prentice-Hall.

Mowrer, O. H., & Jones, H. M. (1943). Extinction and behavior variability as functions of effortfulness of task. *Journal of Experimental Psychology, 33*, 369–386.

32   REESE

Paniagua, F. A., & Baer, D. M. (1982). The analysis of correspondence training as a chain reinforceable at any point. *Child Development, 53,* 786–798.

Parsons, J. A. (1973). The reciprocal modification of arithmetic behavior and program development. In G. Semb (Ed.), *Behavior analysis and education—1972* (pp. 185–199). Lawrence, KS: University of Kansas Press.

Parsons, J. A. (1976). Conditioning precurrent (problem solving) behavior of children. *Revista Mexicana de Análisis de la Conducta, 2,* 190–206.

Parsons, J. A., & Ferraro, D. P. (1977). Complex interactions: A functional approach. In B. C. Etzel, J. M. LeBlanc, & D. M. Baer (Eds.), *New developments in behavioral research: Theory, method, and application. In honor of Sidney W. Bijou* (pp. 237–245). Hillsdale, NJ: Lawrence Erlbaum Associates.

Pepper, S. C. (1942). *World hypotheses: A study in evidence.* Berkeley, CA: University of California Press.

Place, U. T. (1978). Psychological paradigms and behaviour modification. *De Psycholoog, 13,* 611–621.

Reese, H. W. (1962). Verbal mediation as a function of age level. *Psychological Bulletin, 59,* 502–509.

Reese, H. W. (1963). A reply to Youniss and Furth. *Psychological Bulletin, 60,* 503–504.

Reese, H. W. (1971). The study of covert verbal and nonverbal mediation. In A. Jacobs & L. B. Sachs (Eds.), *The psychology of private events* (pp. 17–38). New York: Academic Press.

Reese, H. W. (1976). *Basic learning processes in childhood.* New York: Holt, Rinehart, & Winston.

Reese, H. W. (1979, March). *Verbal self-regulation in historical perspective.* Paper presented at the meeting of the Society for Research in Child Development, San Francisco. (ERIC Document Reproduction Service No. ED 171 398)

Reese, H. W. (1980). A learning-theory critique of the operant approach to life-span development. *Human Development, 23,* 368–376.

Reese, H. W. (1982). Behavior analysis and life-span developmental psychology. *Developmental Review, 2,* 150–161.

Reese, H. W. (1984, May). Historical and philosophical analysis of causality. In H. W. Reese (Chair), *Philosophical foundations and current views of causality in radical behaviorism.* Symposium conducted at the meeting of the Association for Behavior Analysis, Nashville, TN.

Schnaitter, R. (1978). Private causes. *Behaviorism, 6,* 1–12.

Sherman, J. A., & Thomas, J. R. (1968). Some factors controlling preference between fixed-ratio and variable-ratio schedules of reinforcement. *Journal of the Experimental Analysis of Behavior, 11,* 689–702.

Sidman, M. (1952). A note on functional relations obtained from group data. *Psychological Bulletin, 49,* 263–269.

Skinner, B. F. (1938). *The behavior of organisms: An experimental analysis.* New York: Appleton-Century-Crofts.

Skinner, B. F. (1953). *Science and human behavior.* New York: Macmillan.

Skinner, B. F. (1956). A case history in scientific method. *American Psychologist, 11,* 221–233.

Skinner, B. F. (1957). *Verbal behavior.* New York: Appleton-Century-Crofts.

Skinner, B. F. (1968). *The technology of teaching.* New York: Appleton-Century-Crofts.

Skinner, B. F. (1969). *Contingencies of reinforcement: A theoretical analysis.* New York: Appleton-Century-Crofts.

Skinner, B. F. (1971). *Beyond freedom and dignity.* New York: Bantam Books.

Skinner, B. F. (1972). *Cumulative record: A selection of papers* (3rd ed.). New York: Appleton-Century-Crofts.

Skinner, B. F. (1974). *About behaviorism.* New York: Knopf.

Skinner, B. F. (1980, May). Discussion. In D. F. Hake & S. Kendall (Chairs), *Some reflections on the development of behavior analysis.* Symposium conducted at the meeting of the Association for Behavior Analysis, Dearborn, MI.

Spence, K. W. (1941). Operationism and theory in psychology. *Psychological Review, 48,* 1–14.

Spence, K. W. (1948). The postulates and methods of 'behaviorism.' *Psychological Review, 55,* 67–78.

Spence, K. W. (1956). *Behavior theory and conditioning.* New Haven: Yale University Press.

Spiker, C. C. (1956). Stimulus pretraining and subsequent performance in the delayed reaction experiment. *Journal of Experimental Psychology, 52,* 107–111.

Spiker, C. C. (1977). Behaviorism, cognitive psychology, and the active organism. In N. Datan & H. W. Reese (Eds.), *Life-span developmental psychology: Dialectical perspectives on experimental research* (pp. 93–103). New York: Academic Press.

Stoddard, L. T. (1968). An observation on stimulus control in a tilt discrimination by children. *Journal of the Experimental Analysis of Behavior, 11,* 321–324.

Watson, J. B. (1930). *Behaviorism* (rev. ed.). New York: Norton.

Weiner, H. (1970). Human behavioral persistence. *Psychological Record, 20,* 445–456.

Weisberg, P., & Simmons, M. W. (1966). A modified WGTA for infants in their second year of life. *Journal of Psychology, 63,* 99–104.

Wood, W. S. (1978). In defense of descriptive behaviorism, or theories of learning still aren't necessary. *Behavioral and Brain Sciences, 1,* 82–83.

Wozniak, R. H. (1972). Verbal regulation of motor behavior—Soviet research and non-Soviet replications. *Human Development, 15,* 13–57.

Zeaman, D., & House, B. J. (1963). The role of attention in retardate discrimination learning. In N. R. Ellis (Ed.), *Handbook of mental deficiency* (pp. 159–223). New York: McGraw-Hill.

Zuriff, G. E. (1980). Radical behaviorist epistemology. *Psychological Bulletin, 87,* 337–350.

2 The Role of Postulation in the Analysis of Inapparent Events

Linda J. Parrott
Saint Mary's University

INTRODUCTION

Twenty-five years ago, when the principles of behavior derived from animal studies conducted under the auspices of the movement known as the experimental analysis of behavior began to be applied to problems of human adjustment, the future looked bright for the discipline of psychology. A centuries-old barrier to the development of psychology as a natural science—man's dual nature—had been abandoned, and for the first time in the history of the discipline relations among observable and measurable events constituted the focus of study. For the first time relations among behaviors and stimuli were regarded not as mere indices of some more fundamental and intangible entity or process but, instead, as the legitimate subject matter of psychological study. It appeared as though psychology would at last be able to take its rightful place among the natural sciences.

Today, however, we are witnessing a revival of old ways of thinking. The place of behaviorism is being usurped by what has been called the "New Cognitivism," a movement more aptly described as the same old mentalism that has always obstructed the development of psychology as a natural science. What went wrong?

Skinner (1974) has suggested that those who have argued for a return to cognitivism have never fully understood its alternative, and I would agree, as I suspect would most other behaviorists. Apart from sentimentality, misunderstanding has been the most noteworthy feature of both formal (Chomsky, 1959) and informal criticisms of behaviorism since its inception. And it is sentimentality that is at least partially responsible for the failure of behaviorists to guide the misguided in this regard: cherished views are not readily abandoned.

The principal difference between cognitive and behavioral psychologies concerns the concept of knowing and its derivatives, reasoning and remembering. These concepts have always been a source of disagreement in psychology. In fact, the history of the discipline as a whole amounts to little more than a history of interpretations of these concepts. Prior to the advent of behaviorism, though, the disagreements were of another sort. They concerned such things as whether knowledge was all of one piece or of many associated bits; whether it was innate or acquired by way of experience; and where, how, and in what form it was stored for later use. There was never any disagreement over the stuff of which knowledge was made nor was its role in the psychological event disputed: Knowing was assumed to be a mental process of some sort, one which preceded doing, and was further causally responsible for such doing. Behaviorism departed from this tradition, arguing that knowing was doing (or at least talking about doing) and that both were under the causal control of the stimulating environment. (See Parrott, 1983a, for further discussion of Skinner's views on this concept.) Cognitivists have never fully understood the significance of this position nor the reasons for it, and they have not been able to accept what they believed the position to imply: Namely, that man had no mind and, as such, no capacity for knowledge, reason, nor memory; and worse, having no mind, man had neither the power to will his actions nor the freedom to choose one course of action over another. Behaviorism not only contested the wisdom of the ages, which was bad enough; it also denied what was immediately obvious.

These are not the implications of a behavioral perspective. Nonetheless, to blame the failure of behaviorism to compete successfully with more traditional views on the ignorance of its opponents and their emotional attachment to the implications of dualism does little to alleviate the situation. Misunderstanding will not be eliminated merely by identifying it as such. Neither is it reasonable to assume that behaviorism is beyond reproach. On the contrary, it is quite possible that the recent cognitive revival in psychology reflects genuine inadequacies in the behavioral position, despite the failure of its critics to understand the position well enough to articulate them clearly and convincingly. Clear and convincing criticism usually arises from within.

Inadequacies in science may be traced to any number of sources; however, by far the most pervasive and devastating problems have their sources in system-building efforts, or, more precisely, the absence of system-building efforts. Scientific work always involves a set of underlying assumptions of which individual scientists may be more or less aware. These assumptions influence the kinds of problems addressed, the methods employed for their solution, and the manner in which findings are interpreted and related to other findings both within and outside a particular scientific domain. When they are properly articulated and organized into a postulational system they serve as criteria against which the internal consistency and cross-disciplinary compatibility of a given scientific enterprise may be evaluated, as well as provide guidelines for the modification of that enterprise so as to achieve these outcomes. When system-building efforts of this sort are lacking, which is to say, when a system of postulates has not been constructed for these purposes, inconsistency and incompatibility are the rule. This is because assumptions derived from actual confrontations with nature, however remote, are unknowingly intermixed with assumptions having their sources in cultural tradition.

Not all aspects of scientific work are influenced equally by incomplete systemic development. Systemic development is of greatest service when our understanding of some phenomenon requires a considerable degree of methodological and theoretical extension, since it is under these conditions that inconsistency and incompatibility are most likely to arise in its absence. The extremely subtle and transient activities of knowing, reasoning, and remembering are phenomena of this sort and the history of controversy over their proper understanding is a consequence of workers operating on the basis of different assumptions.

Returning to the issue of possible inadequacies in behavior science, to which might be attributed the cognitive revival in psychology, it is my contention that behavior science under Skinner's influence has not and is not likely to advance to the postulational stage of systemic development and, as a result, has not and is not likely to provide a coherent and thoroughly naturalistic account of complex human behaviors that could serve as a viable alternative to the cognitive interpretation of such events. The purpose of this chapter, then, is twofold: to provide support for these claims, and to indicate how complex human behaviors would be understood under the influence of a more fully developed postulational system than has arisen under the auspices of either behaviorism or cognitivism. More generally, the goal of this chapter is to provide a viable alternative to revisionism in psychology.

THE SYSTEMIC DEVELOPMENT OF BEHAVIOR SCIENCE

That behavior science has not reached the postulation stage of systemic development may not be a serious problem. It is possible that what appears to be a problem is only a sign of immaturity. Because the systemic aspects of science are derived primarily from previous investigations and findings, these aspects may not emerge until relatively late in the development of a science. Skinner (1953, p. 14) was well aware of this fact. More importantly, he did not appear to be opposed to developments of this sort, arguing that "experimental psychology is *properly* and *inevitably* committed to the construction of a theory of behavior," because "[a] theory is essential to the scientific understanding of behavior as a subject matter" (1947, emphasis mine). Nonetheless, he questioned the readiness of the science of behavior for even very localized system-building efforts (1950). We might assume, then, that although behavior science will enter the postulational stage eventually and without resistance, it is not likely to do so in the near future.

On the other hand, it is possible that the fragments of a system already developed are serving to thwart further system-making efforts. If the products of earlier system-building work are having this effect, a problem does exist, the seriousness of which depends on whether or not anything can be done about it, regardless of the intention. Assuming that a problem of this sort does exist, we may begin the process of eliminating it by examining the possibility that the effect is unintentional.

Misunderstandings of Skinner

Skinner's objections to particular types of theory building (1950, 1957, p. 12; 1969, preface) may have been misinterpreted as an objection to theory building per se (see Westby, 1966, for example), having the unintended effect of delaying systemic development. Skinner was by no means ambiguous on this issue, however. He explicitly stated that he was opposed only to certain types of theories, specifically, those appealing "to events taking place somewhere else, at some other level of observation, described in different terms, and measured, if at all, in different dimensions" (1950; 1969, preface, p. vii). Misconceptions seem to have arisen nonetheless, and since they can survive only by neglect, it is important to examine their possible sources.

A principal source of Skinner's views on this issue is the article, "Are theories of learning necessary?" (Skinner, 1950), which is long and rather tedious to read, particularly when the answer appears to be provided in a relatively brief conclusion. Skinner's conclusion to this article was not strictly, or solely, a conclusion, however, and to rely too heavily upon it as such invites misinterpretation. Although he did conclude—on the basis of the experimental material he presented—that some types of theorizing are unnecessary, he also introduced the notion that there exists another type of theory that is potentially useful for behavior science, though at some future time. This type of theory, however, is not of the same sort as that which served, in the beginning of the article, as a standard against which the necessity and utility of theories could be evaluated. Consequently, an original premise of this article—that scientific work always involves a set of underlying assumptions and presuppositions called theories—is lost. What remains, as a consequence of concentrating on only the concluding remarks, is the suggestion that most theory building is useless and the science of behavior is not yet ready for what little may be of value.

Misconceptions concerning Skinner's position may stem from another source as well. Numerous passages in Skinner's writings, although presumably addressing only objectionable varieties of theory building, have a certain indiscriminate quality to them that may have contributed to a misinterpretation of his position. The following excerpt from Skinner's *Notebooks* (1981) may serve as an example:

> (Models) evoke contemplation rather than action. The theoretical physicist wants to *represent* reality; the laboratory physicist wants to *do something* about it. One changes a model to produce a different *picture;* the other manipulates independent variables to change a dependent variable. A model is what something is to be done about; it is not what is to be done. *Model* is little more than another word for *idea—* something known by acquaintance. I look forward to greater recognition of the importance of laboratory scientists. The theorists have been sponging on them for decades and getting most of the credit. (pp. 173–174, emphasis his)

To characterize the activities of theoretical scientists, or system-builders, as "sponging" on their experimental colleagues certainly does little to promote theoretical work. Moreover, because this passage appears without a context, whereby the types of theory typically and appropriately criticized by Skinner in this manner may be identified, the passage is damaging to theory-building efforts of any sort.

Skinner's Misunderstandings

Skinner cannot, of course, be faulted for the failure of others to become sufficiently familiar with his position to avoid misinterpreting it. He may, however, be guilty of discouraging system-building efforts intentionally. Skinner was opposed to more than just theories of behavior appealing to inaccessible events. He was opposed to hypothetico-deductive methods of theory construction (1938, p. 437; 1950; 1969, preface), and although he is not alone among positivistic philosophers or empirical scientists in this regard, the reasons for his opposition are somewhat idiosyncratic. For instance, the most commonly cited objection to deductive logic is that it is not productive of new knowledge (Creighton & Smart, 1932, pp. 26–32; Kantor, 1945, pp. 182–183; Russell, 1960, pp. 82–83). In Creighton and Smart's words (1932):

> Its main purpose . . . was to furnish a method by means of which the knowledge we already possess may be so arranged as to be absolutely convincing. (p. 31)

Skinner did not object to the hypothetico-deductive method for this reason. On the contrary, he (1969, preface, p. ix) believed that under circumstances warranting its use (i.e., when a subject matter is very large, very small, or otherwise inaccessible), the hypothetico-deductive method has been productive of brilliant achievements. In the context of behavior science, however, where direct observation is possible, deductive inference is not considered to be necessary or appropriate (Skinner, 1969, preface, p. xi). In essence, Skinner pitted observation and induction against hypothesizing and deduction, arguing that the latter are suitable only for the investigation of not directly observable phenomena. As a result, Skinner believed that if hypotheses are constructed in the course of psychological study, we may assume that observable behavior and the equally observable variables of which it is a function are no longer the focus of investigation. Instead, attention has been turned to not directly observable processes of a neural or mental sort, neither of which Skinner found serviceable to the advancement of an independent, natural science of psychology.

In summary, Skinner objected to hypothetico-deductive methods in psychology because he equates their use with a disserviceable interest in inaccessible events (1969, preface). He objected to hypothetico-deductive methods because they are capable of perpetuating old ways of thinking; not because they are incapable of producing new knowledge, as is more commonly argued.

The difference of opinion on this issue is subtle, but not insignificant. Skinner's objection is formulated with respect to a particular application of deductive logic, and pertains only to this application. In fact, Skinner's objection actually applies to the use of deduction in the psychological domain, not to deduction per se. Further still, his objection applies to a particular usage of the deductive method, because it is by no means a requirement of the method that inaccessible events be the subject of hypotheses. That such has been the case in the psychological domain is a fact about the psychological domain, not about deductive logic. In short, Skinner may be credited with the identification of certain instances of improper hypothesis construction, not with the abstraction of a genuine limitation of hypothetico-deductive methods. The latter is expressed in the statement that such methods are instruments of confirmation, not discovery.

Confirmation of hypotheses or assumptions by means of logical operations is not without value, however. Particularly is this true when the internal consistency of a scientific system is at issue. Under these circumstances, the adequacy of a particular conceptual analysis may be evaluated through the implementation of deductive inferential operations; and should the analysis be found wanting, similar operations may prove useful in the formulation of a new analysis. In short, Skinner's misconception of deductive methods—because it resulted in his abandoning them altogether—prevented him from taking advantage of their regulatory and evaluative functions.

Moreover, by the wholesale rejection of deductive methods, system building is left to proceed solely on the basis of inductive operations, which Skinner regarded as fitting (1938, p. 437; 1947; 1950), but failed to discuss in sufficient detail to provide for their implementation. With regard to system building by induction, Skinner (1947) explained that the first two steps of theory building consist of identifying the basic data and expressing relations among them, respectively. The third step, which he regarded as "theory making in the best sense" is explained by way of an example from the science of mechanics. In this example, however, "theory making" is not discussed. Instead, the products of this activity are simply said to have "emerged" in one instance, and to have "appeared" in another. Other descriptions (1938, p. 45; 1950; 1953, p. 14; 1969, preface) are similarly vague. It is as though Skinner believed, as did Francis Bacon (as cited in Kantor, 1969a, p. 320; Russell, 1960, p. 82; and Watson, 1979, p. 5), that a scientific system would automatically emerge from the mere collection of facts, although a more severe condemnation of the "mere collector of facts" than appears in the following passage (Skinner, 1947) is hard to imagine:

> Most of the facts entered in our scientific handbooks are virtually hack work. Some were collected in the course of more rewarding scientific pursuits, but the tables were filled out only by the type of man who might otherwise be found collecting stamps or old coins. There is no more pathetic figure in psychology today than the mere collector of facts, who operates, or thinks he operates, with no basis for selecting one fact as against another. In the end he is usually to be found doing something else, or perhaps nothing at all.

Skinner went on to argue that we must go beyond the collection of facts to the development of a theory; whereupon he hastened to add that not just any theory will do. It must be a theory based upon facts. "Theories," he argued (1947), "are statements about organizations of facts." Although he did not say how facts are to be organized, one may assume that organization will be achieved on the basis of certain underlying postulates that "most psychologists respect" and that "constitute the beginning of an implicit theory". However, he did not explain the nature of these underlying postulates, nor the manner in which they are to be derived. The end result is confusion: Theory building is both praised and disparaged with no clear indication as to when, how, and to what end valid system-making efforts are to proceed.

Furthermore, it is questionable whether or not the final stage of scientific system building envisaged by Skinner is, in fact, a postulational system. He seems to have regarded the ability to predict and control events as the hallmark of a mature science (1953, p. 14). By this criterion the science of behavior is devoid of responsibility for further systemic development. Consequently, the future of behavior science promises to be one of more accurate prediction and more precise control. In this regard, Skinner looked forward to the time when behavior science may "move on from the study of frequencies to a consideration of the probability of a single event" (1957, p. 28).

Prediction and control are not indicative of the maturity of a science, however. They are characteristic outcomes of less advanced systemic arrangements concerned with clarifying and formalizing investigative procedures. The science of behavior, therefore, is destined for the stage of operations, not postulates. The latter stage is achieved with the articulation of postulates derived from confrontations with events arranged by way of investigative operations (Kantor, 1953, pp. 72–75).

In conclusion, there is reason to doubt that the science of behavior will enter the postulational stage as a matter of course. Some attempt is made to articulate the assumptions underlying this science (Skinner, 1974, p. 207); however, the list is far from complete and no attempt is made to relate these assumptions to those of other sciences or to science as a whole. Likewise, references to the general nature and operation of postulation are vague and infrequent, indicating a lack of appreciation for the significance of this aspect of scientific work. Further, Skinner's objections to hypothetico-deductive methods in science seem to indicate a confusion about how postulates are derived and how they might be of service once they are derived. And, finally, there is no evidence to suggest that behavior science is advancing beyond the stage of operations, nor is there evidence to suggest that it has any desire to do so.

THE NATURE AND ROLE OF POSTULATION

A postulational system constitutes a collection of formal assumptions or postulates concerning such issues as the kinds of events worthy of study and how knowledge of them might be obtained. The postulates making up such a system are organized, hierarchically, in accordance with the generality or scope of the issue addressed. This organization makes for levels of assumptions wherein assumptions at the lowest level (i.e., those concerning issues of least generality) are influenced by more general assumptions at the next higher level, and these, in turn, are influenced by even more general assumptions, and so on.

Postulates are derived from observations of the things and events of nature and, as such, are changed or modified as new observations permit. Once derived, however, they influence all aspects of scientific work, including event selection, investigative practices, and theory construction. Moreover, their explicit articulation allows for periodic evaluations of their scientific serviceability, a task undertaken by philosophers of science.

The task of evaluating the assumptive bases of a scientific enterprise has three major components, identified by Kantor (1981, p. 116) as monitorial, coordinative, and semantic. The first of these entails a critical examination of the origins and validity of established premises. The second involves coordinating the findings and interpretations of the various sciences so as to eliminate contradictions among them, as well as to guard against other kinds of problems. The third component, that of semantic supervision, is concerned with the way terms are used in the sciences, and serves to prevent semantic confusion and to repair the damage done should it prevail.

If the assumptive bases of a scientific enterprise are not explicitly articulated, they cannot, of course, be evaluated in this way. Hence contradictions among the findings and interpretations of the various sciences may not be readily detected, and if detected, no guidelines exist by which they may be eliminated. Likewise, semantic confusion may prevail without notice, and, further, because scientists always operate upon a foundation of assumptions, even if they are not explicitly acknowledged, premises of questionable origins may be allowed to exert a disserviceable influence upon the decriptive, investigative, and explanatory phases of scientific work. The end result is disharmony among the postulates, practices, and products of a particular scientific enterprise, ineffective interdisciplinary contacts, and slow progress toward a comprehensive understanding of the universe.

Postulational Problems in the Behavioral Interpretation of Inapparent Events

Skinner's analyses of complex human activities are marked by three problems. Certain implicit assumptions have their sources in cultural and religious traditions rather than observation; inferences regarding the nature of complex activities implicate the science of biology without proper regard for the subject matter of this science; and descriptions of psychological events embody an unacceptable degree of metaphor. The purpose of this section is not to provide an exhaustive critique of Skinner's analyses of complex human behavior. Critical commentaries on several classes of such behavior, among them knowing, listening, understanding, and private events in general, are available elsewhere (Parrott, 1983a, 1983b, 1984). Instead, I attempt to show how these problems arise as a function of inadequate system building and how they might have been prevented.

Problems of Origin of Implicit Premises.   Scientific enterprises arise under the auspices of particular cultures, only some of which are favorable to the development of science. Kantor (1963, 1969), for example, has argued that the two periods of most rapid expansion of scientific knowledge in the history of the Western World, the Hellenic Age of Greece and the Renaissance of Europe, were characterized by cultural conditions not shared to the same extent by the intervening period of civilization during which science failed to flourish. Among the conditions most favorable for scientific development is the disassociation of spiritual and scientific concerns. In this regard, the Hellenic Age preceded the rise of Christianity and its influence upon scientific thinking. Likewise, political power struggles between sacred and secular leaders during the Renaissance served to disassociate science from theology, at least to a moderate degree. It was during the intervening period that many of the obstacles to the evolution of psychology as a natural science arose and continue to exert a disserviceable influence. The major obstacle to the development of a natural science of psychology was the theologically inspired conceptualization of man as a composite of soul and flesh. This conceptualization, although having no basis in observation, served a number of religious purposes. First, it separated man from beast: Man alone had a soul. Second, it provided an explanation for man's most complex actions, among them knowing, reasoning, and remembering. These were the activities of the soul, which, like God, required no further explanation of where it was located, of what stuff it was made, and how it operated with respect to the material world. Third, it localized the agent of control over action within the actor: The power of the will was a power of the soul. And, finally, in giving the soul power to will action, a doctrine of personal responsibility could be maintained.

Over time, the duality of soul and flesh gave way to the duality of mind and body. The terminological change did not involve a significant change in dogma, however. Animals were still believed to have limited mental capacities relative to man. Complex activities were still held to originate in and be enacted by the mind. And the mind was still regarded as the agent of control over man's actions, through its power of the will, thereby perpetuating the belief in personal responsibility. And, inasmuch as the mind was conceptualized as a spaceless, timeless entity, it did not admit to observation and did not thereby spring from observational sources. Instead, like the concept of the soul, it arose out of religious belief and cultural tradition.

In still more recent times, the dichotomy of mind and body has given way to that of brain and behavior. This was more than a terminological change; however, vestiges of tradition are still apparent in brain-behavior dogma. For example, although the brain is possible of observation, the powers and activities attributed to the brain are not; and since these are the same powers and activities previously attributed to the mind and soul, one can only conclude that much of what we think we know about the brain has its sources in tradition, not observation. From an observational standpoint, the brain is a biological organ having integrative and coordinative functions with respect to the rest of the body. What we presume to know about the brain's involvement in the psychological events of knowing, reasoning, remembering, and willing is pure speculation. In summary, the current psychological assumptions that complex activities are enacted by the brain and that activities occurring in this part of the organism exert a causal influence over the activities of other parts, including the muscular and glandular systems, have their origins in religious speculation, not confrontation with events.

Given this analysis of the origins of current beliefs concerning the brain and its participation in complex human performances, we may now examine Skinner's views in this regard. Skinner (1953, 1969, 1974) dichotomized psychological performances into what he calls public and private events on the criterion of their accessibility to external observers. Private events are described as psychological occurrences taking place "within the skin" of the organism. Such events are sometimes conceptualized as stimulus events sustaining a variety of relations with response events, among them relations of elicitation, discrimination, and automatic reinforcement (Skinner, 1953, pp. 257–258). Private events are also conceptualized as response events, their privacy a function of their small magnitude (Skinner, 1953, p. 282; 1957, p. 141; 1969, p. 242; 1974, p. 27) or fractional nature (Skinner, 1974, p. 82). And, finally, there are references to events of unclear dimensions, which are not readily classified as either stimuli or responses. For the most part, these events are classified as responses although they do not involve muscular action. Among them are acts of feeling and activities occurring at a neurological level (Skinner, 1957, p. 371, p. 435; 1969).

Skinner was careful to point out in his discussions of private events that such events are distinguished only by their limited accessibility and not by any special structure or nature (1953, p. 257). This assertion is somewhat problematic, however, because his postulation with respect to private events differs markedly from the assumptions underlying his accounts of public events. For example, in the context of public events, Skinner assumed that behavior is the action of the whole organism as opposed to its muscles, organs, or glands considered separately. Moreover, behavior is conceptualized as "that part of the functioning of an organism which is engaged in acting upon or having commerce with the outside world" (Skinner, 1938, p. 6). Behavior is, in this sense, described as "adaptive" (Skinner, 1953, p. 90). These statements imply a postulate concerning the subject matter of psychological study having the following form: Psychology is the study of the actions of the whole organism in its contact with the stimulating environment. A postulate of this or of any other sort is not explicitly stated, however. As a result, the assumptions underlying the interpretation of apparent activities are at odds with those underlying inapparent activities. The latter are assumed to be enacted by parts of an organism as opposed to the organism conceptualized as a whole, and further, the parts in question include, among others, the brain. Had a postulate concerning the subject matter of psychology been derived from observations of apparent interactions between organisms and their environment, its articulation would have steered speculations concerning inapparent actions away from traditional pronouncements of this type. Inapparent interactions would not have been conceptualized as "private events" but, instead, as "subtle interactions of the whole organism in commerce with the stimulating environment." A subtle event is not distinguished by any special structure or nature; it is simply an event posing difficulties of observation. An event occurring "within the skin" implies a different type of event altogether: It implies a biological as opposed to a psychological occurrence, and a hypothetical one at that. Scientists always operate upon a set of assumptions. When new assumptions are not articulated for the purpose of guiding scientific work, older assumptions fill the void. Skinner's analysis of "private events" is a good illustration of this principle.

Relations with Other Sciences.   The sciences are distinguished one from the other on the basis of the kinds of events isolated by each as their unique subject matters. This is not a matter of intellectual territoriality or legislation. It is simply a comment on the evolution of the specialized sciences as it is observed to occur. Simple observations of a particular set of events evolve into more rigorous and methodical observational strategies or investigative methods suited to that particular type of event. These developments, in addition to producing a body of findings, establish conditions under which the orgainzation of those findings becomes necessary. As a result, generalizations and abstractions derived from specific findings are articulated in the form of principles, laws, and theories. These theoretical products, like the specific findings and their methods of discovery, pertain to the particular set of events from which they were derived, and no other set. The end result is a specialized science, distinguished from all others on the basis of the type of event around which it was erected.

Improper postulation with respect to relations among the various sciences—a consequence of failing to appreciate the circumstances of their origins and with that, an understanding of their fundamental differences—inevitably results in unproductive interdisciplinary contacts. Nowhere is this more apparent than in current views concerning the relation of biology to psychology. Improper postulation in this regard had its origins in the burgeoning of the biological sciences during the early part of the 18th century (Kantor, 1969). Up until that time, psychology had been relegated to the social science domain on the grounds that a natural science of man, given his embodiment of a supernatural essence (i.e., the soul), was impossible of accomplishment. With the reawakening of science in Europe, however, attempts began to be made to naturalize the soul by way of neural parallelism, and the belief arose that a natural science of man's actions could be predicted on the science of biology. In other words, the events isolated for specialized study by the science of psychology came to be regarded as capable of reduction to the events isolated by the science of biology. Descriptions of happenings at a biological level of analysis came to be regarded as descriptions of psychological phenomena.

This practice not only undermined the development of a natural science of psychology, but, by attributing to biological structures the mythical powers of the soul, it had the effect of distorting the science of biology. This is not to suggest, of course, that biological events do not participate in psychological performances. A psychological performance is, after all, enacted by a biological organism. However, a series of neural impulses, for example, is a series of neural impulses—a biological event. It is not an act of thinking or remembering. Likewise, glandular secretions are glandular secretions, not acts of rage or love. Unlike biological activities, psychological performances are not strictly organismic events; they involve a commerce with the stimulating environment, and no quantity of description at a biological level of analysis can ever add up to a psychological phenomenon.

It is important to maintain this distinction; and the formulation of postulates concerning the nature of science, the differences among the sciences, and the kinds of relations productivity sustained among them may serve in this regard. In their absence, disserviceable intellectual traditions may exert an undue influence, particularly in the face of difficult problems. The result is inconsistency of interpretation: Relatively simple activities from the standpoint of their accessibility to observers are analyzed in accordance with a set of postulates derived from observation, whereas more complex activities are interpreted in accordance with traditional pronouncements. Skinner's theory may be characterized in this way. On one hand, he argued that a science of behavior may proceed in the absence of information concerning the biological state of the behaving organism (1953, p. 36). Such information, he believed, may be expected to complement what behavior scientists have already discovered with respect to relations among behavior and stimuli, but it can never change what they have discovered. Likewise, he has argued that measures of biological activities taking place as an organism thinks are not themselves measures of thinking (Skinner, 1969, p. 226). On the other hand, Skinner argued that psychology is a branch of biology (1969, p. 221), and that the observational problems posed by private events of psychological significance will eventually be solved by technologies designed to amplify biological occurrences (1953, p. 282). It is this sort of inconsistency that postulation is designed to correct.

Semantic Confusion.   As previously argued, the special sciences are relatively independent, given their focus on different kinds of data. Nonetheless, the data of one science may overlap with the data of another, giving rise to interdisciplinary enterprises such as biochemistry and astrophysics. Under these conditions, technical terms established in the course of investigating one phenomenon tend to be borrowed by another enterprise to describe only similar or related events. One outcome of this practice is that aspects of the original phenomenon become improperly attached to the new set of events. That is, the new set of events is misinterpreted.

For example, the terms *stimulus* and *response* originated in the biological sciences. In a biological context, *stimuli* refer to the bare qualities or conditions of objects that interact with organismic structures (Kantor, 1982, pp. 66–67). Given qualities impinge upon given structures in standard ways across organisms of the same species, i.e., their effects on structures do not ordinarily vary from individual to individual or from time to time with respect to the same individual. As such, stimulus objects, and the nature of their coordination with organismic events (i.e., their functions), are not differentiated. In a biological context, they amount to the same thing. Likewise, in biological perspective, responses refer to the whole or some part of a neuro-musculo-glandular configuration. That is, they are constituted exclusively of organismic actions or movements. Such movements, moreover, are invariant with respect to particular forms of stimulation: A particular tissue will react to a particular form and intensity of stimulation in precisely the same way from one occasion to the next.

Psychological events, on the other hand, have an entirely different character. The psychological organism does not interact with sheer objects as does the biological organism. A given object may stimulate a variety of psychological performances, acquired over the course of prior interactions of particular organisms with those objects. Consequently, the relatively stable structural characteristics of stimuli must be differentiated from their numerous and changing functional properties. Otherwise there is no possibility of correlating psychological responses with stimuli (Kantor, 1933). Accordingly, from a psychological perspective, a response is not exclusively an organismic performance. It is a phase of a larger, unitary, adjustmental event that includes, as well, the stimulational functions of objects.

These distinctions tend to be overlooked, however, owing to the fact that the same terms are used to describe different sets of events across the two fields. The effect of this confusion is not felt in biology, as it was in this field that the terms were originally coined. Instead, the effect is felt in psychology. Specifically, objects, which may only be regarded as sources of stimulation from an observational standpoint, are taken to be stimuli; and biological reactions are interpreted as psychological performances. The outcome is to assume that psychological stimuli and responses are independent entities capable of independent occurrence.

As instances of this confusion, Skinner has argued that individual responses may be identified by their forms alone (1957, p. 20); that "seeing," for example, may occur in the absence of the thing seen (1969, p. 253); that stimuli may be regarded as exerting causal control over responding (1953, p. 23); and that stimulus control may be weak or defective (1957, p. 254). Responses described in these ways have a biological, not a psychological, character; and it is only when stimuli are interpreted as physical objects that they may be sufficiently isolated from responding to allow for hypotheses concerning their causal efficacy—however adequate—with respect to response events. Had the nature of psychological stimuli and responses and the differences between these events and only similar events of the biological domain been formally articulated in postulational form, semantic confusions of this sort would not have arisen.

In summary, when a science lacks adequate systemic development, the monitorial, regulatory, and semantic benefits of postulation cannot be realized. In their place are misinterpretations of the events isolated by a particular science as its unique subject matter, inconsistencies in descriptive and explanatory practices, and disjunctions among the data and constructs of related sciences. In the case of Skinner's behaviorism, assumptions having nonscientific sources are permitted a disserviceable influence on theoretical work; disciplinary boundaries are not respected, giving rise to reductionistic interpretations of psychological events; and biological events are confused with psychological events as a consequence of an unacknowledged borrowing of terms from the biological sciences.

An Example of Adequate Postulation for the Interpretation of Inapparent Events

Kantor's (1924, 1926) formulation of complex human behavior provides an example of the benefits to be derived from proper postulation. The underlying assumptions of Kantor's interbehavioral psychology are neither ignored nor taken for granted. They constitute a formal feature of his system from which all more specific analyses of psychological conduct follow, including the analysis of inapparent activity. To illustrate the role of postualtion in Kantor's analysis of inapparent events, it will be necessary to provide some detail as to the postulates themselves, to which we may now turn.

The assumptions underlying Kantor's interbehavioral psychology (Kantor, 1958; Kantor & Smith, 1975) are organized hierarchically, such that the postulates at each higher level of more limited scope are articulated in accordance with those at each lower level of broader scope. At the lowest level are the civilizational circumstances prevailing where scientific work is performed. These circumstances are regarded as the ''matrix of scientific interest and labor'' (Kantor & Smith, 1975, p. 409). Kantor held that some civilizational circumstances are more conducive to scientific work than others, owing to the types of social institutions making up those circumstances, and their relative powers of authority and influence. Civilizations characterized by powerful religious institutions are assumed to be less favorable for scientific work than those characterized by powerful industrial institutions, for example. This assumption is derived from a study of cultural conditions and scientific developments over a period of 24 centuries (Kantor, 1963, 1969).

As for the nature of the scientific enterprise itself, Kantor assumes that it is cumulative and corrigible, and as such, it is completely free from all absolutes, ultimates, and universals (Kantor & Smith, 1975, p. 413). Scientific knowledge accumulates as particular individuals interact with particular materials under particular cultural circumstances eventuating in theoretical products (i.e., laws, theories, hypotheses, etc.) bearing the unavoidable stamp of these particulars. The corrigibility of scientific enterprises, in turn, depends upon how theoretical products are constructed. To whatever extent constructions are not continuous with crude data, that is the extent to which they resist change under the influence of new findings, and this resistance is regarded as an obstruction to scientific progress. Therefore, Kantor assumed that serviceable theoretical constructions have their sources in confrontable events. They must constitute generalizations or abstractions derived from interactions with those events, and must not make reference to factors not found among the events. References of this sort have their sources in nonscientific and thereby disserviceable cultural traditions (Kantor & Smith, 1975, p. 413). By implication, theoretical constructions in science constitute descriptions of confrontable events, not explanations for them. Consequently, all conceptions of inapparent psychological performances in which such events are explained by reference to hypothetical mental or bodily processes must be rejected as examples of improper constructional practices.

At the next more specific level of postulation are assumptions concerning the nature of psychology as a science, including its relations with other sciences. Kantor (1958, p. 66) distinguished the science of psychology from other sciences on the basis of its unique subject matter. The principal implication of the assumptions articulated at this level is that the events of the psychological domain cannot be reduced to the events of any other domain, including biology. Neither can the events of any other science, such as sociology, be reduced to psychological happenings. Moreover, because scientific constructions are derived from observations of particular subject matters, they cannot be regarded as descriptions or explanations for the events isolated as the subject matter of any other science. For instance, the laws of physics or biology do not generally apply to psychological occurrences. With regard to the interpretation of inapparent psychological performances, the implication of this postulate is obvious: No interpretation of such performances articulated in biological terms may be tolerated, as such would simply not constitute an account of the psychological aspects of these events.

Kantor was not assuming a total lack of relation among the various sciences by this postulate. On the contrary, all of the special sciences are regarded as participating factors in an interacting whole. He argued further that some sciences are also related by way of overlapping subject matters, in which case findings and theories developed in one science may be relevant to an understanding of the subject matter of another. These are special cases, however. For the most part, each science undertakes the study of a unique set of events and these boundaries must be respected. With regard to the relation between biology and psychology, his postulation is quite explicit: psychological events are enacted, in part, by biological organisms, hence biological factors participate in psychological events. This does not mean, however, that the psychological event may be reduced to biological occurrences because a psychological event is not strictly an organismic occurrence. In short, Kantor's point with regard to relations among the various sciences is not that they are not related but that some ways of interpreting those relations are more fruitful than others.

The assumptions at the next higher level are regarded as the system postulates proper. They concern the definitions of subject matters and the nature and products of investigative and theoretical practices. Four assumptions at this level are particularly relevant to the interpretation of inapparent events. First, Kantor (Kantor & Smith, 1975, p. 416) assumed that, from a psychological perspective, the organism always acts as an integrated whole. The *psychological* response is conceptualized upon the prior occurrence of biological happenings involving special organs or tissues and constitutes an action of the whole organism. This postulate rejects the commonly held view that inapparent activities are localized in parts of organisms, such as the brain or nervous system. In Kantor's (1976) words:

> We never make only one kind of contact with a stimulating object. We do not hear through our ears alone, but through our eyes, also. And conversely we see things through our ears and touch reactions too. In all cases we do nothing less than act as a complete and complex person with all the numerous reaction systems which make a complex response to a stimulus situation, and which moreover may be influenced by a very elaborate setting. (p. 127)

A second postulate suggests that all psychological events are ontogenic, which is to say, they originate in the lifetimes of individual organisms as they interact with specific stimulus objects (Kantor & Smith, 1975, p. 416). This ontogenesis applies even to the so-called unconditioned relfexes. Actions of this sort are held to originate in the organism's first contact with particular stimulus objects, as a result of the natural properties of those objects and the biological structures of organisms (Kantor, 1924, pp. 131–133). With regard to inapparent events, this postulate makes it necessary to reject all explanations of such events articulated in terms of inherited drives, innate capacities, and instincts of various sorts.

A third postulate states that psychological events occur without any internal or external determiners. That is, from an interbehavioral perspective "cause" and "causal relations" are regarded as interrelations of multiple field factors. As such, causal knowledge is simply knowledge of the pattern or organization of those factors (Kantor, 1950, p. 174). This assumption removes the necessity to explain inapparent events by reference to internal or external causal agents, including "mental states or processes" as well as such constructs as "eliciting" or "reinforcing" stimuli.

A final postulate deals with the units of analysis in psychological study. For Kantor these units are composed of functional relations sustained among stimuli and responses. In other words, it is not responses and stimuli, conceptualized as independent events, that constitute units of analysis for Kantor; rather it is the interrelations sustained among these events that have this status. Kantor (1933) explained:

> A response is only one of two mutually necessary factors of a stimulus-response interaction. The response is an adjustmental function of an organism, a dynamic factor in a complex situation and not merely a fixed and static configuration of bodily activity. (p. 86)

Likewise, a stimulus is a functional affair. It is not conceptualized as an object, but as an action of an object occurring with respect to some action on the part of an organism. The principal implication of this postulate for the analysis of inapparent action is that such actions cannot be conceptualized as strictly organismic events: A psychological occurrence is not localized in an organism.

With this expansion of the assumptive bases of Kantor's interbehavioral psychology and the implications of these assumptions for the analyses of inapparent events behind us, we may turn now to Kantor's specific formulations of the nature of these events.

INAPPARENT EVENTS FROM AN INTERBEHAVIORAL PERSPECTIVE

When psychological events are conceptualized as interdependent stimulus-response relations, nothing short of a functional relation has psychological significance. Hence, what may be inapparent, and thereby problematic, are not the responses of an organism but rather the functional relations sustained between responses and stimuli. As such, the stimulational phases of such functions may be as inapparent as the response phases, and often are. In fact, so common are inapparent stimulational phases in complex human activity that it is on this criterion that these activities are isolated and organized for analysis.

Implicit Interbehaviors: Inapparent Stimulus Functions

The class of activities occurring under circumstances of inapparent stimulation are called implicit interbehaviors. Implicit interbehaviors are defined as actions occurring in the absence of the stimulus objects with which they were originally coordinated (Kantor, 1924, p. 295). More accurately, then, the stimulus objects, in which stimulational functions with respect to presently occurring actions originally inhered, are more than inapparent in such cases; they are absent from the fields in which such actions are taking place.

The notion of responding in the absence of stimulation violates the interbehavioral assumption concerning the units of analysis in the psychological domain, however. Accordingly, Kantor introduced the concept of substitute stimulation: Actions occurring with respect to absent stimulus objects do so by way of stimulation arising from other objects in the immediate situation. For example, one may react to an absent individual by a mention of his name. Moreover, in having postulated that all psychological events originate in the lifetimes of particular organisms, Kantor is obligated to account for the genesis of substitutional functions, as explained in the following section.

The Development of Substitutional Functions.   Substitute stimulus functions develop when reactions become detached from the stimulus situations in which they were first acquired and attached to new stimuli. Stimulus function transfers of this sort are by no means uncommon and their occurrence is acknowledged in other psychological systems by the principle of stimulus generalization. Stimulus generalization is typically explained by appeal to similarities among the qualities of stimulus objects (for example, see Skinner, 1953, p. 132). Other relations between stimuli may also serve as a basis for the transfer of functions, namely, their proximity in time and space. Metonymical extensions of the "tact" relation in Skinner's (1957, pp. 92–102) analyses of verbal behavior exemplify events of this type.

That stimuli share properties or occur proximally with respect to one another, as a fact about the physical world, does not explain stimulus function transfer from Kantor's perspective, however. Purely physical relations between stimuli are not the psychological events of transfer. Psychological events are conceptualized as interdependent stimulus-response relations, and stimulus events considered apart from these relations have no psychological significance. For Kantor then, relations of similarity or proximity among stimulus objects are merely conditions under which the psychological events of stimulus functions transfer may take place, and their consideration in the analysis of stimulus transfer is warranted only because such objects and their relations are sources of stimulation for specific forms of behavior (Kantor, 1924, pp. 316–319). In other words, the similarity and proximity of stimulus objects provide for a similarity and proximity of responses with respect to them, and it is through a consideration of similar and proximal relations among stimuli and responses that an explanation for the events of stimulus function transfer may be constructed. For example, if the name of some object, encountered as an auditory stimulus, frequently occurs simultaneously or in close temporal proximity to encounters with the object itself, then the acts of hearing the name and manipulating the object also frequently occur simultaneously or in close temporal proximity. As such, hearing the name of the object becomes a feature of the setting in which manipulating the object occurs, and vice versa. As a result, hearing the name of the object may give rise to reactions originally occurring with respect to the object itself, such as feeling its texture. Likewise, manipulating the object may give rise to hearing the name of the object—a reaction originally occurring with respect to the name as a stimulus. This development is what Kantor regards as the transfer of stimulus functions from one stimulus object to another. Its significance is in the opportunities it affords for reacting to things in their absence, that is, for the occurrence of implicit behavior.

In the previous example, the events acquiring substitute stimulus functions were those making up the setting in which stimulus-response relations originally occurred. Among these setting factors Kantor included organismic conditions of various sorts (1924, p. 503). For example, if a condition of violent illness had accompanied one's visit to India, a current bout of violent illness may give rise to thoughts of India in the absence of any mention of India, or other more direct form of stimulation. Moreover, the acquisition of substitutional functions is not restricted to setting factors, be they proximal stimulus objects or organismic conditions. The common element in past and present circumstances may be some aspect of the stimulus with which action was originally coordinated, or it may constitute some current action. As an example of the former, a person may react to a whole object, in the sense of seeing it, when only a part of it is visible at the moment. Likewise, an act of stretching to reach a book on a high shelf may share features in common with actions taken on a badminton court, and as such may serve as a substitute stimulus for actions normally occurring under conditions of playing badminton. For example, one may snatch up the book in a somewhat peculiar manner or think of one's badminton partner for no apparent reason.

Varieties of Implicit Behavior.   Having discussed the nature of implicit behavior and its operation by way of substitute stimulation, we may now turn to the varieites of such events. Before doing so, however, it will be helpful to clarify the distinction Kantor maintained between *implicit* and *explicit* activity. Technically, these terms refer to the characteristics of the field in which stimulus-response relations are occurring. When a field contains the stimulus object originally coordinated with a presently occurring response, the relation between stimulus and response is considered to be direct or explicit. When the field does not contain the stimulus object originally coordinated with a presently occurring response, the stimulus-response relation occurring under those conditions is said to be implicit, indirect, or substitutive. Given this distinction, it should be clear that the term implicit does not imply that the response phase of an implicit functional relations is inapparent, private, or covert. An implicit response may be quite apparent and readily observable. Likewise, an explicit response may be inapparent and not readily observable. In short, implicit and explicit refer to the stimulational characteristics of psychological events, not to the response phases of those events.

As for the varieties of implicit relations, Kantor (1924, pp. 305–312) began by suggesting that such relations are morphologically and functionally continuous with explicit relations. To illustrate this continuity, he suggested that between fully implicit and fully explicit relations are perceptual activities characterized as semi-implicit. In the case of seeing, for example, action is stimulated by objects as they are encountered in the immediate present, as well as by features of those objects not immediately present but encountered on previous occasions. For example, one may see a whole object even though only part of it is currently visible. In such cases the object participates in both an explicit and an implicit relation with the act of seeing: the object directly stimulates action with respect to that part of the object that is currently visible; and that part of the object that is currently visible serves as a substitute stimulus for that part that is not currently visible.

Of the fully implicit class, Kantor identified three distinct types: representative, substitutional, and referential relations. This classification is made on the basis of whether or not the action occurring with respect to substitute stimulation resembles that which might have occurred in coordination with stimulation arising from the substituted-for object. Implicit actions of the representative type are those that *do* resemble actions performed with respect to the substituted-for stimulus. These actions are vestiges or repetitions of previous explicit performances. Seeing an object in its absence by way of stimulation arising from some other object (i.e., imagining) would be an example of representative implicit action. Motor actions may also be representative, as when one kisses a photograph of a lover. In this case, the photograph has acquired the stimulative function of the lover such as to give rise to an action that closely resembles the action stimulated by the lover.

Substitutive reactions, on the other hand, do not resemble the actions performed when the original stimulus object is present. This lack of resemblance is because the implicit action is made up of several component actions, each of which has previously occurred with respect to a different stimulus object. When the functions of these various stimulus objects are acquired by a single substitute stimulus, the action taken with respect to this stimulus is unlike any of the individual actions occurring with respect to the substituted-for stimuli. It is a new form of action. In this regard, Kantor mentioned acts of a conceptual nature, of reverie, dreaming, thinking, and planning (1924, p. 299).

Between fully representational and fully substitutional acts of the implicit category are referential or linguistic acts. Referential acts are representative in the sense that one may say "chair" in the presence of an actual chair, as well as in the presence of a stimulus substituting for a chair, such as a picture of a chair. In another sense, however, referential acts are substitutive in that one is unlikely to sit on a picture of a chair, which is to say one's actions with respect to a substitute stimulus may be quite unlike one's reaction to the original stimulus object.

Psychological Events Characterized by Inapparent Responding

In accordance with Kantor's postulate concerning the units of analysis in psychological study, inapparent events of the psychological domain may be categorized as those involving inapparent stimulation, inapparent responding, or both. The activities discussed previously were those involving inapparent stimulation, called implicit acts. We may now examine Kantor's formulation of psychological events involving inapparent responding.

Responding to which observers other than the person responding have no direct access has been the subject of many fanciful theories throughout the history of psychology. For most of that history these acts have been assumed to be activities of the mind, taking place somewhere inside the person. As activities of the mind, they were not regarded as having physical dimensions and, as such, were not regarded as being possible of observation. Hence, theorists were free to postulate whatever they thought useful concerning the nature and operation of these activities without fear of contradiction from observational sources.

Opposition to this view arose as psychologists began to approach their subject matter from the standpoint of natural science. Skinner (1953, 1957, 1969, 1974), for example, argued that response events taking place within the skin of the responding organism, called "private events," were to be distinguished only by their more limited accessibility to observers, not by any special structure or nature. They were regarded as overt activities that had become so reduced in magnitude as to be obscured from view of external observers (1953, p. 282; 1957, p. 141; 1969, p. 242; 1974, p. 27); or as fractional components of overt responses (1974, p. 82). As such they were regarded as being executed with the same musculature as their overt counterparts, and for this reason they were thought possible of direct observation by way of amplifying technologies of various sorts (Skinner, 1974, p. 215). Skinner also allowed for reductions in magnitude beyond the point of muscular involvement. In the context of verbal behavior (Skinner, 1957, p. 438), and particularly self-editing (Skinner, 1957, p. 371), he argued that private events may be occurring at a neurological level.

Kantor's position regarding the nature and operation of inapparent response events was at odds with both the traditional and the behavioral positions. Like the behaviorist, he rejected the traditional view as unscientific. No science can be concerned with events that transcend the boundaries of scientific investigation. His rejection also extended to those theories in which hypothetical mental processes were not regarded as having ontological status, but instead were postulated only for their utility in directing research efforts. From Kantor's perspective the study of mental processes is useful only to those who regard mental processes as legitimate objects of study in the first place. For theorists operating from a foundation of confrontable things and events, investigations into the nature and operation of the objectively nonexistent are not regarded as having any utility in the accumulation of objective knowledge. Further, such theorizing Kantor regarded as impervious to change as warranted by new discoveries and, as such, constitutes an obstruction to scientific progress.

The rejection of traditional views on the grounds of their questionable scientific status marks the only point of agreement between Kantor's position and that of the behaviorists, as articulated by Skinner. In the first place, Kantor assumed that psychological events cannot be reduced to the events of any other scientific domain. Hence, he could not accept the view that psychological performances may be understood as biological occurrences. What is occurring in an organism's musculature or central nervous system is a biological not a psychological event, and no study of biological activities is held to reveal anything about what is distinctly psychological in nature. Second, the agent of psychological action from Kantor's standpoint is the whole organism, not its parts considered separately. And finally, for Kantor it did not make sense to talk about responding apart from stimulation, or vice versa. The units of analysis in his system are functions, involving both responding and stimulation.

To understand Kantor's formulation of psychological events involving inapparent response phases, we must review his conceptualization of the organismic phase of psychological events in general. In this regard, it should be noted that the response phase of a psychological event constitutes only an aspect of a larger unitary event that includes, as well, a stimulational phase. Hence, from Kantor's perspective, the response phase may be conceptualized apart from its relation to stimulation, but it has no genuine psychological significance apart from stimulation and cannot, thereby, be studied in isolation. More accurately, the response phase may be studied in isolation but that study is not of a psychological sort. With this clarification in mind, we may examine the nature and constituents of the organismic component of a psychological event.

Kantor (1924, p. 56) introduced the concept of the reaction system as a means of describing organismic action. Reaction systems are sequential activities of the biological organism including activities of a neural, muscular, and glandular sort, among others. A psychological response, at least with respect to its form, is conceptualized upon the occurrence of some configuration of these biological events. Different responses are conceptualized as involving different degrees of participation by these various reaction systems. For example, one response form may be characterized by more glandular involvement than another. Despite this admission of prominence, Kantor did not regard any reaction system as possible of independent action. That is, in no case does the nervous system, for example, operate independently or in isolation from the other systems of the body. Moreover, as previously suggested, these systems do not constitute units of analysis from a psychological perspective. They constitute biological components of a larger conceptual unit, which, in turn, is only a phase of an even larger genuinely psychological unit involving stimulation. In short, the concept of the reaction system is introduced as a means of illustrating the participation of biological factors in psychological happenings.

Psychological events involving inapparent response functions may be distinguished in part from those involving more apparent functions by the types of reaction systems constituting response forms. Response forms in which muscular and skeletal reaction systems have prominence constitute readily confrontable stimulus objects for observers to interact with; whereas those involving considerable glandular reactions, for example, may not be as readily confronted. However, for Kantor it is not response form but response function that has psychological significance, and response functions are not constituted of organismic action alone. As such, the observational problems posed by inapparent response functions will not be resolved by amplifying organismic occurrences such as to make them more readily apparent to observers. Observers have difficulty observing inapparent response functions because they have not had sufficient prior contacts with the person on the part of whom such functions are taking place and they do not thereby know how that person is stimulated by the objects making up his or her surrounds. For example, we may know what an intimate acquaintance is thinking on some particular occasion because we have observed that person's more apparent action under similar circumstances in the past. On the other hand, we do not know what an unfamiliar person is thinking because we have not observed that person's actions in the past and do not know how they are stimulated by the events of the present situation. In summary, psychological events characterized by inapparent response phases are not private response events. They are subtle functional relations to be understood not by the "physiologist of the future," but through a study of an individual's psychological history.

Subtle Implicit Action

A psychological event may not only be subtle, in the sense of involving an inapparent response function, it may also occur with respect to substitute stimulation. Much complex human activity is of this sort, making it extremely difficult to observe. Kantor did not believe it to be impossible of observation, however. As previously discussed, subtle but explicit action was regarded as confrontable to observers with sufficient knowledge of an individual's psychological history. The additional complication of substitute stimulation, in the case of action that is both subtle *and* implicit, is only a matter of there being an observer who not only knows how an individual is stimulated by objects but also which objects have acquired the stimulational functions of other objects for that individual. Needless to say, in order to know what someone is thinking in concert with substitute stimulation, we must have had frequent opportunities to observe that person's action under a variety of circumstances over an extended period of time. And this is precisely why we know what our intimate acquaintances are thinking and have no such knowledge of a stranger.

CONCLUSION

The cognitive revival in psychology at the present time testifies to the failure of behaviorism to revolutionize the discipline. That failure, I believe, is owing, at least in part, to the fact that behavior scientists have never dealt with inapparent psychological events in a manner consistent with their naturalistic interpretations of more apparent events. Instead, they have adopted a subtle form of dualism— the dichotomy of public and private—as a solution to the problem of inapparence. A misstep of this magnitude would not go unnoticed had behavior scientists developed the systemic aspects of their science. However, this has not occurred, nor is it likely to occur, due in part to Skinner's misunderstandings of the nature of postulation and its role in science.

The aim of this chapter has not been to suggest that one set of postulates is more adequate than another. The relative value of a given set of postulates is an issue to be decided on other criteria, among them the extent to which the postulates of one science do not contradict those of other sciences, the extent to which they are productive of new discoveries, and so on. Although it is necessary to make such an evaluation in the course of system building, it has not been my purpose to make such an evaluation here.

Instead, I have attempted to show how an absence of postulation may lead to problems of inconsistency of interpretation and how these problems may be eliminated by more extensive system-building efforts. My purpose has been to suggest that *a* set of postulates is better than none at all, and any well-developed set of postulates would have been useful for this illustration. I have not selected just any set of postulates, however. I have selected Kantor's postulates and I have done so for several reasons. First, Kantor's systematics are more fully developed than are those of any other psychologist, making them particularly useful in illustrating the role of postulation in science. Second, Kantor's postulates contrast sharply with those underlying the current cognitive revival in psychology. As such, they allow not only for an illustration of the role of postulation, but also for the presentation of an alternative viewpoint of the nature and operation of inapparent events. And lastly, I assume that when behavior scientists finally do articulate and organize their assumptions, they will duplicate those already formulated by J. R. Kantor. May this exposition of Kantor's postulates facilitate that process and redirect psychology toward the path of natural science.

REFERENCES

Chomsky, N. (1959). Verbal behavior. By B. F. Skinner. *Language, 35,* 26–58.
Creighton, J. E., & Smart, H. R. (1932). *An introductory logic* (5th ed.). New York: Macmillan.
Kantor, J. R. (1924). *Principles of psychology* (Vol. 1). Chicago: Principia Press.
Kantor, J. R. (1926). *Principles of psychology* (Vol. 2). Chicago: Principia Press.
Kantor, J. R. (1933). In defense of stimulus-response psychology. *Psychological Review, 40,* 324–336.
Kantor, J. R. (1945). *Logic and psychology* (Vol. 1). Chicago: Principia Press.
Kantor, J. R. (1950). *Logic and psychology* (Vol. 2). Chicago: Principia Press.
Kantor, J. R. (1953). *The logic of modern science.* Chicago: Principia Press.
Kantor, J. R. (1958). *Interbehavioral psychology.* Chicago: Principia Press.
Kantor, J. R. (1963). *The scientific evolution of psychology* (Vol. I). Chicago: Principia Press.
Kantor, J. R. (1969). *The scientific evolution of psychology* (Vol. 2). Chicago: Principia Press.
Kantor, J. R. (1976). *Psychological linguistics.* Chicago: Principia Press.
Kantor, J. R. (1981). *Interbehavioral philosophy.* Chicago: Principia Press.
Kantor, J. R. (1982). *Cultural psychology.* Chicago: Principia Press.
Kantor, J. R., & Smith, N. W. (1975). *The science of psychology: An interbehavioral survey.* Chicago: Principia Press.

Parrott, L. J. (1983a). Perspectives on knowing and knowledge. *The Psychological Record, 33,* 171–184.

Parrott, L. J. (1983b). Systemic foundations for the concept of private events: A critique. In N. W. Smith, P. T. Mountjoy, & D. H. Ruben (Eds.), *Reassessment in psychology: The interbehavioral alternative.* Washington: University Press of America.

Parrott, L. J. (1984). Listening and understanding. *The Behavior Analyst, 7,* 29–39.

Russell, B. (1960). *An outline of philosophy.* New York: Meridan.

Skinner, B. F. (1938). *The behavior of organisms.* New York: Appleton-Century-Crofts.

Skinner, B. F. (1947). *Current trends in experimental psychology.* Pittsburgh: University of Pittsburgh Press.

Skinner, B. F. (1950). Are theories of learning necessary? *Psychological Review, 57,* 193–216.

Skinner, B. F. (1953). *Science and human behavior.* New York: Free Press.

Skinner, B. F. (1957). *Verbal behavior.* New York: Appleton-Century-Crofts.

Skinner, B. F. (1969).*Contingencies of reinforcement.* New York: Appleton-Century-Crofts.

Skinner, B. F. (1974). *About behaviorism.* New York: Knopf.

Skinner, B. F. (1981). *Notebooks.* Englewood Cliffs, NJ: Prentice-Hall.

Watson, R.I. (1979). *Basic writings in the history of psychology.* New York: Oxford University Press.

Westby, G. (1966). Psychology today: Problems and directions. *Bulletin of the British Psychological Society, 19,* No. 65.

3 Response Patterns

Dennis J. Delprato
Eastern Michigan University

Observers and theorists agree that the behavior of organisms is organized, structured, or configurational simply because lawfulness or predictability of a subject matter is axiomatic to a scientific approach. Therefore, it is not surprising that behavioral scientists have maintained an interest in organization throughout the history of the science. However, it has been only recently that some researchers and theorists have begun to treat the topic in radically different ways from earlier views, which promise fresh approaches to several psychological issues. The purpose of this chapter is to address some of the major empirical and theoretical advances that have been made in behavioral organization in recent years.

Table 3.1 presents an overview of several matters of central relevance to the thesis that behavioral organization is part of an alternative to traditional approaches to behavioral theory. Because the items in the table will be addressed, there is no need to comment on most of them here except for a few introductory remarks.

First, Table 3.1 makes a distinction between an earlier approach, labeled response independence theories, and the more recently developed organizational approach, labeled response pattern theories. This distinction is founded on differences in two working assumptions regarding the interrelationships between and among concurrent (simultaneous) and sequential (serial) responses. One of these assumptions is that responses are independent; hence, any correlations between responses are attributable to organizing factors external to the responses. These organizing factors may be in the external environment or intraorganismic (e.g., biological states and processes, hypothetical cognitive structures). According to the assumption of response independence, responses are always dependent upon external, organizing independent variables. In contrast,

TABLE 3.1
Overview of Major Features of an Approach to Behavior that
Does Not Give Theoretical Status to Response Patterns
(Response Independence Theories) Compared with
Response Pattern Approaches

Feature	Response Independence Theories	Response Pattern Theories
General Scientific Thinking	Mechanism or Statistical-Correlational	Integrated-Field Theory
Methodological/Interpretative Activity	Inferential or Indicator Analysis	Descriptive Functional Analysis
Investigative Strategy	Single-Response Analysis	Multiple Response Analysis
Basic Theoretical Constructs	Intraorganismic States and Processes	Response Patterns
Subclasses of Basic Theoretical Constructs	Numerous and Varied	Concurrent and Sequential Response Patterns
Empirical Phenomena	Laboratory and Extra-Laboratory Events	Laboratory and Extra-Laboratory Events

response pattern theories begin from the assumption that it is meaningful and necessary to consider response interdependencies or response interactions. This alternative assumption to that of independent responses holds that responses are conditionally organized, and it follows that the search for organizing principles must include responses themselves. Responses are no longer strictly dependent variables subject to external control, but they can function as independent variables in their own right (Henton & Iversen, 1978; Honig, 1959; Ray & Brown, 1975). This latter point has far-reaching implications for behavioral theory, and this chapter touches on some of these.

A second introductory point that pertains to the overview in Table 3.1 is that response pattern approaches are associated with a way of going about science that is drastically different from that of response independence theories. Above all else, integrated-field thinking appears to be at the heart of rejections of response independence in favor of response patterns. Furthermore, recognition of response interdependencies entails reconsideration of traditional methodological/interpretative and investigative strategies and their implications for theoretical activity.

Third, response independence and response pattern approaches revolve around the same empirical phenomena—the events of behavior in the laboratory and elsewhere remain pristine. However, insofar as the approaches imply different investigative strategies, it is not surprising that they are frequently associated with different emphases as regards behavioral events. This is especially the case in relation to the single-response versus multiple-response investigative strategies. The latter reveal events in the form of response patterns that would otherwise remain undetected. Thus is established the common circumstance in science whereby general statements (theory) and events interact in the progression of the science.

BEHAVIORAL ORGANIZATION: SOME EARLY VIEWS

Organismic Biology

Organismic thinking in biology provided an important background for contemporary response pattern approaches. Theorists proposed this development as an alternative to two earlier ways of handling biological organization—vitalism and mechanistic reflex chain theory. Some biologists, such as Driesch (1914), assumed that the coordinated activities of living organisms imply the operation of a supernatural organizing force such as soul, *élan vital,* vital force, or *entelechy.* The vitalistic argument was countered by the mechanistic viewpoint that the integration of organismic activity was reducible to physicochemical causal chains (Loeb, 1912; Sherrington, 1906).

The organismic position arose in opposition to both vitalism and mechanism. On the one hand, this theory included the contribution of environmental conditions, as data seemed to require despite the vitalistic view. On the other hand, in contrast to the mechanistic view, organismic theorists did not set apart the organism and environment, and they included the organism itself as a source of influence in determining structure and function (Haldane, 1917, 1921, 1936; Irwin, 1932; Ritter, 1919; E. S. Russell, 1945). I have noted that response pattern theories emphasize interdependencies among responses. Ritter's (1919) call for an organismic approach to biological phenomena shows the recognition of such a view in biological science:

> The task now before us is that of examining closely and systematically the interdependencies among the parts of the individual organism. Although these interdependencies are among the most obvious and general of all organic phenomena such an examination of them biology has not yet made systematically. (p. 93)

Thus, biological theory early in the 20th century was beginning to include concepts that were compatible with response pattern theory in psychological science. Integrated-field thinking was beginning to work its way into the life sciences (see Irwin, 1932). It was to be a while, however, before theorists developed field thinking to the point where they would consider response patterns in their own right as legitimate components of the unit psychological event. In the meantime, behavioral organization was treated in a manner similar to the way nonorganismic biologists dealt with biological integration.

Chains and Internal Structure

Chains.   Psychological theories of response independence have approached behavioral organization in one of two ways. According to one approach, temporally coordinated responses are accounted for by sensorimotor chains. Theorists postulated that the external environment and response-produced stimulation (proprioception) were sources of stimuli for successive response components of the temporally extended pattern (e.g., Hull, 1930; Keller & Schoenfeld, 1950; S. S. Smith & Guthrie, 1921; Watson, 1907, 1914). According to chaining theory, sequentially related responses are independent, and they are organized by hypothetical stimulus-response chains. Such causal chains are perfectly consistent with the mechanical chains of biological theory mentioned above.

Internal Structure.   Another class of psychological theory again is based upon the assumption of response independence, but it treats spatially and temporally integrated responses as prima facie evidence of underlying mental, cognitive, or neural (i.e., internal) structure. The avowed behaviorist, Tolman (1932), did not trust self-reports as a route to mental processes, but he did not question that his rats' overt response patterns revealed mental processes that served as intermediators "in the causal equation between environmental stimuli and initiating physiological states or excitements, on the one side, and final overt behavior, on the other" (p. 2). Many writers have readily inferred mental structures from the events of response patterns. Notice how subtly the following authors (G. A. Miller, Galanter, & Pribram, 1960) slip back-and-forth between events (patterning) and constructs (cognitive representation):

> The problem is to describe how actions are controlled by an organism's internal representation of its universe. If we consider what these actions are in the normal, freely ranging animal, we must be struck by the extent to which they are organized into patterns . . . . The configurations of behavior . . . tend to be predominately temporal—it is the *sequence* of motions that flows onward so smoothly as the creature runs, swims, flies, talks, or whatever. What we must provide, therefore, is some way to map the cognitive representation into the appropriate *pattern* of activity. (pp. 12–13)

Mandler (1962), likewise, uncritically infers internal structure from the events of response patterning: "Once a response sequence has been integrated and acts as a unit, it develops a structural representation, a 'central' analogue of this new

response unit which can function independently of the overt response sequence"
(p. 417). I have pointed out that theorists have inferred cognitive or neural
structure from response patterns. Mandler's "central analogue" could be either.
Actually, there has been much translation back and forth between cognitive and
neural terminology; this is not surprising in view of the appeal of anchoring
hypothetical mental structure in brain structures (Delprato, 1979; Kantor, 1947).
Hebb (1949) and Lashley (1951) stand out here in their attempts to relate response organization to neural patterns.

Chaining and internal structural approaches to response patterns assume response independence, keep responses as dependent variables, and attribute patterning to the causal influence of independent variables. The dispute between the
two traditional positions is over the nature of the crucial independent variable:
stimuli, cognitions, or brain structure. Thus, the conventional experimental
model of scientific activity is preserved. This model is a basic feature of a pattern
of scientific thinking handed down from the 19th century, viz., mechanism. In
contrast, recent developments concerning the organization of behavior substitute
response interdependence for response independence, and they follow from the
integrated-field alternative to mechanism. As outlined below, response interdependence (or response pattern) theory is consistent with developments in the
history of science.

EVOLUTION OF INTEGRATED-FIELD THINKING

Several authoritative historical analyses of the evolution of scientific thinking
agree that it is useful to identify three stages. These stages are summarized in
Table 3.2, which presents the different terms Einstein and Infeld (1938), Kantor
(1946), and Dewey and Bentley (1949) have used to refer to the successively
evolved ways of thinking.

Substance-Property and Mechanical Approaches to Science

The first stage in the evolution of scientific thinking regarded natural events as
acting under self-contained powers. Dewey and Bentley (1949) point out that to
the time of Galileo the learned view was "that there exist things which completely, inherently, and hence necessarily, possess Being; that these continue
eternally in action (movement) under their own power—continue, indeed in
some particular action essential to them in which they are engaged" (p. 110).
Thinkers created various substances with unique, inherent properties to account
for phenomena such as heat, combustion, light, and psychological behavior
(e.g., caloric, phlogiston, ether, and mind, respectively).

TABLE 3.2
Three Stages in the Evolution of Scientific Thinking Identified
by Three Historical Analyses

Analyst(s)	Stage		
	I[a]	*II*[b]	*III*[c]
Einstein & Infeld (1938)	Substance Theory	Mechanical View	Field Theory
Kantor (1946)	Substance Property	Statistical-Cor-relational	Integrated-Field-Theory
Dewey & Bentley (1949)	Self-Actional	Interactional	Transactional

[a]Natural events act under self-contained powers
[b]All natural phenomena are described in terms of simple forces between unalterable objects; substances retained
[c]Substances and inherent properties rejected; events described in terms of components in dynamic event-fields

Galileo's accomplishments marked the beginning of the second stage and of classical science. Substances were retained but now thinkers accounted for naturalistic phenomena in terms of forces acting between unalterable objects. Newton's gravitational laws connecting the motion of the earth with the action of the distant sun exemplify this stage: "The earth and the sun, though so far apart, are both actors in the play of forces" (Einstein & Infeld, 1938, p. 152). Theorists advanced the energy concept as a new substance and used it as the basis for transformational descriptions expressed in statistical-correlational laws. The second stage was the era of the world-machine, mechanism, materialism, causal determinism, and reductionism. The independent-dependent variable model of experimentation became accepted as the framework for empirical and conceptual analysis.

Integrated-Field Stage

No longer do modern physical scientists compare the world to a machine. The world-machine viewpoint has gradually declined (Frank, 1955), although the decline has been complex and is not yet complete (Holton, 1973). Einstein and Infeld (1938) point to the transition from classical mechanics (e.g., Newton's gravitational laws) to Maxwell's equations as a critical development in the evolution of the third stage of thinking in physics. Now there are no material actors; the mathematical equations "do not connect two widely separated events; they do not connect the happenings *here* with the conditions *there*" (Einstein & Infeld, 1938, pp. 152–153). Maxwell's theory introduces the field concept, according to which events *here* or *now* are not connected to conditions *there* or *then*. As Einstein and Infeld (1938) put it, "The field *here* and *now* depends on the field in the *immediate neighborhood* at a time *just past*" (p. 153). Although the mechanical theorist attempted "to describe the action of two electric charges only by concepts referring directly to the two charges, . . . in the new field language it is the description of the field between the two charges, and not the charges themselves, which is essential for an understanding of their action" (Einstein & Infeld, 1938, p. 157). The field conception has taken physics far away from the mechanistic stage with its bifurcations of nature (e.g., mass and energy, matter and force, gravitational mass and inertial mass) to the inertial-energy concept and the equivalence of mass-energy and gravitational-inertial mass.

Although the biological and psychological sciences lagged behind physics in progression through the three stages of science (Kantor, 1946), field thinking now is definitely a factor in behavioral science. Kantor (1969) suggests that for psychology the field is

> the entire system of things and conditions operating in any event taken in its available totality. It is only the entire system of factors which will provide proper descriptive and explanatory materials for the handling of events. It is not the reacting organism alone which makes up the event but also the stimulating things and conditions, as well as the setting factors. (p. 371)

Field thinking has directed explanatory efforts in physics away from the search for ultimate causes suggested by the mechanical view. Modern physical scientists no longer consider their science in the cause-effect framework (e.g., Feigl, 1953; Holton, 1973; B. Russell, 1953). According to Feigl (1953), the field alternative to the terms *cause* and *effect* of ordinary language "is the entire *set* of conditions [event-field]" (p. 410), and this set represents "the" cause of an event. Kantor (1959) makes the same point for psychological science and further clarifies the field concept:

> The alternative to the causal construction is the *interbehavioral field*. All creative agencies, all powers and forces, are rejected. An event is regarded as a field of factors all of which are equally necessary, or, more properly speaking, equal participants in the event. In fact, events are scientifically described by analyzing these participating factors and finding how they are related. (p. 90)

The integrated-field approach regards the psychological event as a field or system of interacting factors that is changing from moment to moment. At the investigational level, the researcher abstracts events of study (e.g., stimuli, responses, setting factors) out of the complex matrix of event-fields. We now reach a critical implication of integrated-field theory for descriptions of psychological behavior—*the single response is an abstraction.* A response occurs in a field or stream of events, including other responses. The psychological field and its continuous nature make the reaction system a configurational affair (Henton & Iversen, 1978; Kantor & N. W. Smith, 1975). The investigative strategy that yields the most complete description of the field organization of responses is multiple-response analysis in contrast with single-response strategies. And the interpretative approach that comports with the field alternative to causal analysis and with multiple-response analysis is descriptive functional analysis.

DESCRIPTIVE FUNCTIONAL ANALYSIS

Although it is a truism that all science is the search for relationships between variables and that the power of experimentation is found in the functional relationships that result from such activity, contemporary psychologists follow two classes of rules for interpretative activity (see Table 3.1). On the one hand, functional relationships between responses and stimuli and between one response and other responses are used as indicators of underlying causes that the theorist infers are either outside the organism or inside the organism in the form of global states and processes. This is the interpretative activity labeled "inferential or indicator analysis" in Table 3.1 that is associated with the second stage of scientific thinking (mechanism) and with response independence theories. It is inferential analysis that has provided the foundation for chaining and internal structural approaches to response patterning.

The second class of rules for interpretative activity follows from integrated-field thinking (in which there is no place for underlying causes) and it is labeled "descriptive functional analysis" in Table 3.1. Descriptive functional analysis and integrated-field thinking have evolved in a mutually reciprocal progression in the history of science. As internal substances (such as phlogiston, caloric, and the ether) previously presumed to be the causes of worldly phenomena became the exuviae of physical science, experimentation and functional relationships remained. But now the attainment of explanation by interpreting established relationships as indicators of internal substances and properties gave way to explanation in terms of descriptive mathematical laws between observables, i.e., functional relationships (*cf.* Holton, 1973).

Because the distinction between inferential and descriptive functional analysis is not always appreciated and because it is so important for the response interdependence alternative to response independence, I briefly consider some issues bearing on the distinction. First, although it is somewhat redundant to modify "functional analysis" with "descriptive," this is recommended because psychological science has been retarded in moving to the third stage of scientific thinking (Kantor, 1946). The result has been that description and explanation are used to refer to different classes of scientific behavior, as implied by substance-property and mechanistic thinking. According to traditional thinking, explanation is to identify "higher level" substantive causes of described phenomena, and the essence of the distinction between description (observation) and explanation (law) is that "explanation somehow transcends events, [and] provides certain and *a priori* knowledge concerning their nature" (Kantor, 1953, pp. 33–34). With the evolution of integrated-field thinking, explanation became a matter of expressions of relationships between events, i.e., there is no division between description and explanation (Frank, 1955; Holton, 1973; Kantor, 1953).

Second, one source of contemporary psychologists' objections to explanation and theory as descriptive very likely is found in the ancient view that theory be in accord with supervening philosophical or theological precepts. In contrast, the modern approach to theory is an attempt to correlate sets of observations, and the value of a theoretical scheme is judged against its ability to account for available data and the degree to which it is concordant with subsequent observations (Holton, 1973).

Third, within the integrated-field perspective the number and complexity of the explanatory set of relational statements varies with the particular phenomenon under analysis and the particular question asked. For example, little remains to be said about simple falling bodies *in vacuo* once it is found that they move according to a particular mathematical statement (Holton, 1973). More complex phenomena such as projectile motion require additional equations (the general law of projectile motion), which, in this case, involve application of the mathematics of parabolas. If we go on and ask why trajectories are parabolic, laws of gravitational force, themselves statements of relationships between variables, can be cited. Contrary to the views sometimes heard that descriptive functional analysis in behavioral science impedes development of abstracted concepts and therefore obviates the formulation of integrative theory, this has not been the case in physical science. Rather, functional analysis increases the likelihood that abstract concepts used in explanations will be derived from experimentation and other controlled observations (relationships between events), not from everyday experience and culturally transmitted notions (Holton, 1973; Kantor, 1953).

Finally, it should be emphasized that the present distinction between indicator or inferential analysis and descriptive functional analysis is not made because the former eschews functional relationships. As recognized above, functional relationships have provided the cornerstone of science since its inception, for all properly conducted experimentation yields functional relationships. The key feature of descriptive functional analysis is that it refers to a set of rules for using data in order to achieve scientific products. These rules are the same as those followed by any other scientist whose behavior is in accord with the integrated-field stage of science (e.g., Bijou & Baer, 1978; Henton & Iversen, 1978; Holton, 1973; Johnston & Pennypacker, 1980; Kantor, 1953; Schafer, 1976; Sidman, 1960).

In summary, descriptive functional analysis encourages response pattern theory with the emphasis on interdependencies between responses, as opposed to response independence theory, especially because it permits the investigator to include relationships between responses as legitimate findings in their own right. Such relationships refer to response patterns.

MULTIPLE-RESPONSE ANALYSIS AND RESPONSE PATTERNS

Response patterning refers to characteristics of the performances of individual subjects; thus, patterning always refers to within-subject measurement. In the broadest sense and speaking negatively, response patterns will not be observed if the researcher analyzes but a single response measure (score) of the subject. This circumstance is quite common. For example, experimenters may take a single measure on each of several subjects or they may, in fact, record several measures from each subject but collapse (average) the scores in an attempt to obtain a representative score. It follows that pattern identification requires more than one data point per subject. Given more than a single score, the only other state of affairs not involving response patterning is a random relationship between the scores. Thus, in order to talk of response patterns we require (a) multiple scores from the subject (i.e., multiple-response methodology) and (b) a nonrandom relationship between scores. More detail concerning patterning is taken up below in a discussion of two classes of pattern analysis: concurrent and sequential analyses.

Concurrent Response Patterns

In concurrent pattern analysis, the investigator records more than one response during an observation period. The response codes may or may not be mutually exclusive, but in the final analysis of the data the responses are treated as nonmutually exclusive. At a minimum, concurrent pattern analysis requires a measure (e.g., probability, duration) on two responses within at least one time interval.

Figure 3.1 depicts three concurrent response patterns reported by Henton and Iversen (1978, pp. 195–203). These patterns were obtained from a rat during steady state responding under three experimental conditions in which three responses were recorded throughout 30-min sessions. The responses were lever pressing, observing (spatial location 1.0 cm or less away from a wall with a light that signaled reinforcer availability), and food tray entry. The pattern seen in Panel A was obtained during a signaled reinforcer phase. The light blinked when a reinforcer was available on a variable-interval 1-min schedule, and the first lever press following onset of the signal was followed by a food reinforcer. The

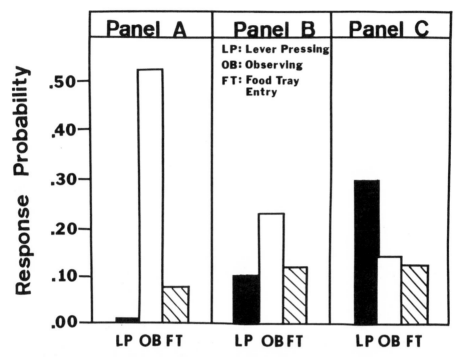

FIG. 3.1.   Concurrent response patterns obtained from a rat under three experimental conditions. (Adapted from Henton & Iversen, 1978, p. 197, Rat 2.)

response pattern is characterized by a very low probability of lever pressing concurrently with a relatively high probability of observing and a much lower probability of food tray entry.

Panel B of Fig. 3.1 shows a change in the concurrent response pattern as a function of introducing an unsignaled variable-interval 1-min schedule that ran concurrently with the signaled variable-interval 1-min schedule. Probability of lever pressing increased over that of the signaled reinforcer phase and observing probability decreased; the probability of food tray entry slightly increased. Panel C reveals still another decrease in probability of observing in conjunction with an increase in the probability of lever pressing brought about by adding to the unsignaled variable-interval 1-min schedule the requirement that four lever presses occur within 2.0 sec. In short, Fig. 3.1 depicts three different concurrent response patterns that resulted from variations in the experimental conditions used by Henton and Iversen. The patterns supply a far more complete description of the subject's performance than does any one isolated response.

Figure 3.2 presents an example of concurrent response patterns across several observation intervals. These data were reported by Dunham (1971), and the subject (a food- and water-deprived gerbil) was in a condition in which the onset

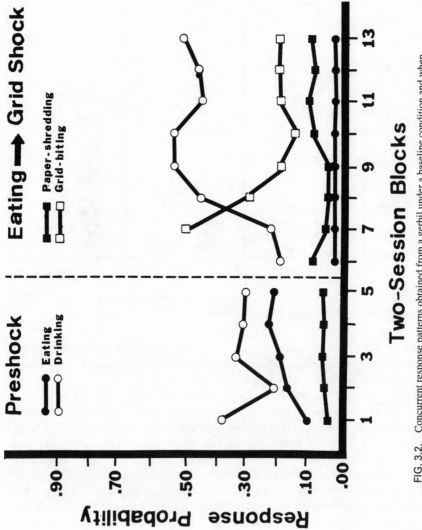

FIG. 3.2. Concurrent response patterns obtained from a gerbil under a baseline condition and when grid-shock was contingent upon eating. (Adapted from Dunham, 1971, Fig. 2, Subject 1 of Group E.)

72

of eating was followed by onset of grid-shock. Dunham recorded four responses before and after introduction of the eating-shock contingency. One of these responses (grid-biting) did not occur prior to the eating-shock phase, whereas the others (eating, drinking, and paper-shredding) occurred during both experimental phases. Clearly, the response pattern changed across blocks of sessions within phases, and it changed between phases. Especially noteworthy is the concurrent pattern change across the eating-shock phase sessions: grid-biting and paper shredding increased in probability when eating decreased.

As exemplified by the above instances, concurrent response patterns are defined as nonrandom interrelationships among multiple responses that are measured during the same period of time. The continuous nature of behavior through time (Kantor & Smith, 1975; Ray & Brown, 1975; Schoenfeld & Farmer, 1970) is ignored by concurrent pattern analyses. It is sequential response analysis that focuses on the flow of behavior.

Sequential Response Patterns

It appears that much of the discussion concerning such notions as "personality," "self-percept," and "character traits" is based upon identification of intraindividual serial dependencies in global measures of performances (e.g., Kelly, 1955). However, as Kantor (1938) pointed out, theorists typically accounted for such observations in terms of underlying mental organization. Thus, early social, personality, and clinical psychologists tended to assume response independence, and they accounted for sequential patterning with hypothetical underlying structures.

Contemporary sequential response analyses are considerably more complex than those relying upon casual observation and global measures of personality. They are also more intricate than concurrent response analyses. The basic principle of sequential pattern analysis, however, is rather straightforward. This is that the analyst looks for serial dependencies over successive responses. Quantitative techniques of serial pattern analysis fall into two categories: conditional probability analysis and correlational analysis. Figure 3.3 presents the outcome of one analysis of the former category. Ray, Upson, and Henderson (1977) observed a killer whale residing in an oceanarium environment in an investigation of the circadian structure of behavior and respiration, and the figure represents a portion of their findings. This kinematic diagram uses connecting arrows of proportional widths to depict the probability of occurrence of each type of response sequence. In contrast to the concurrent pattern analysis, the reader can examine the kinematic diagram and study the flow of responses through time. For example, the animal went from submerged floating to head-bob breathing with a probability of .50, and once he thus sequenced, he virtually always returned directly to submerged floating ($p = .92$).

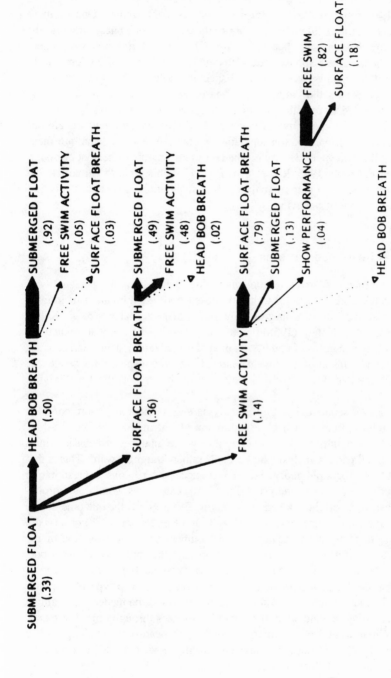

FIG. 3.3.   Sequential response patterns obtained from a killer whale in an oceanarium. (From Ray et al., 1977, Fig. 11.)

An example of the analysis of sequential response relationships via correlational methodology is seen in Fig. 3.4, which presents a correlogram for a subject's repetitive performances of a psychophysical task. Weiss, Coleman, and Green (1955) asked subjects to bisect an angle (without knowledge of results) on the basis of kinesthetic cues. The basis of the analysis was the autocorrelation coefficient (Abelson, 1953; Frick & G. A. Miller, 1951; Weiss, Laties, Siegel, & Goldstein, 1966). Computation of an autocorrelation requires multiple scores that are time-ordered from a single subject. Coefficients are calculated on these scores at various lags. Thus, the autocorrelation at lag 1 is obtained between the series $X_1, X_2, \ldots, X_{n-1}$, and the series $X_2, X_3, \ldots, X_n$, where each pair of scores consists of X_t and X_{t+1}. Autocorrelations for lags greater than 1 are obtained in a similar way, e.g., for lag 2 the pairs of scores are X_t and X_{t+2}. The correlogram (as seen in Fig. 3.4) is a plot of autocorrelation coefficients at various lags. The coefficients provide estimates of sequential dependencies, not only between adjacent responses (lag 1), but between responses separated by other responses in the time series. The data in Fig. 3.4 suggest that interresponse dependencies extend beyond adjacent responses, and that response-response correlations die out with increases in lag.

The previous examples of concurrent and sequential response patterns provide the final introduction to a consideration of selective problems and research areas in terms of response pattern research and theory.

GENERAL ACTIVITY

If an experimenter places an animal into an open field, running wheel, or stabilimeter cage and records movement scores that are not specifically related to intruded stimuli, the experiment may be described as involving general activity (Baumeister, Hawkins, & Cromwell, 1964; Gross, 1968). Some researchers have used multiple-response recording under conditions of the activity experiment and response patterns emerged in the data. Shettleworth (1975) found that relative to nondeprived animals, food-deprived hamsters showed decrements in several responses (yawning and stretching, standing in nest, scratching, grooming sides, face washing, scent marking, freezing) concurrently with increases in other responses (manipulating paper, picking up sawdust, rearing, sniffing, digging). Wong (1979) reported similar results when rats' food deprivation levels were varied.

Bolles (1960) noted that one may attempt to predict rats' grooming responses from physiological or external stimulus conditions, or from previous responses. Bolles observed rats in their home cages and found first-order sequential dependencies (different types of grooming were predictable from the immediately preceding response event). In a much more detailed analysis of interbehavioral fields with rats, Wong (1979) discovered various first-order sequential depen-

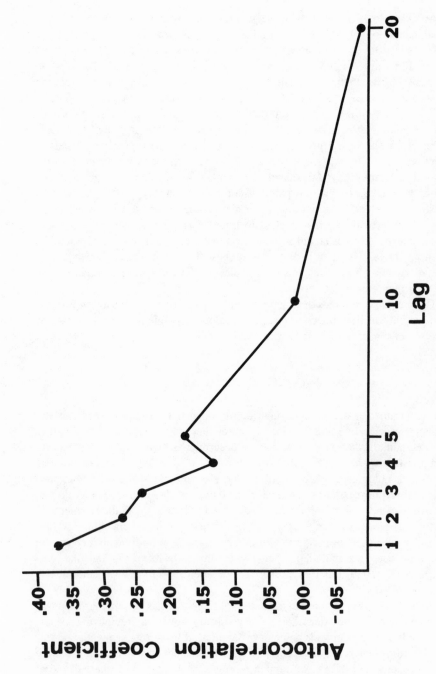

FIG. 3.4. Sequential response relationships from a human subject performing a psychophysical task. (Drawn from data presented by Weiss et al., 1955, Table 2, Subject 2.)

76

dencies involving different manipulatory responses, as well as immobility and grooming.

Bindra (1961) argued that because general activity is composed of specific, identifiable responses, it should be profitable to analyze behavior in terms of its components. Patterning such as that mentioned previously supports Bindra's argument.

CLASSICAL CONDITIONING

According to textbook lore, classical conditioning is a matter of modifying single, isolated responses. Possibly no area of behavioral science is more associated with the mechanistic stage of science than is the work stimulated by Pavlov's solution for objectifying the study of behavior. It was the mechanistic S-->R model of reflexology, as exemplified by the classical conditioning paradigm, that provided early behaviorists such as Watson (1924) and Smith and Guthrie (1921) with their interpretative framework.

Concurrent Response Patterns

In light of the emphasis in this chapter on the relationship between integrated-field thinking and response interdependencies, it is noteworthy that the first convincing data regarding the prevalence of response interactions in this "model" preparation of response independence were stimulated by an early version of field thinking in behavioral science. Zener (1937) took the position that "conditioned response behavior will vary with any variation in the organization of the psychological field" (p. 387), since "behavior is considered to be directly determined by the organization of the whole psychological organism-environment field" (p. 387). It was argued previously that multiple-response procedures follow from the integrated-field view, and this is supported by Zener's radical departure from the vast majority of previous classical conditioning experiments. Zener (1937) and Zener and McCurdy (1939) simultaneously observed dogs' secretory and overt motoric responses and found that standard appetitive (food unconditional stimulus, UCS) and negative (acid UCS) conditioning procedures did not yield simple, elementary conditional responses (CRs) that were independent of other responses. Instead, they found complex patterns of secretory and motoric responses that varied across deprivation levels, stages of conditioning and extinction, changes in the position of the dogs in the conditioning situation, and subjects.

The results of the early experiments of Zener (1937) and Zener and McCurdy (1939) are consistent with the integrated-field view that classical conditioning is always a matter of the modification of response patterns, as opposed to the alteration of isolated responses. Zener's concurrent response analyses were not quantitative; experimenters who have undertaken quantitative concurrent multiple-response analyses have found a wide variety of concurrent patterning in appetitive and aversive conditioning. Such patterns are especially easy to detect with unrestrained subjects. This procedural alternative to the restrained subject of orthodox classical conditioning techniques represents another deviation from the investigative strategies of the response independence approach. For example, pairings of a white noise conditional stimulus (CS) and food UCS resulted in food-deprived hamsters displaying increases in frequency of open rearing and decreases in grooming and scrabbling (a type of wall-oriented activity) to the CS; no changes in digging, wall rearing, and sniffing occurred to the appetitive CS (Shettleworth, 1978). However, when Shettleworth (1978) measured these same six responses following pairings of the CS with shock, open rearing increased to the CS, and the other five responses did not show clear changes in conjunction with CS-shock pairings. Shettleworth's experiments were similar to those of Bindra and Palfai (1967) who reported that water-deprived rats exhibited increases in perambulation, decreases in grooming, and no change in sitting to a CS that had been paired with water. The same rats decreased perambulation and grooming responses and increased sitting to a CS that had been paired with shock.

Staddon and Simmelhag (1971) used an observation system of 16 mutually exclusive responses to record food-deprived pigeons' performances during the course of temporal conditioning (response-independent presentation of food every 12 sec). Systematic response interactions over the 12-sec UCS-UCS interval developed. During steady-state performance, the probabilities of orientation and pecking toward the UCS wall were low immediately following a UCS presentation and these responses increased in probability of occurrence as the UCS-UCS interval progressed. Other responses that varied from animal to animal (e.g., orienting to a non-UCS wall, wing flapping, circle-turning) were unlikely immediately following the UCS, increased to a maximum approximately 2–6 sec into the UCS-UCS interval, then decreased in probability as the interval further progressed. Staddon and Ayres (1975) obtained similar patterning of multiple responses with rats under a 30-sec temporal conditioning schedule. Valuable related analyses also are provided by Anderson and Shettleworth (1977) and Innis, Simmelhag-Grant, and Staddon (1983).

Henton and his collaborators have been some of the most productive researchers of response interactions. Henton's classical conditioning experiments reveal the development, stabilization, and restructuring of concurrent response patterns in the context of delay conditioning, external inhibition, extinction, various concurrent conditioning schedules, compound CS conditioning, compound UCS conditioning, and conditioning with cyclical food deprivation regimens (Henton, 1981a; Henton & Fisher, 1981; Henton, Fisher, & Spohn, 1981; Henton & Iversen, 1978; Henton & Spohn, 1980).

A particularly elegant example of the descriptive-explanatory power of the response pattern framework is demonstrated in Henton and Iversen's (1978, pp. 314–325) treatment of the data from a delay conditioning experiment. By analyzing successively higher order relationships between interacting responses, Henton and Iversen were able to approach with increasing accuracy a description of a target response selected out of the response matrix. In this case, duration of UCS approach during the CS was poorly accounted for (underestimated) by concurrent changes in one response. Adding a second response to the analysis increased the accuracy of the description of the target response, and including yet a third response resulted in an overestimation. When the analysis was expanded to include a fourth response, UCS approach responses were accounted for with a considerably higher degree of accuracy over that yielded by the lower order interactional analyses. Such a finding is not surprising if psychological phenomena are components of event-fields, for the analyst is taking more of the field into account as the analysis progresses to higher orders of interactions.

Sequential Response Patterns

It is now clear that classical conditioning procedures alter the sequential organization of responses in addition to concurrent patterns. Many researchers have conducted concurrent and sequential analyses within the same experiment. As is the fact with concurrent patterns, sequential patterns are more easily identified with unrestrained subjects than with the orthodox procedure of restrained subjects. Indeed, the latter procedure virtually ensures preservation of the response independence position.

Staddon and Simmelhag (1971) found clearly identifiable response sequencing of their pigeons during steady-state performance under conditions of the temporal conditioning schedule discussed above (response-independent food on a fixed-time 12-sec schedule). The patterning did develop with the conditioning treatment, as indicated by comparison of sequencing early and later in training, i.e., sequential regularities evident during steady-state were not apparent earlier (when interresponse relationships were much more variable).

Modifications in sequential response patterning have been obtained with unrestrained subjects in a wide variety of classical conditioning experiments, including those with compound UCSs (Henton & Spohn, 1980), compound CSs (Henton et al., 1981), two concurrent CS-UCS pairings (Henton, 1981a), and stimuli paired (CS+) and consistently unpaired (CS−) with UCSs (Ray & Brown, 1976). One of the most detailed sequential analyses of classical conditioning was conducted by Ray and Brown (1976) who recorded 11 responses made by water-deprived rats yoked to animals that participated in an operant discrimination experiment. One analysis, similar to that depicted in Fig. 3.3, in part, revealed that some patterns (e.g., head exploration-->gross motor movement-->head movement) were transferred intact from an apparatus adaptation to a conditioning phase, but were replaced by new patterns elicited by the CS and water UCS. Another sequential measure obtained by Ray and Brown, labeled behavioral flow, specifies the rate of flow or change from one type of response to another. A general finding was that flow rate increased as a function of increases in CS-UCS pairings. The authors also analyzed the number of response sequence variations (behavioral pattern variability) and found that this measure increased then decreased in frequency as a function of increases in CS-UCS pairings. Yet another sequential measure that Ray and Brown examined was the proportion of elicited behavior changes accounted for by each specific initial (base) response. This analysis revealed that certain initial or base responses (e.g., head exploration) more readily came to sequence with the drinking CR than did other base responses (e.g., scratching).

Ray and Brown's (1976) analysis of base response-CR sequences suggested that not all such sequences are equally likely. If so, this would mean that the CR is not isolated from the interbehavioral flow; however, conventional classical conditioning procedures do not control the base response at CS onset, except by restraint of the subject, and thus do not permit evaluation of the role of the base response in CR performance. The Kupalov conditioning procedure (Henton, 1981b; Kupalov, 1969; Ray, 1977), on the other hand, provides experimental control over the base response in the CS-elicited sequence because the experimenter makes CS onset contingent upon a specified response. Henton (1981b) and Ray (1977) used Kupalov's procedure and demonstrated that variability in the detailed molecular structure of CRs was a function of variability of the base response at onset of the CS. As Henton (1981b) points out, traditional global analyses typically lead analysts to interpret CR variability in terms of random variations in cognitive and associative processes. Alternatively, and of much more value, is the substitution of multiple-response and descriptive functional analysis for speculations regarding mental processes and other unknowable sources of variation.

Response-Pattern Theory and Classical Conditioning

Response pattern theory promises a new approach to the theoretical understanding of classical conditioning phenomena. It appears that CS-UCS presentations are superimposed upon a field of concurrently and sequentially interdependent responses. "Conditioning" is not a matter of modifying a single response that resembles the UCS, of arousing mediating cognitive or motivational states, or of substitutively eliciting responses via activation of neural centers. The question is not whether S-S or S-R associations are formed. Instead of "a response" being conditioned, a matrix of concurrently and sequentially patterned responses is altered. As is the general case with response patterns, they do not provide an underlying explanation of conditioning effects. Rather, patterning theory establishes a framework for more complete and generally applicable descriptions of conditioning phenomena than mechanistically inspired substantive theory has offered.

Several aspects of the classical conditioning experiments cited in this section bespeak radical departures from the standard approach. These features include (a) rejection of mechanical descriptions, (b) unrestrained subjects, (c) multiple-response recording, (d) failure to restrict classical conditioning to autonomic responses, and (e) emphasis on interdependent responses. It is encouraging that these apparent deviations from orthodoxy are continuous with developments having a foundation in earlier events. For example, Pavlov (1927) clearly noted effects of his procedures on multiple responses: secretory and motor. He did not measure salivation because of a belief that only the autonomic system was influenced. The secretory reflex was selected because of ease of measurement and to minimize interpretation of data in "an anthropomorphic fashion" (Pavlov, 1927, p. 18). A 20-year program of research with unrestrained subjects was conducted under the supervision of Kupalov, Pavlov's closest collaborator and second in command of Pavlov's laboratory up to the time of Pavlov's death (Kupalov, 1969). And there are Pavlov's distinctly less mechanistic terms—*unconditional* and *conditional*—as opposed to the more mechanistic Western translations of *unconditioned stimulus* and *conditioned stimulus* (Gantt, 1966).

Finally, response pattern and integrated-field theory are consistent with views expressed by a number of theorists who have examined classical conditioning. Anokhin, known as one of the most productive of Pavlov's students (Corson, 1974), pointed out that "any one of the components of the conditioned alimentary reaction, as well as of any other reaction, regardless of the number of components, is not isolated and independent of the nature of the general reaction" (Anokhin, 1974, p. 399). Wickens (1940) recommended that we look at conditional response data in terms of the holistic point of view of the Gestaltists. Others have suggested that classical conditioning procedures condition "an entire behavior system" (Timberlake & Grant, 1975) or "a pattern of functionally related behaviors, not a single response" (Hearst, 1975). Perhaps the present account of classical conditioning is best terminated with a summary statement from a researcher who reviewed in almost 100 pages a large body of intricate research on the relationship between autonomic and skeletal responses in conditioning. The researcher makes no reference to integrated-field theory per se, but his data do take him to the conclusions that single-response measures are inadequate and "it might be more profitable to focus on how autonomic and skeletal responses are organized during conditioning than to worry about testing theoretical notions concerning classical and operant conditioning which are either outmoded or better studied by some other means" (Black, 1971, p. 96).

OPERANT (INSTRUMENTAL) CONDITIONING

A procedural alternative to classical conditioning is for the experimenter to make reinforcer presentations contingent upon responses. In such cases, the subject is an integral participant in the reinforcement process (Ray & Brown, 1976), and the procedure is referred to as instrumental or operant. As is true with classical conditioning, instrumental conditioning experiments typically have been conducted via single-response measurement. Thus, experimenters have analyzed single, isolated responses such as running in a straight alley, hurdle jumping, turns in a maze, lever presses, and key pecks. Despite the preponderant tendency for researchers to implicitly assume response independence, instrumental conditioning does contain a large literature with implications for the issue of response independence versus interacting responses, and it is to a portion of this literature that we now turn.

Concurrent Response Patterns

Concurrent Schedules.   The multiple-response concurrent schedules procedure consists of two (or more) schedules that are simultaneously and independently in effect, each for a different response (Ferster, 1957; Ferster & Skinner, 1957). Responses in concurrent schedules do not behave the way they do in isolation (Catania, 1966). Not only is each response influenced by its schedule, but each is influenced by the schedule associated with the other response as well. Therefore, it is appropriate to refer to this typical effect of concurrent schedules as one of "schedule interaction." But what of *response* interaction? Indeed, the major way in which concurrent schedules interactions are observed is that increased reinforcement for one concurrent response increases the rate of that response and simultaneously decreases the rate of the other response (Catania, 1963, 1966; Herrnstein, 1961, 1970; Rachlin, 1973). This appears to be response interaction or response interdependence; however, until recently theorists (e.g., Catania, 1966) favored reinforcement interaction:

> Interactions in concurrent schedules are produced directly by reinforcement rather than by interference or competition of concurrent responses. Concurrent performances, therefore, may be described as the product of reinforcement interaction, in that the rate of each operant is determined not only by its own rate of reinforcement but also by the concurrent rates of reinforcement of other operants, and response independence, in that the rate of each operant is not determined by the concurrent rates of other operants. (p. 248)

Catania (1963) developed the signaled reinforcement procedure to experimentally evaluate the issue of response versus reinforcement contributions to concurrent schedule interactions. This procedure permits the experimenter to manipulate the rate of reinforcement under one concurrent schedule while the associated response rate is held at a constant, low level. Catania (1963, Experiment 2) found that pigeons' overall rate of one response maintained by a constant reinforcement schedule (20 reinforcers per hour) decreased as an alternative schedule yielded increased numbers (0–40) of signaled reinforcers per hour. These results are considered to demonstrate that the response rate decreases on the constant schedule were determined directly by the signaled reinforcers; i.e., they do not implicate interacting responses because of the constant, low rate of responding at all reinforcement rates of the alternative schedule (Catania, 1963, 1969; Rachlin & Baum, 1969).

The results of subsequent work with the signaled reinforcement procedure indicate serious limitations with the conclusion that this procedure is not associated with concurrent response interactions. Guilkey, Shull, and Brownstein (1975) varied the reinforcement rate yielded by one schedule and recorded response rate to a constant schedule when reinforcer availability on the varied (alternative) schedule was unsignaled or signaled. Overall response rate in the constant schedule (30 reinforcers per hour) decreased as the reinforcement rate of the varied schedule increased (10, 30, and 90 reinforcers per hour) in both unsignaled and signaled reinforcement conditions. However, overall response rates of five out of six pigeons were consistently higher to the response key in the signaled condition than when the reinforcers were unsignaled. Thus, these findings demonstrate response interaction, because signaled reinforcement reduced response rate to the varied schedule and concomitantly increased rate of responding to the constant schedule.

The Guilkey et al. (1975) finding is supported by the outcomes of similar experiments with pigeons by Pliskoff and Green (1972) and with humans by Bradshaw, Szabadi, Bevan, and Ruddle (1979). These experiments demonstrated response interactions in concurrent variable-interval variable-interval schedules when reduced response rates produced by signaled reinforcers on one schedule were associated with increased response rates to the other schedule, independently of reinforcement rate. Duncan and Silberberg (1982) extended the generality of this finding to procedural manipulations of alternative response rate in addition to the signaled reinforcement procedure. A changeover in the concurrent schedules preparation refers to a response that takes the subject from one schedule to another; changeover delay (COD) refers to a period of time following a changeover response during which reinforcers are not available on the schedule to which the subject switched. Duncan and Silberberg (1982) found that pigeons' overall response rates under a constant schedule (60 reinforcers per hour) decreased as training was changed from a 2-sec COD (COD 2 sec) requirement into each of the two variable-interval schedules to when the reinforcers available on the 60 reinforcers per hour schedule were signaled (COD 2 sec + signaled reinforcers). Rate of responding further decreased when the response requirement on the schedule was eliminated by providing 60 reinforcers per hour independently of responding on a variable-time schedule. Concomitant with the decreased response rates in the 60 reinforcers per hour schedule across the COD 2 sec, COD 2 sec + signaled reinforcers, and variable-time conditions were increased overall response rates to a concurrently available schedule that consistently provided 15 reinforcers per hour. Given that relative reinforcement rates were unchanged, these results offer strong support for response interactions (interdependencies) in concurrent schedules.

Researchers recognized that concurrent schedules interactions could have occurred as a result of changes in the rate of unmeasured responses, and some looked for interfering responses such as observing and orienting directed toward the stimulus signaling reinforcement in the signaled reinforcement procedure. However, the role of such responses was rejected after experimenters failed to observe them (Catania, 1969; Rachlin & Baum, 1969). On the other hand, Henton and Iversen (1978) suggested that earlier methods used to identify observing responses were insensitive, and they reevaluated the question. Indeed, the rather extensive literature on subjects' orienting and approach responses to stimuli paired with particular response-independent reinforcers (sign-tracking) suggests that it is highly likely that similar responses would occur to the signal with signaled reinforcement (Hearst & Jenkins, 1974). Henton and Iversen (1978) report several experiments in their monograph that show an inverse relationship between variable-interval responding and concurrent observing responses. Iversen's (1981) additional confirmatory data reiterate that rejection of interacting responses on the basis of limited observational methods is a hazardous maneuver.

The research that is now available on concurrent schedule interactions no longer warrants adherence to the original reinforcement interaction-response independence position (Catania, 1966). It appears that many instances of concurrent schedule interactions are described by patterns of ongoing responses. Given the distinction made in this chapter between the mechanical and integrated-field approaches to science and its relationship to response independence and response pattern theories (Table 3.1), it is worthwhile to consider the early resistance to concurrent responses as independent variables. The initial accounts of concurrent schedule interactions may have stressed reinforcement as the critical independent variable, not because empirical evidence favored reinforcement over concurrent responses, but because the former more readily fit the classical mechanical framework. Reinforcement seems to be more under the control of the experimenter than do concurrent responses; thus, reinforcement is a more obvious choice for the independent variable (cause) half of the classic cause-effect model of mechanism. Such a view ignores that reinforcement is not independent of the responding organism. For example, a response-independent schedule of food presentation merely describes a rule for delivery of food; it does not imply that the subject will not respond to the food when it is delivered. Whatever the schedule of reinforcement, the variable controlled by the experimenter's response will be behaviorally effective to the extent that the subject's behavior is changed by the reinforcer (Denny & Adelman, 1955; Dunham, 1977; Glickman, 1973; Glickman & Schiff, 1967; Henton et al., 1981; Killeen, 1975; Staddon, 1977). In concurrent variable-interval variable-time schedules, for example, food-elicited responses apparently can provide the foundation for responses that interfere with variable-interval performance (Hearst & Jenkins, 1974; Henton & Iversen, 1978). In these cases, more generalizable functional relationships seem to hold for the subject's concurrent response-ongoing response relationship than between the experimenter's food-delivery response and the subject's ongoing response. From the integrated-field perspective, the subject's responses are legitimate components of the event-field under analysis and, as such, are acceptable candidates for all components of functional relationships that describe the event-field. In short, integrated-field theory, in contrast with the earlier mechanistic approach, finds acceptable explanation in organisms' interbehavioral relationships.

Collateral Responses. The literature contains numerous instances of responses that (a) were not explicitly reinforced and (b) occurred concurrently with response-dependent and response-independent schedules of reinforcement (Dunham, 1971; Falk, 1977; Hearst & Jenkins, 1974; Henton & Iversen, 1978; Lyon, 1982; Staddon, 1977; Staddon & Simmelhag, 1971; Wilson & Keller, 1953). Some of the response interactions already mentioned (e.g., Staddon & Simmelhag, 1971) have involved these collateral responses. It appears that collateral responses enter into patterns of interdependency with ongoing, reinforced responses.

If the concurrent schedules experiment is modified such that the schedules, each with a discriminable stimulus, are successively alternated by the experimenter, a multiple-schedules experiment is defined (Ferster & Skinner, 1957). Like concurrent schedules, multiple schedules yield schedule interactions (Reynolds, 1961). One of these interactions, positive behavioral contrast, is of interest here because researchers evidently have implicated interactions between concurrent collateral responses and reinforced responses in this type of multiple-schedule interaction. Suppose pigeons are first trained in multiple schedules with identical reinforcement densities, e.g., multiple variable-interval 1-min variable-interval 1-min, until response rate stabilizes. Next, one schedule remains unchanged but the other is changed to extinction, i.e., multiple variable-interval 1-min extinction. Positive contrast refers to the common finding of an increased response rate in the unchanged schedule component that accompanies the decreased response rate to the changed (now extinction) component. This is the pattern of response rate change that occurs when the same schedule change is made with concurrent schedules, and it now seems that time allocated to one response subtracts from the time available for responding to the other concurrent response (see previous). However, because multiple schedules are programmed sequentially, the time allocated to responding in one component cannot directly influence the time available for responding in the other temporally adjacent component. Thus, response interactions between the reinforced responses in the two components of multiple schedules are perforce impossible.

Henton and Iversen (1978, pp. 227–235) hypothesized that collateral responding would covary with reinforced response changes in multiple variable-interval extinction schedules. To test this, rats' lever-press responses were reinforced on a variable-interval 1-min schedule in the presence of a houselight throughout the experiment, and the collateral response of wheel running was recorded concurrently. The major finding was that when a single variable-interval schedule was changed to multiple variable-interval extinction, probability of lever pressing in the variable-interval component increased (positive contrast) and wheel running decreased in this component, but wheel running increased in the extinction component concomitantly with the decrease in probability of lever pressing. On the other hand, when wheel running was restricted to the variable-interval component in another phase when the wheel was locked during the extinction component, wheel running competed with variable-interval lever pressing and positive contrast was attenuated. Results such as these suggest that schedule interactions across sequential components of multiple variable-interval extinction schedules may be functionally related to interactions between the reinforced response and concurrent collateral responses within each schedule component. This conclusion is supported by the outcome of Hinson and Staddon's (1978) procedurally similar experiment.

Experimenters have obtained concurrent interactions between operant and collateral responses when they simultaneously recorded both types of response within simple reinforcement schedules. In an experiment by Skinner and Morse (1957), rats' collateral wheel running predominated during low rates of lever pressing reinforced on a fixed-interval schedule. Conversely, rate of wheel running was low when high rates of lever pressing occurred. An elementary question raised by such findings is whether collateral responses enter into relationships with reinforced responses as independent variables (response interdependence) or merely by way of changes in reinforcement schedules or underlying states. The results of several experiments favor the former. The distinguishing features of these experiments is that experimenters directly manipulated collateral responding and obtained systematic variations of concurrent, reinforced responses. In one experiment, Iversen (1976) manipulated rats' collateral licking by varying the contents of a bottle that subjects could access by way of a tube located in the experimental chamber. Rate of lever pressing, reinforced on a fixed-ratio schedule, was inversely related to duration of collateral licking. In another experiment, Henton and Iversen (1978, pp. 263–268) manipulated collateral licking by means of a retractable drinking tube that was inserted at different locations within a fixed-ratio schedule. The effect of varying opportunity for licking in this way was that the "post-reinforcement pause" that typically occurs in periodic reinforcement schedules was shortened, and pauses occurred at the location of experimenter-determined collateral licking in the schedule. Thus, fixed-ratio lever pressing was functionally related to collateral licking.

Other researchers have obtained increased rates of reinforced lever pressing when collateral drinking rates were suppressed by making the water mildly aversive (Wayner & Greenberg, 1972) or by preventing access to water (Clark, 1962; Colotla & Keehn, 1975; Segal & Bandt, 1966). Decreased rates of lever pressing occurred concomitantly with increased licking rates when access to water was restricted to the final 10 sec of a fixed-interval schedule (Gilbert, 1974).

Demonstrations of concurrent interactions between reinforced and collateral responses in multiple and simple operant schedules greatly extend the scope of response pattern theory and the associated integrated-field approach. Whatever the eventual outcome of the notion of collateral responses, their recognition very much typifies field analyses. As long as experimenters at least perused their data, and especially when they observed their subjects, it became clear that referent responses are always components of integrated multiresponse contexts. This observation has led to some of the most radical departures to date from orthodox methodological and investigative strategies that are especially evident in work treating responses as independent variables. Associated with this has been descriptive functional analysis wherein experimenters described systematic relationships between responses.

Sequential Response Patterns

Sequences of instrumental responses have provided a classic research and theoretical problem in behavioral science. The problem is inherent in the theory of associationism, which became regarded as a universal principle for all psychological phenomena (Kantor, 1924). Early researchers studied the development of serial response sequences with human verbal responses (Ebbinghaus, 1885/1913) and with rats in mazes (Small, 1900). It was the continuous and integrated nature over time of organismic acts that stimulated theorists to apply the biological notion of reflex chains (e.g., Sherrington, 1906) to psychological behavior (e.g., Hull, 1930, 1931; Skinner, 1934; Smith & Guthrie, 1921; Watson, 1907, 1914). And some early theorists (e.g., Hunter, 1920; Lashley, 1917; Schlosberg & Katz, 1943) did consider the possibility that some sequences of action are better viewed as patterned rather than as composed of individual stimulus-response units.

Theorists have objected to the chaining hypothesis on several grounds. Morse (1966) alleged that it requires hypothetical stimuli, and Kelleher (1966) followed with the objection that the theory is inherently untestable because it is based on purely inferred stimuli. Lashley (1917) rejected the general applicability of chaining on the basis that certain organized movements may be executed so quickly that there is insufficient time for impulses from one movement component to get back to the brain before the next component is initiated. Lashley (1951) added that the number of combinations of individual components was often too great to be organized by combinations of direct associations. Others pointed to data that indicate precise movement sequences do not require interoceptive and exteroceptive feedback (Lashley, 1917; Taub & Berman, 1968).

The chaining hypothesis of sequentially patterned responses maintains the individual response as the basic unit. It follows that in operant conditioning, reinforcement acts on the immediately preceding response. Alternatively, it may be that reinforcement operates on units that are patterns of responses (e.g., Morse, 1966; Shimp, 1975, 1976, 1979, 1981, 1982; Zeiler, 1977). Shimp (1976) has argued that patterning is but one subclass of response organization and that other classes are found in phenomena such as "subjective organization" in human free-recall experiments (Tulving, 1962, 1964) and "chunking" in tests of immediate memory (G. A. Miller, 1956).

Unrequired Emergence and Alteration of Sequences. Miller and Frick (1949) proposed that when investigators ignore sequential realtionships, this is tantamount to assuming that successive responses are independent. Frick and G. A. Miller (1951) argued that analysis of response rate alone in a typical operant conditioning experiment may leave important data undetected, and they proceeded to examine response sequences of rats' bar presses and approaches to the food tray during successive baseline, conditioning, and extinction phases. Frick and Miller's analysis revealed orderly patterns and changes in patterns of bar presses and food-tray approach responses within and between sessions even though the reinforcement contingency did not require such patterns and changes. For example, during baseline, perseveration (e.g., bar press followed by bar press) generally occurred. When food was made contingent on every bar press, not only did rate of bar pressing increase but sequential patterning also drastically changed. Specifically, bar-press to tray-approach and tray-approach to bar-press sequences increased in probability during conditioning. Extinction was accompanied by a gradual approach to random sequencing of the two responses prior to a return to a pattern somewhat approximating that of baseline. The reproducibility of Frick and Miller's results was confirmed by Millenson and Hurwitz (1961).

The tendency for serially related responses to pattern despite the requirements of reinforcement contingencies receives strong support from experiments that required a specified number of responses (key pecks) to each of two keys for reinforcement. Although the order of the two responses was unrelated to the reinforcement contingency, with continued training pigeons developed stereotyped sequences of pecking each key the three (Vogel & Annau, 1973) or four (Schwartz, 1980) times required for reinforcement. Schwartz (1980) also tested for extinction effects and found decreases in patterning.

The literature shows many additional instances of the development and alteration of sequential patterning irrespective of the requirements of reinforcement contingencies. Some of most familiar of these patterns are seen in the cumulative record generated by different reinforcement schedules. Even though reinforcement is contingent upon the occurrence of a specific response (not upon a pattern) in interval and ratio schedules, distinctive patterns, such as the fixed-interval scallop, develop (e.g., Ferster & Skinner, 1957; Kelleher, 1966; Zeiler, 1977). Although the cumulative record provides a useful picture of patterned responding, molecular analyses of performance reveal even more detailed sequential response patterns. For example, Williams (1968) examined rats' fixed-interval and fixed-ratio responding only at steady rate performance (at the "terminal rate" toward the end of interreinforcement intervals) and found that serially adjacent interresponse times (the time between two successive responses) were sequentially dependent. Wertheim (1965) reported similar sequential dependencies in unsignaled avoidance with rats. In other words, the microanalysis of responding uncovered sequential patterns not evident in even the cumulative record (also see Weiss, 1970; Weiss, 1981; Weiss et al., 1966).

The fine structure of behavior as revealed in Williams' and Wertheim's data is of particular significance if the science of behavior is to continue on the road to ever more complete descriptive accounts of its subject matter. This point is exemplified by work evaluating molecular sequential response patterns as possibly critical factors in matching. The matching problem considered here derives from the two-response concurrent schedules experiment discussed above. Specifically, Herrnstein (1961) found that when several different pairs of variable-interval schedules were used with a brief changeover delay and overall session data were analyzed (molar analysis), pigeons matched the relative frequency of reinforcement on the two keys. That is, the proportion of responses to a key equaled or matched the proportion of reinforcements the key delivered (the number of responses to a key divided by the total number of responses to both keys equaled the number of reinforcements delivered by the key divided by the total number of reinforcements delivered by both keys). A large number of experiments have reproduced Herrnstein's original finding, and the matching law appears to be an accurate description of choice in concurrent intervals performance over a wide variety of conditions and species (de Villiers, 1977; Timberlake, 1982). But is the matching law as complete a description of choice as presently possible?

Shimp (1966) proposed that in the concurrent schedules and other probability learning situations "there exists a unique [maximizing] sequence of choices [responses] such that each choice is of the alternative that momentarily has the greater probability of reinforcement" (p. 449), and it is this sequence that develops and produces overall matching. Thus, Shimp's view is that choice is more completely described by the molecular maximizing response sequence than by molar matching. If this is so, it should be possible to detect sequential response patterns that track the changing probabilities of reinforcement during experiments. Experimenters have reported patterning consistent with the maximizing sequence (Shimp, 1966; Silberberg, Hamilton, Ziriax, & Casey, 1978; Silberberg & Ziriax, 1982). Even though there is by no means universal agreement with the maximizing sequence description of choice (e.g., Nevin, 1969, 1979, 1982), continued work on the issue should prove exciting for response pattern theory in general.

Reinforced Sequences. The numerous cases in the literature of the emergence of sequential response patterns in the absence of reinforcement contingency requirements are supplemented by demonstrations of the modification of sequential patterning via explicit contingencies. Early views of Hunter (1920) and Lashley (1917) suggested that it should be possible to treat sequences of individual response occurrences as units in and of themselves, and Skinner (1938) applied this thinking in a discussion of extinction (cf. Denny, Wells, & Maatsch, 1957; Mowrer & Jones, 1945).

The tendency noted previously for many theorists to infer brain or mental structures from response patterning is clearly evident in discussions regarding one of the first classes of experiment on reinforced sequential patterns. Hunter (1920) attempted to directly attack experimentally the chaining hypothesis with the double alternation problem. With the temporal maze, in which each arm of the T-choice point lead back to the starting point, and the appropriate manipulation of its doors, the experimenter could require the subject to complete a sequence of turns at the choice point prior to the presentation of a reinforcer. In the double alternation problem, the subject is required to complete a circuit or sequence of turning right, right, left, left. Since exteroceptive and interoceptive cues are irrelevant in such a task, it seemed that successful performance must be the outcome of symbolic, brain, or at least some lingering physiological states (Hunter, 1920; Hunter & Hall, 1941; Schlosberg & Katz, 1943). Such dreary theorization did stimulate researchers to demonstrate that sequential response patterns could function as reinforceable units. For example, successful double alternation performance was accomplished by raccoons (Hunter, 1928), monkeys (Gellermann, 1931), cats (Karn & Patton, 1939), and rats—when they lever pressed (Schlosberg & Katz, 1943).

Many operant experiments demonstrate the alteration of response sequences as a function of contingent reinforcement. Interresponse time is a reinforceable unit (e.g., Morse, 1966; Wilson & Keller, 1953; Zeiler, 1977). In a spaced interresponse time schedule, reinforcement is contingent on a response that follows a specified period of time without the response. The spaced interresponse time schedule and the double alternation problem represent the reinforcement of what have been referred to as complex operants (Catania, 1968). The notion of complex operants recognizes sequential response patterns, because it simply means that the reinforcement contingency is based on the occurrence of sequences of responses as a unit. Second-order schedules also have been used to investigate response sequences. Kelleher (1966) defined a second-order schedule as "one in which the behavior specified by a schedule contingency is treated as a unitary response [complex operant] that is itself reinforced according to some schedule of primary reinforcement" (p. 181). Reviews of second-order schedules by Kelleher (1966) and Gollub (1977) should be consulted by the reader interested in sequential patterning in relation to conditioned reinforcement.

Experimenters have modified various other patterns of response sequences via explicit reinforcement contingencies. Ferster (1958) successfully trained a chimpanzee to press two keys in the sequence left, left, left, right. Grayson and Wasserman (1979) showed that pigeons varied the sequences of pecking two keys in correspondence with the particular two-peck sequence that was followed by food reinforcement. Shimp (1981) and Fetterman and Stubbs (1982) varied the frequencies with which various two-peck sequences were followed by reinforcement and found that pigeons' relative performances of the different sequences depended on the relative reinforcement rates for the sequences. The output of the sequential patterns tended to follow the relative frequencies of reinforcement. In another example of sequential patterns defined by combinations of discrete responses, Shimp (1982) reinforced on a variable-interval schedule pigeons' changeover responses from the left to the right key following either two or four pecks on the left or following either two or eight pecks on the left. Changeovers were likely to occur only when they terminated sequences approximating the lengths of reinforced ones.

Shimp (1973) treated pigeons' interresponse times as units and reinforced with different frequencies four sequences of short (1.0–2.0 sec) and long (3.0–4.5 sec) times. Examination of relative frequencies indicated that the complex sequences defined by temporal duration occurred more frequently when they were more frequently reinforced, and conditional relative frequency analyses suggested that successive interresponse times were not independent.

The emergence of the fixed-interval scallop even though unrequired by the reinforcement contingencies was mentioned above. Hawkes and Shimp (1975) explictly reinforced sequential patterns similar to "scallops." Specifically, they required pigeons to approximate a constant rate of change (either increasing or decreasing) of key pecking within 5-sec trials. The birds' performance varied as a function of the particular pattern that was reinforced. Wasserman (1977) obtained results in agreement with those of Hawkes and Shimp.

Response Pattern Theory and Operant Conditioning. It is possible to distinguish between response independence and response pattern approaches to operant conditioning on the basis of several points of emphasis. Although response pattern thinking has been evident in the area virtually since its inception, the predominant position has been one of response independence; thus, general adoption of response interdependencies entails departures from orthodox practices and views. A fundamental difference in emphasis from that of conventional operant thinking suggested by response pattern theory is further movement away from the reflexological foundations of the area. At the least, the Response = f(Stimulus) formula is enlarged to include Response = f(Response).

Given that science is a search for functional relationships, an elementary question pertains to the units that we use to define behavior. The conventional operant unit is the instantaneous response (e.g., lever press, key peck). Response pattern theory, on the other hand, suggests that patterns of responding can function as fundamental units in their own right (Hearst, 1975; Morse, 1966; Shimp, 1975, 1979). Actually, because operant researchers and theorists follow the position of radical behaviorism that units are always functionally defined (Branch, 1977; Marr, 1979), response patterns have gradually entered into operant theory as units, beginning with Skinner (1938, p. 300ff.). Nonetheless, writers have not always taken into account the full implications of patterning. The conventional operant framework is stimulus-response-consequence (S-R-C). Response pattern theory suggests that this be expanded to at least S-(R-R)-C to recognize the multiple-response nature of the fundamental action unit.

Another aspect of operant analysis is need of further development should response interdependence be substituted for response independence is the microanalysis of behavior (Henton & Iversen, 1978; Shimp, 1975, 1978, 1979; Weiss, 1970). The typical operant analysis is of averaged data whereby responses are sampled and averaged over time. Shimp (1975, 1978, 1979, 1982) has strongly argued that analysis of mean rates of instantaneous responses presupposes response independence and shields the assumption from discordant observations. Shimp suggests the substitution of microanalysis of the local patterning of responding for averaged data is compatible with Skinner's original emphasis on precise analyses rather than inferential analyses—''Skinner's well-known warning that a curve averaged over Ss may be unrepresentative of individual Ss is, in generalized form, appropriate here: A curve averaged over responses from a single S may be unrepresentative even of that S's individual responses'' (Shimp, 1969, p. 101). Clearly, it is only possible to evaluate the role of response patterns if the proper measurements are taken. The availability of sophisticated observational tools such as computers (e.g., Weiss et al., 1966) that no longer make impossible or extremely tedious the recording of detailed patterns, in combination with the functional orientation noted above, no doubt will contribute greatly to the development of response pattern theory in operant work. According to response pattern theory, reinforcement operates on sequential and concurrent patterns of responses, not instantaneous responses. Rather than strengthening stimulus-response bonds, expectancies, or isolated responses, when reinforcers are intruded into the behavioral field they restructure concurrent and sequential patterns of responses. The effect of reinforcers varies as a function of ongoing responses, setting factors, and the subject's developmental history. Reinforcement is no longer viewed as a unique force or power. Instead, it is one of the many kinds of conditions that alter the interbehavioral field (Kantor, 1970). This is a terse statement regarding reinforcement in relation to response pattern theory, but it is compatible with other positions more fully developed elsewhere that offer alternatives to the conventional accounts of reinforcement (e.g., Denny & Adelman, 1955; Glickman, 1973; Killeen, 1975; Morse & Kelleher, 1977; Premack, 1959; Ray & Brown, 1975; Schoenfeld, 1978).

BEHAVIORAL DECREMENTS

Behavioral decrements not attributable to physical impairments represent one of the most persistent problem areas in behavioral science. Theories of behavioral decrements fall into two classes. One postulates global intraorganismic states and/or processes that singly or in interaction with one another mediate decrements. This class of theory has predominated in the history of psychological theorizing in the form of motivational, emotional, cognitive, and other substantive constructs. The other approach to decrements emphasizes response interdependencies. According to this alternative to traditional theory, a decrement in a measured response implicates at least one other potentially measurable response. For example, although typical accounts of punishment and extinction have treated these only as response decrementing procedures, the response patterns view emphasizes that decremental effects associated with these procedures are accompanied by increments in antagonistic or alternative responses that are observable with sufficiently refined techniques (Henton & Iversen, 1978).

The foundations for a response patterns analysis of behavioral decrements are in the two basic patterns—concurrent and sequential ones. Decrements, like increments, represent the reorganization of the interbehavioral field. Simply put, one consequence of certain intrusions into the field is the systematic alteration of concurrent and sequential response patterns and included in these alterations are decrements in certain component responses. This thinking provides a truly behavioral approach to decremental phenomena. An example of this is seen in the inhibition construct, long offered as a substantive causal force underlying decrements. Kantor (1924) presented the integrated-field view of inhibition and, hence, an early statement of the response pattern analysis of decrements:

> The process of inhibition is always a case of preferential reaction and never one of non-action. The non-action situation is a definite and unique sort of activity, involving a replacement action by elementary reflexes. Such a non-action situation is, therefore, a relatively simple sort of behavior. In fact as long as the organism is complete and not disintegrated it is never inactive, no matter what the stimulating conditions may be. (pp. 8–9)

Multiple-response analyses of contemporary response pattern research in several ways have contributed to the overcoming of problems associated with early versions of this approach to decremental phenomena. One glaring flaw of what were typically identified as competing response or interference theories is that they usually were offered without confirmatory data in the form of quantitative measures of the responses that were alleged to compete with or replace the decremented response. Such merely inferred competing responses were of no different status than other illegitimate inferential constructs such as those of other theories (see critiques by Azrin & Holz, 1966; Mackintosh, 1974; Razran, 1939). Although some early experimenters did report observing such responses (Kantrow, 1937; N. E. Miller & Stevenson, 1936; Wendt, 1936), the data were not convincing. The crux of the problem was researchers' reliance on the single-response model, which obviated the accumulation of a body of findings that would provide the foundations for response pattern theory. Only after researchers adopted multiple-response analyses did the pervasiveness and complexity of interacting responses become evident (e.g., Henton & Iversen, 1978; Ray & Brown, 1975).

In revealing the field organization of behavior, multiple-response analyses have addressed another major problem of earlier versions of this completely behavioral account of decrements. Specifically, some critics correctly questioned the interacting response view by noting that the theory did not provide a believable analysis of the origin and maintenance of alternative responses (Kimble, 1961; Spence, 1951). Multiresponse research now reveals that alternative responses were always available to replace decremented responses, for they are components of the matrix of events comprising the interbehavioral field. One example here is the interdependent relationship between collateral responses and concurrently reinforced responses, as previously discussed.

Another criticism of competing response theory has been that it is "merely descriptive" and not explanatory because it only relies on other (alternative) responses to explain diminutions in referent responses (e.g., Azrin & Holz, 1966; Hilgard & Marquis, 1940; Mackintosh, 1974). However, as was pointed out earlier, response pattern theory is within the stream of the third stage of scientific thinking (integrated-field perspective), according to which there is no longer a division between description and explanation. Descriptive functional analysis is substituted for the search for "explanatory" powers and forces via inferential analysis and for the traditional view that experimentation involves true independent variable (cause) and dependent variable (effect) relationships.

There exists a large literature on behavioral decrements that supports response pattern theory and which patterning in turn helps to clarify. A small sampling of this literature is overviewed in the following sections.

Stimulus Change

Decrements in an animal's general activity may be discussed in terms of a corresponding diminution in an underlying, substantive energizing force such as drive or motivation (cf. Bolles, 1975). Bindra (1959, 1961) introduced the notion of the general activity matrix, which suggested that the components of what is referred to as general activity are sequentially patterned actions. Bindra further hypothesized that the common empirical finding of response decrements associated with stimulus change (e.g., "novelty" effects) is systematically related to increases in frequency of occurrence of alternative actions, not to decreases in hypothetical intraorganismic forces. This analysis led Bindra to conduct multiple-response analyses that supported the predicted covariation between referent and other concurrent responses (e.g., Claus & Bindra, 1960). Migler and Millenson's (1969) multiple-response discrimination paradigm yielded results consistent with the patterning account when they recorded rats' responses on an alternative lever during tests of stimulus generalization.

Extinction of Appetitively Maintained Responding

It is not absolutely necessary to record multiple responses to find evidence that implicates interdependent responses in decrements. Contrary to Mackintosh's (1974) assertion that researchers have not independently manipulated competing responses, several experimenters concerned with the extinction of appetitively reinforced responses have done this, and their results are compatible with response pattern theory, even though they did not undertake multiple-response analysis. Denny (1971b) reviewed several tests of a version of a competing response analysis of decrements in which experimenters primarily recorded rats' runway performance during extinction of previously food-reinforced running. According to Denny (1971b), Denny and Adelman (1955), and Maatsch (1954), the removal of a reinforcer from an established response sequence functions as an unconditional stimulus for withdrawal responses that typically compete with referent responses and mediate extinction decrements. However, all withdrawal responses to the nonpresentation of the reinforcer need not compete equally with running to the goal area. For example, Adelman and Maatsch (1955) demonstrated that it is possible to experimentally control the topographical relationship between the referent running response and the withdrawal response to the absence of food reinforcement and to thereby manipulate rate of extinction. Specifically, these experimenters found that when rats were permitted to perform a withdrawal response compatible with running to the goal (jumping out of the end of the goal box in the same direction as the running response), resistance to extinction was much greater than when the withdrawal response to nonfood was less compatible with running (e.g., simple confinement to the goal box). This finding is supported by several experiments reviewed by Denny (1971b), as well as by the recent study of Johnson and Denny (1982). It appears that the removal of a food reinforcer has no inherent effects on behavior. Instead, the consequences of this alteration of the interbehavioral field especially vary as a function of response-response relationships (cf. Amsel, 1962; Spence, 1960, pp. 97–100; Wong, 1971).

Related to the complete removal of appetitive reinforcers from the testing setting (as in the typical extinction experiment) is the omission procedure in which a phase of contingent reinforcement is followed by a schedule in which the reinforcer is now presented whenever the referent response has not occurred for a specified period of time. Thus, omission is similar to ordinary extinction in that the reinforcer is no longer available following response occurrences; it is different because the reinforcer is available after a period in which the referent response does not occur. The typical consequence of the omission procedure is a decrement of the referent response (Lane, 1961; Sherman, 1965; Skinner, 1938). Theoretical interpretations of omission effects vary. Anger's (1983) approach represents an excellent example of contemporary research and theory based on the assumption of response independence and associated strategies as discussed in this chapter. Anger attempts to explain omission decrements with the substantive inhibition construct. On the other hand, the procedural aspects of omission seem ideally suited for analysis in terms of interacting responses, as was recognized by Reynold's (1961) reference to omission as differential reinforcement of other behavior (DRO). Reynold's widely accepted terminology implies that alternative responses are inadvertently or adventitiously (Herrnstein, 1966) reinforced during omission training.

A response pattern analysis does not depend upon reinforcement as the only source of alternative responses but allows for the alteration of concurrent and sequential patterning via any of a variety of other means. For example, the conditions of omission would seem to be optimal for collateral responses to enter into patterns of interdependency with the referent response, as happens with concurrent schedules. The application of response pattern theory to the omission situation is supported by clear evidence of the maintenance of responses themselves on an extinction schedule during omission training (Harman, 1973; Zeiler, 1970).

Inhibition of Fear and Avoidance Behavior

Historically, theorists have juxtaposed fear behavior and avoidance responding. The classic instance of this is the application of two-process learning theory to avoidance behavior (N. E. Miller, 1951; Mowrer, 1939, 1947). According to two-process theory, fear is respondently conditioned and serves as a substantive-like source of motivation for avoidance responding that in turn is reinforced by fear reduction. This influential theory's account of decrements of fear and avoidance responses is oriented around the constructs of inhibition and demotivation. Pavlovian inhibitory factors are assumed to override fear and once fear is inhibited, avoidance responding diminishes due to decreased motivation (decreased fear).

Response pattern theory takes a very different view of what is often referred to as the inhibition of fear and avoidance. All decrements are considered as matters of preferential reaction and never of nonaction (Kantor, 1924). Therefore, diminutions in both avoidance responding and what is traditionally referred to as fear are related to performances of other, antagonistic responses. Denny's (1971a, 1976) relaxation hypothesis is the most developed alternative response account of fear and avoidance inhibitory effects. Briefly, Denny's position gives no special status to fear; instead, fear is related to fear responding. Thus, fear responding and the response classified as avoidance both refer to response (no substantive-like constructs are postulated). Denny emphasizes that avoidance has withdrawal and approach components and argues the corollary that responses occurring under aversive conditions are not fundamentally different from those occurring under nonaversive conditions (Delprato & McGlynn, 1984). The most common response that competes with fear and avoidance is relief/relaxation. Relief/relaxation occurs following termination of aversive and conditioned aversive stimuli, mediates approach to safe areas and thus avoidance of aversive events, and is modifiable. From the response pattern framework, relief/relaxation responding disrupts concurrent and sequential response patterns in which fear and avoidance responding are involved. But just as response pattern theory permits no universal, immutable powers and forces of reinforcers and withdrawal responses to the removal of food (see above), the consequences of relief/relaxation responding are relative to where in the behavioral stream they occur. For example, if relief/relaxation occurs in a place associated with shock, approach may compete with withdrawal to interfere with ("inhibit") avoidance. On the other hand, if relief/relaxation occurs in a place subsequent to shock, approach to this place may facilitate avoidance (Denny, 1971a, 1976; Grelle & James, 1981).

Conditioned Suppression and Punishment

If response-independent shocks are intruded into a baseline of ongoing responding (e.g., rats' food-reinforced lever pressing), decrements in the rate of the baseline response frequently occur. Experimenters often present a signal prior to each shock and the decrements are evident during the signal after a relatively small number of shocks (Estes & Skinner, 1941). This phenomenon has been referred to as conditioned suppression and used as an index of anxiety. The decrement in responding is commonly thought to reflect a motivational decrement that is attributable to inhibiting conditioned fear (Estes, 1969; Millenson & de Villiers, 1972).

In contrast to the search for internal states as substantive causes of suppression, response pattern theory directs the analyst to observed and recorded responses (e.g., Brady & Hunt, 1955). The newer theory no longer assumes that suppression is a manifestation of underlying nonbehavioral states or processes. Henton and Iversen (1978) reviewed the conditioned suppression research literature in depth and concluded that the strongest supported position was the patterning one. As Frick (1953) demonstrated, pattern measures reveal that suppression is a component of a disrupted pattern of responding that may not, in fact, inevitably include decrements in response rate per se. Some other noteworthy findings that implicate patterning in suppression include the variation of suppression as a function of the baseline schedule (Brady, 1955), the failure for suppression of the baseline response to be associated with corresponding decrements in another supposed measure of motivation—eating (Jackson & Delprato, 1974)—and multiple-response analyses that show relationships between defensive responses (freezing) and the baseline response (Bouton & Bolles, 1980).

It is worthwhile to note here that the response pattern position also is readily applicable to data on positive conditioned suppression or decrements in baseline responses to signals paired with response-independent appetitive reinforcers. For example, signals distant from an operant manipulandum were associated with greater degrees of suppression than were closer signals, and measurements of rats' approach to the signals showed that the differing degrees of suppression were related to responses directed toward the signal (Karpicke, 1978; Karpicke, Christoph, Peterson, & Hearst, 1977).

Conditioned suppression refers to decrements associated with noncontingent presentations of stimuli. The punishment procedure is similar, except decrements occur in conjunction with response-contingent onset of stimuli (aversive reinforcers). Mechanistic thinking is applied to punishment when it is assumed that response decrements are attributable to the unique, inherent substantive property of "aversiveness" that certain stimuli possess (e.g., Azrin & Holz, 1966). Alternatively, we can view the punishment procedure as yet another way of intruding into interbehavioral fields with the consequential alteration of patterns of responding. According to this latter position, punishers are not uniquely different from reinforcers. The effects of both punishers and reinforcers are dependent upon where they intrude in the interbehavioral stream and the previous interbehavioral field at a time just past. The field nature of punishment is nicely supported by Dunham and Grantmyre's (1982) data showing that when electric shock was contingent on a specific response, the alternative response that was most sequentially dependent upon the referent response was most likely to be suppressed in subsequent sessions. Dunham and Grantmyre (1982) also found that when the referent response was simply prevented from occurring by removal of the opportunity for the response to occur, the change in multiple-response patterning was indistinguishable from when the referent response was followed by shock. Furthermore, just as reinforcers do not strengthen responses or stimulus-response bonds, punishers do not possess the inherent property of weakening responses or bonds. Morse and Kelleher's (1977) review of the varied effects of response-contingent electric shocks is particularly pertinent here. For example, these authors discuss many findings demonstrating the facilitative effects on responding of response-contingent shock (see also, Brown, 1969, and Melvin, 1971).

That what are commonly thought to be only decrementing procedures are, consistent with response pattern theory, also incrementing procedures is well documented by the results of multiple-response analyses of punishment. Dunham has reported numerous instances in which increments in certain responses accompanied decrements in punished or prevented responses (Dunham, 1971, 1972, 1978; Dunham & Grantmyre, 1982).

Short-Term Forgetting by Nonhumans

Forgetting is one of the classic sub-areas of response decrements. Forgetting phenomena, of course, have been associated with memorial behavior, and memory is taken up later. At the present time, I simply mention some considerations that are relevant for the application of response pattern theory to the description of forgetting. Specifically, contemporary research on forgetting by nonhuman subjects over short time intervals has yielded significant findings that are consistent with the patterning approach. It is an aspect of this work that I briefly consider.

Theorists have attributed response decrements said to represent instances of forgetting to numerous intraorganismic states and processes, e.g., decayed memory traces, proactive and retroactive inhibition, rehearsal failure, retrieval failure, and unlearning. Given the tenor of traditional thinking regarding memory, the implication of response pattern theory that forgetting is just as much an incremental as a decremental phenomenon is quite radical. Of course, competition theory (Wickelgren, 1976) has been the classical theory that comes closest to such a position.

The role of interbehavioral relationships in forgetting has recently become clearer as a result of research with directed forgetting in the delayed matching-to-sample task in which presentation of a sample stimulus is followed by a delay interval. At the end of the delay interval, the sample and comparison stimuli are presented. A response to the sample stimulus produces a reinforcer, and a response to the other (nonsample) stimulus produces a timeout period. In the directed forgetting paradigm, the experimenter introduces one of two cue stimuli into the delay interval. During training, a forget cue signals that the sample and comparison stimuli will not be presented following the end of the delay period, whereas a remember cue indicates that the stimuli will be presented at the end of the delay interval. On occasional test trials, the sample and comparison stimuli are presented following the forget cue, contrary to training. The basic directed forgetting effect is the inferior matching performance on forget cue test trials relative to performance on remember cue trials (Kendrick, Rilling, & Stonebraker, 1981; Maki & Hegvik, 1980). Observations of pigeons' behavior suggest that analysis of response patterns may be fruitfully applied to these cases of forgetting. On remember cue trials, the birds remain oriented to the key throughout the delay interval and usually key peck; however, after the forget cue is presented, the birds move away from the key and perform other responses (Rilling, Kendrick, & Stonebraker, in press; Stonebraker & Rilling, 1981). In fact, matching efficiency is directly proportional to the rate of key pecking in the delay interval (Stonebraker & Rilling, 1981). Furthermore, decrements in matching performance increase with increases in the duration of the post-cue interval (Stonebraker & Rilling, 1981); it appears that the forget cue is more disruptive as the time in which to perform collateral responses increases.

According to a response-oriented analysis of directed forgetting, the crucial responses should be those occurring at the end of the delay interval when the test stimuli are presented, as opposed to those occurring prior to this point. Kendrick et al. (1981) demonstrated that this is indeed the case. In view of this and other findings, Rilling et al. (in press) proposed a behavioral context hypothesis that especially is compatible with an emphasis on the role of sequential response patterns. The major assumption of the behavioral context hypothesis is that forgetting is likely to occur when the response preceding the referent response does not occur. Rilling et al. (in press) reviewed research on directed forgetting and other short-term forgetting situations that suggests that these classes of forgetting are functionally related to the occurrence of responses incompatible with criterion responses, and it appears these competing responses are themselves functionally related to the absence of the appropriate behavioral context at the time of the retention test.

COGNITION

If any topic in behavioral science is in need of reevaluation within the context of integrated-field thinking, it is the area of cognition. This has been done to some extent by certain interbehavioral analysts (Blewitt, 1983; Delprato, 1983; Parrott, 1983; N. W. Smith, 1983). In this section, I consider a few contributions of response pattern theory to the reassessment of cognition.

Kantor's (1924, 1926, 1933) long-held position that problems of psychology are best approached from an integrated-field perspective led him to propose the centrality of cognitive activities in virtually all psychological activity in conjunction with the analysis of the complete behavioral event in terms of sequential and concurrent response patterning. Kantor's analysis of performance in a reaction-time experiment exemplifies the interbehavioral view (also see Kantor & N. W. Smith, 1975). First, a distinction is made between precurrent and consummatory reaction systems. The main point here is that typically only the consummatory reaction system is emphasized in analysis, perhaps because, in part, it gives the name to the entire psychological event. Thus, the consummatory reaction system refers to final component of a particular behavioral segment under analysis; in the case of the reaction-time experiment, this may be the final act of key pressing. But we have not completely described the behavioral segment by referring only to the signal or stimulus and the consummatory act. A more detailed analysis suggests that the consummatory act is preceded by two other major reaction systems on which it is dependent. In general terms, these precurrent systems may be referred to as attending and perceiving. Thus, the more complete description of the behavioral segment under analysis is: Stimulus‹--›Response Pattern (Attending—Perceiving—Final Act). (Kantor's analysis also recognizes that concurrent [collateral-type] responses may be involved in the event in the form of a "by-play" response pattern [verbal reactions, affective reactions, strain, etc.]; however, I will emphasize sequential patterning.) According to this analysis, "cognitive" refers to certain precurrent responses in sequential response patterns, e.g., attending (getting set) and perceiving (seeing the signal) in the reaction-time experiment. There are no nonresponse processes such as attention or perception that intervene between stimulating things and organismic actions. Variations in the consummatory reaction are not attributable to cognitive or any other mental or substantive states/processes such as inhibition or motivation. Instead, the final reaction is a component of a pattern of other responses.

The present approach to cognition supplies an alternative to the conventional account of apparently cognitively mediated responses. No longer do we find acceptable such statements as "cognition has causal influence on behavior" (Bandura, 1977, p. 10), "knowledge of results . . . enhances performance" (Bandura, 1977, p. 28), and "beliefs or expectancies [are] better predictors of human behavior than external variables" (Mahoney, 1977, p. 8). The dualism evident in such positions can be rejected. The dualistic statements can be substituted for with a statement that *responses are frequently related to other responses*. This way of discussing apparently mediated responses does not deny any events; it simply brings the response pattern framework to bear on the issue.

It is useful to consider the cognitive construct of memory within the response patterns perspective. Instead of the traditional substantive approach to memory, the integrated-field alternative is that memory in a behavioral system refers only to sequential dependencies between responses and other responses and between responses and prior stimulus conditions. There has been a definite tendency for observers to identify such dependencies and then go on to infer an explanation for them in the form of a substantive memory construct. For example, Altmann (1965) found sequential dependencies between monkeys' responses and preceding social events in group activity. He then suggests that the stochastic contingencies are a measure of (indicator methodology) social memory. Shimp (1976, 1979, 1981) displays much the same behavior after citing evidence in support of sequential response patterns. Shimp follows mechanistic thinking and implies that because responding occurring through time can function as a reinforceable unit, the subject must hold the events in memory, which is separate from responding. If we shed the mechanistic approach to science with the need for independent causes and the like, it becomes clearer that memory is not independent of responding, but a potentially fruitful way of talking about sequential dependencies. The functional relationships are taken as legitimate data in their own right. Thus, Shimp's (1976) apparently controversial position that for a more complete understanding of behavior the experimental analysis of behavior must include the concept of memory is taken as an argument for response pattern over response independence approaches.

It is encouraging that the present position on cognition and intraorganismic states and processes in general receives support from what might appear to be a surprising source. Roy Schafer has long been one of the most productive writers in the area of psychoanalysis. Schafer (1975, 1976, 1978) has called for a revolutionary modification of psychoanalytic theory that substitutes action language for Freudian metapsychology. As a result of his examination of contemporary thinking in science and philosophy, Schafer seeks to move psychoanalysis from the second (mechanism) to the third (integrated-field theory) stage. The outcome is a proposed new beginning for psychoanalysis on the basis of an action language. This means that since psychological phenomena can only refer to actions, only active verbs and adverbs are properly used to designate the basic phenomena of psychology. All dualisms are rejected and "the traditional distinction between description and explanation is discarded" (Schafer, 1976, pp. 210–211). Schafer's substitution of action language for substantive internal powers, forces, structures, capacities, and so forth takes him directly to response pattern theory; e.g., inhibition "is one action through which a person has refrained from taking another" (Schafer, 1976, p. 137). Schafer's rejection of chaining and intraorganismic causes in favor of a sequential patterning approach to apparently mediated responding is evident in the following:

> We need not assume that each action must be triggered by something. We view actions historically, that is, as following one another in a sequence that is intelligible in a number of related ways; the sequence is more than a chaotic chronicle whose only organizing principle is the passage of time. (p. 232)

SELF-CONTROL

Integrated-field thinking takes us to a very different view of self-control than that of earlier approaches. Modern theorists from Skinner (1953) to Schafer (1978) have promoted self-control as action rather than a manifestation of a substantive-like intraorganismic self. The above analysis of the role of response patterns in cognition generalizes to self-control. Many instances of self-control are readily analyzed in terms of sequential response dependencies in which precurrent response components of the pattern substitute for a presumptive self. The final component of the behavioral segment, consummatory reaction system, comprises what is often referred to as the controlled response (Kanfer, 1971). Thus, to lose or acquire self-control is a matter of the development or disruption of sequential response patterns, depending on the specific circumstances.

SUMMARY AND CONCLUSIONS

The organization of behavior traditionally has been approached in terms of hypothetical stimulus-response chains or equally hypothetical underlying mental or neural structure. Although theorists have offered chaining and structural viewpoints as antagonistic to one another, a thesis of this chapter is that both are consistent with the mechanistic (or statistical-correlational) stage in the evolution of scientific thinking. Chaining and intraorganismic structural positions are based on the assumption of response independence, whereby responses always retain their role as dependent on organizing independent variables. Response independence theories maintain the classic cause-effect model of mechanistic science. On the other hand, the portions of contemporary research and theorizing examined in the present chapter support the position that when behavioral organization is approached from the more recently evolved integrated-field perspective, organization, in the form of concurrent and sequential response patterns (or interdependencies), emerges as a fundamental description of behavior in its own right. Response pattern theories are based upon descriptive functional analysis rather than the inferential (or indicator) analysis of response independence theories. Therefore, no distinction is made between description and explanation, and response patterns function as descriptive explanations of phenomena, in contrast to their earlier treatment as indicators of underlying causal chains or internal mental or neural structure. An important difference in investigative strategies differentiates response independence from response interdependence approaches. Response independence has been maintained, in part, because the strategy of single-response analysis makes identification of patterning possible only indirectly; hence, response interdependencies typically are obscured. The more recently developed multiple-response analytic strategies have been indispensable in revealing the shortcomings of response independence and the descriptive advantages of response patterns.

Response pattern theory is supported by findings from, and is useful for organizing, a wide variety of areas, ranging from studies of the general activity of nonhumans to human cognition and self-control. Perhaps the most developed research on patterning is in classical and operant conditioning. It now appears that classical and operant conditioning entail the intrusion of stimuli into fields of concurrently and sequentially interdependent responses. Conditioning does not seem to involve the modification of isolated, independent responses; instead, response patterns change and indeed can be modified by explicit reinforcement contingencies. Multiple-response analysis and the response patterns construct have provided alternatives to interpretations of behavioral decrements in terms of inhibition and similar substantive constructs. The more recently developed viewpoint emphasizes that procedures such as extinction, punishment, and conditioned suppression are associated just as much with increments in responding as with decrements; i.e., decremented referent responses are components of patterns of interdependent responses.

In conclusion, response pattern research and theory may represent one of the first substantially developed areas in behavioral science that exemplifies the type of scientific thinking necessary to move the field to the next stage of advancement—integrated-field theory.

REFERENCES

Abelson, R. P. (1953). *Spectral analysis and the study of individual differences in the performance of routine, repetitive tasks.* Princeton, NJ: Educational Testing Service.

Adelman, H. M., & Maatsch, J. L. (1955). Resistance to extinction as a function of the type of response elicited by frustration. *Journal of Experimental Psychology, 50,* 61–65.

Altmann, S. A. (1965). Sociobiology of rhesus monkeys. II: Stochastics of social communications. *Journal of Theoretical Biology, 8,* 490–522.

Amsel, A. (1962). Frustrative nonreward in partial reinforcement and discrimination learning: Some recent history and a theoretical extension. *Psychological Review, 69,* 306–328.

Anderson, M. C., & Shettleworth, S. J. (1977). Behavioral adaptation to fixed-interval and fixed-time food delivery in golden hamsters. *Journal of the Experimental Analysis of Behavior, 25,* 33–49.

Anger, D. (1983). Reinforcement of inhibition, *Journal of the Experimental Analysis of Behavior, 39,* 213–226.

Anokhin, P. K. (1974). *Biology and neurophysiology of the conditioned reflex and its role in adaptive behavior.* Oxford: Pergamon Press.

Azrin, N. H., & Holz, W. C. (1966). Punishment. In W. K. Honig (Ed.), *Operant behavior: Areas of research and application* (pp. 380–447). New York: Appleton-Century-Crofts.

Bandura, A. (1977). *Social learning theory.* Englewood Cliffs, NJ: Prentice-Hall.

Baumeister, A., Hawkins, W. F., & Cromwell, R. L. (1964). Need states and activity level. *Psychological Bulletin, 61,* 438–453.

Bijou, S. W., & Baer, D. M. (1978). *Behavior analysis of child development.* Englewood Cliffs, NJ: Prentice-Hall.

Bindra, D. (1959). Stimulus change, reactions to novelty, and response decrement. *Psychological Review, 66,* 96–103.

Bindra, D. (1961). Components of general activity and the analysis of behavior. *Psychological Review, 68,* 205–215.

Bindra, D., & Palfai, T. (1967). Nature of positive and negative incentive-motivational effects on general activity. *Journal of Comparative and Physiological Psychology, 63,* 288–297.

Black, A. H. (1971). Autonomic aversive conditioning in infrahuman subjects: In F. R. Brush (Ed.), *Aversive conditioning and learning* (pp. 3–104). New York: Academic Press.

Blewitt, E. (1983). The computer analogy in psychology: Memory as interbehavior or information processing? In N. W. Smith, P. T. Mountjoy, & D. H. Ruben (Eds.), *Reassessment in psychology: The interbehavioral alternative* (pp. 381–407). Washington, DC: University Press of America.

Bolles, R. C. (1960). Grooming behavior in the rat. *Journal of Comparative and Physiological Psychology, 53,* 306–310.

Bolles, R. C. (1975). *Theory of motivation* (2nd ed.). New York: Harper & Row.

Bouton, M. E., & Bolles, R. C. (1980). Conditioned fear assessed by freezing and by the suppression of three different baselines. *Animal Learning and Behavior, 8,* 429–434.

Bradshaw, C. M., Szabadi, E., Bevan, P., & Ruddle, H. V. (1979). The effect of signaled reinforcement availability on concurrent performances in humans. *Journal of the Experimental Analysis of Behavior, 32,* 65–74.

Brady, J. V. (1955). Extinction of a conditioned "fear" response as a function of reinforcement schedules for competing behavior. *Journal of Psychology, 40,* 25–34.

Brady, J. V., & Hunt, H. F. (1955). An experimental approach to the analysis of emotional behavior. *Journal of Psychology, 40,* 313–324.

Branch, M. N. (1977). On the role of "memory" in the analysis of behavior. *Journal of the Experimental Analysis of Behavior, 28,* 171–179.

Brown, J. S. (1969). Factors affecting self-punitive locomotor behavior. In B. A. Campbell & R. M. Church (Eds.), *Punishment and aversive behavior* (pp. 467–514). New York: Appleton-Century-Crofts.

Catania, A. C. (1963). Concurrent performances: Reinforcement interaction and response independence. *Journal of the Experimental Analysis of Behavior, 6,* 253–263.

Catania, A. C. (1966). Concurrent operants. In W. K. Honig (Ed.), *Operant behavior: Areas of research and application* (pp. 213–270). New York: Appleton-Century-Crofts.

Catania, A. C. (Ed.) (1968). *Contemporary research in operant behavior.* Glenview, IL: Scott, Foresman.

Catania, A. C. (1969). Concurrent performances: Inhibition of one response by reinforcement of another. *Journal of the Experimental Analysis of Behavior, 12,* 731–744.

Clark, F. C. (1962). Some observations on the adventitious reinforcement of drinking under food reinforcement. *Journal of the Experimental Analysis of Behavior, 5,* 61–63.

Claus, H.-J., & Bindra, D. (1960). Reactions to novelty and stimulus-change induced response decrement. *Canadian Journal of Psychology, 14,* 101–110.

Colotla, V. A., & Keehn, J. D. (1975). Effects of reinforcer-pellet composition on schedule-induced polydipsia with alcohol, water, and saccharin. *Psychological Record, 25,* 91–98.

Corson, S. A. (1974). Editor's preface. In P. K. Anokhin, *Biology and neurophysiology of the conditioned reflex and its role in adaptive behavior* (pp. vii–viii). Oxford: Pergamon Press.

Delprato, D. J. (1979). The interbehavioral alternative to brain-dogma. *Psychological Record, 29,* 409–418.

Delprato, D. J. (1983). An interbehavioral alternative to cognitive-behaviorism: In N. W. Smith, P. T. Mountjoy, & D. H. Ruben (Eds.), *Reassessment in psychology: The interbehavioral alternative* (pp. 137–160). Washington, DC: University Press of America.

Delprato, D. J., & McGlynn, F. D. (1984). Behavioral theories of anxiety disorders. In S. M. Turner (Ed.), *Behavioral theories and treatment of anxiety disorders* (pp. 1–49). New York: Plenum.

Denny, M. R. (1971a). Relaxation theory and experiments. In F. R. Brush (Ed.), *Aversive conditioning and learning* (pp. 235–295). New York: Academic Press.

Denny, M. R. (1971b). A theory of experimental extinction and its relation to a general theory. In H. H. Kendler & J. T. Spence (Eds.), *Essays in neobehaviorism* (pp. 43–67). New York: Appleton-Century-Crofts.

Denny, M. R. (1976). Post-aversive relief and relaxation and their implications for behavior therapy. *Journal of Behavior Therapy and Experimental Psychiatry, 7,* 315–321.

Denny, M. R., & Adelman, H. M. (1955). Elicitation theory: I. An analysis of two typical learning situations. *Psychological Review, 62,* 290–296.

Denny, M. R., Wells, R. H., & Maatsch, J. L. (1957). Resistance to extinction as a function of the discrimination habit established during fixed-ratio reinforcement. *Journal of Experimental Psychology, 54,* 451–456.

de Villiers, P. (1977). Choice in concurrent schedules and a quantitative formulation of the law of effect: In W. K. Honig & J. E. R. Staddon (Eds.), *Handbook of operant behavior* (pp. 233–287). Englewood Cliffs, NJ: Prentice-Hall.

Dewey, J., & Bentley, A. F. (1949). *Knowing and the known.* Boston: Beacon Press.

Driesch, H. (1914). *The problem of individuality.* London: Macmillan.

Duncan, H. J., & Silberberg, A. (1982). The effects of concurrent responding and reinforcement on behavioral output. *Journal of the Experimental Analysis of Behavior, 38,* 125–132.

Dunham, P. J. (1971). Punishment: Method and theory. *Psychological Review, 78,* 58–70.

Dunham, P. J. (1972). Some effects of punishment upon unpunished responding. *Journal of the Experimental Analysis of Behavior, 17,* 443–450.

Dunham, P. J. (1977). The nature of reinforcing stimuli. In W. K. Honig & J. E. R. Staddon (Eds.), *Handbook of operant behavior* (pp. 98–124). Englewood Cliffs, NJ: Prentice-Hall.

Dunham, P. J. (1978). Changes in unpunished responding during response-contingent punishment. *Animal Learning and Behavior, 6,* 174–180.

Dunham, P. J., & Grantmyre, J. (1982). Changes in a multiple-response repertoire during response-contingent punishment and response restriction: Sequential relationships. *Journal of the Experimental Analysis of Behavior, 37,* 123–133.

Ebbinghaus, H. (1913). *Memory: A contribution to experimental psychology* (H. A. Ruger & C. E. Bussenius, Trans.). New York: Teachers College, Columbia University. (Originally published, 1885)

Einstein, A., & Infeld, L. (1938). *The evolution of physics.* New York: Simon & Schuster.

Estes, W. K. (1969). Outline of a theory of punishment: In B. A. Campbell & R. M. Church (Eds.), *Punishment and aversive behavior* (pp. 57–82). New York: Appleton-Century-Crofts.

Estes, W. K., & Skinner, B. F. (1941). Some quantitative properties of anxiety. *Journal of Experimental Psychology, 29,* 390–400.

Falk, J. L. (1977). The origin and functions of adjunctive behavior. *Animal Learning and Behavior, 5,* 325–335.

Feigl, H. (1953). Notes on causality. In H. Feigl & M. Brodbeck (Eds.), *Readings in the philosophy of science* (pp. 408–418). New York: Appleton-Century-Crofts.

Ferster, C. B. (1957). Concurrent schedules of reinforcement. *Science, 125,* 1090–1091.

Ferster, C. B. (1958). Intermittent reinforcement of a complex response in a chimpanzee. *Journal of the Experimental Analysis of Behavior, 1,* 163–165.

Ferster, C. B., & Skinner, B. F. (1957). *Schedules of reinforcement.* New York: Appleton-Century-Crofts.

Fetterman, J. G., & Stubbs, D. A. (1982). Matching, maximizing, and the behavioral unit: Concurrent reinforcement of response sequences. *Journal of the Experimental Analysis of Behavior, 37,* 97–114.

Frank, P. (1955). Foundations of physics. In O. Neurath, R. Carnap, & C. Morris (Eds.), *Foundations of the unity of science* (Vol. 1, pp. 423–504). Chicago: University of Chicago Press.

Frick, F. C. (1953). The effect of anxiety—A problem in measurement. *Journal of Comparative and Physiological Psychology, 46,* 120–123.

Frick, F. C., & Miller, G. A. (1951). A statistical description of operant conditioning. *American Journal of Psychology, 64,* 20–36.

Gantt, W. H. (1966). Conditional or conditioned, reflex or response? *Conditional Reflex, 1,* 69–73.

Gellermann, L. W. (1931). The double alternation problem: I. The behavior of monkeys in a double alternation temporal maze. *Journal of Genetic Psychology, 39,* 50–72.

Gilbert, R. M. (1974). Ubiquity of schedule-induced polydipsia. *Journal of the Experimental Analysis of Behavior, 21,* 277–284.

Glickman, S. E. (1973). Responses and reinforcement. In R. A. Hinde & J. Stevenson-Hinde (Eds.), *Constraints on learning* (pp. 207–241). New York: Academic Press.

Glickman, S. E., & Schiff, B. B. (1967). A biological theory of reinforcement. *Psychological Review, 74,* 81–109.

Gollub, L. (1977). Conditioned reinforcement: Schedule effects. In W. K. Honig & J. E. R. Staddon (Eds.), *Handbook of operant behavior* (pp. 288–312). Englewood Cliffs, NJ: Prentice-Hall.

Grayson, R. J., & Wasserman, E. A. (1979). Conditioning of two-response patterns of key pecking in pigeons. *Journal of the Experimental Analysis of Behavior, 31,* 23–29.

Grelle, M. J., & James, J. H. (1981). Conditioned inhibition of fear: Evidence for a competing response mechanism. *Learning and Motivation, 12,* 300–320.

Gross, C. G. (1968). General activity. In L. Weiskrantz (Ed.), *Analysis of behavioral change* (pp. 91–106). New York: Harper & Row.

Guilkey, M., Shull, R. L., & Brownstein, A. J. (1975). Response-rate invariance in concurrent schedules: Effects of different changeover contingencies. *Journal of the Experimental Analysis of Behavior, 24,* 43–52.

Haldane, J. S. (1917). *Organism and environment as illustrated by the physiology of breathing.* New Haven: Yale University Press.

Haldane, J. S. (1921). *Mechanism, life and personality.* New York: E. P. Dutton.

Haldane, J. S. (1936). *The philosophy of a biologist* (2nd ed.). Oxford: Clarendon Press.

Harman, R. E. (1973). Response elimination in concurrent and single operant situations with pigeons. *Learning and Motivation, 4,* 417–431.

Hawkes, L., & Shimp, C. P. (1975). Reinforcement of behavioral patterns: Shaping a scallop. *Journal of the Experimental Analysis of Behavior, 23,* 3–16.

Hearst, E. (1975). The classical-instrumental distinction: Reflexes, voluntary behavior, and categories of associative learning. In W. K. Estes (Ed.), *Handbook of learning and cognitive processes* (Vol. 2, pp. 181–223). Hillsdale, NJ: Lawrence Erlbaum Associates.

Hearst, E., & Jenkins, H. M. (1974). *Sign tracking: The stimulus-reinforcer relation and directed action.* Austin, TX: Psychonomic Society.

Hebb, D. O. (1949). *The organization of behavior.* New York: Wiley.

Henton, W. W. (1981a). Concurrent classical conditioning. *Psychological Record, 31,* 395–411.

Henton, W. W. (1981b). Kupalov conditioning: Molecular control of response sequences. *Psychological Record, 31,* 489–509.

Henton, W. W., & Fisher, B. R. (1981). Cyclical food deprivation and classical conditioned response patterns. *Psychological Record, 31,* 377–393.

Henton, W. W., Fisher, B. R., & Spohn, W. D. (1981). Acquisition and retention of response patterns in compound classical conditioning. *Psychological Record, 31,* 165–181.

Henton, W. W., & Iversen, I. H. (1978). *Classical conditioning and operant conditioning: A response pattern analysis.* New York: Springer-Verlag.

Henton, W. W., & Spohn, W. D. (1980). Classical conditioning with compound unconditioned stimuli. *Psychological Record, 30,* 47–60.

Herrnstein, R. J. (1961). Relative and absolute strength of response as a function of frequency of reinforcement. *Journal of the Experimental Analysis of Behavior, 4,* 267–272.

Herrnstein, R. J. (1966). Superstition: a corollary of the principles of operant conditioning: In W. K. Honig (Ed.), *Operant behavior: Areas of research and application* (pp. 33–51). New York: Appleton-Century-Crofts.

Herrnstein, R. J. (1970). On the law of effect. *Journal of the Experimental Analysis of Behavior, 13,* 243–266.

Hilgard, E. R., & Marquis, D. G. (1940). *Conditioning and learning.* New York: D. Appleton-Century.

Hinson, J. M., & Staddon, J. E. R. (1978). Behavioral competition: A mechanism for schedule interactions. *Science, 202,* 432–434.

Holton, G. (1973). *Introduction to concepts and theories in physical science* (2nd ed.). Reading, MA: Addison-Wesley.

Honig, W. K. (1959). Perspectives in psychology XII. Behavior as an independent variable. *Psychological Record, 9,* 121–130.

Hull, C. L. (1930). Knowledge and purpose as habit mechanisms. *Psychological Review, 37,* 511–525.

Hull, C. L. (1931). Goal attraction and directing ideas conceived as habit phenomena. *Psychological Review, 38,* 487–506.

Hunter, W. S. (1920). The temporal maze and kinaesthetic sensory processes in the white rat. *Psychobiology, 2,* 1–17.

Hunter, W. S. (1928). The behavior of raccoons in a double alternation temporal maze. *Journal of Genetic Psychology, 35,* 374–388.

Hunter, W. S., & Hall, B. E. (1941). Double alternation behavior of the white rat in a spatial maze. *Journal of Comparative Psychology, 32,* 253–266.

Innis, N. K., Simmelhag-Grant, V. L., & Staddon, J. E. R. (1983). Behavior induced by periodic food delivery: The effects of interfood interval. *Journal of the Experimental Analysis of Behavior, 39,* 309–322.

Irwin, O. C. (1932). The organismic hypothesis and differentiation of behavior. I. The cell theory and the neurone doctrine. *Psychological Review, 39,* 128–146.

Iversen, I. H. (1976). Interactions between reinforced responses and collateral responses. *Psychological Record, 26,* 399–413.

Iversen, I. H. (1981). Response interactions with signalled delay of reinforcement. *Behaviour Analysis Letters, 1,* 3–9.

Jackson, D. E., & Delprato, D. J. (1974). Aversive CSs suppress lever presses for food but not the eating of free food. *Learning and Motivation, 5,* 448–458.

Johnson, C. M., & Denny, M. R. (1982). Inhibition of performance as a function of withdrawal from nonreinforcement in a partial reinforcement situation. *Psychological Record, 32,* 315–327.

Johnston, J. M., & Pennypacker, H. S. (1980). *Strategies and tactics of human behavioral research.* Hillsdale, NJ: Lawrence Erlbaum Associates.

Kanfer, F. H. (1971). The maintenance of behavior by self-generated stimuli and reinforcement. In A. Jacobs & L. B. Sachs (Eds.), *The psychology of private events* (pp. 39–59). New York: Academic Press.

Kantor, J. R. (1924). *Principles of psychology* (Vol. 1). Chicago: Principia Press.

Kantor, J. R. (1926). *Principles of psychology* (Vol. 2). Chicago: Principia Press.

Kantor, J. R. (1933). *A survey of the science of psychology.* Chicago: Principia Press.

Kantor, J. R. (1938). Character and personality: Their nature and interrelations. *Character and Personality, 6,* 303–320.

Kantor, J. R. (1946). The aim and progress of psychology. *American Scientist, 34,* 251–263.

Kantor, J. R. (1947). *Problems of physiological psychology.* Granville, OH: Principia Press.

Kantor, J. R. (1953). *The logic of modern science.* Chicago: Principia Press.

Kantor, J. R. (1959). *Interbehavioral psychology.* Granville, OH: Principia Press.

Kantor, J. R. (1969). *The scientific evolution of psychology* (Vol. 2). Chicago: Principia Press.

Kantor, J. R. (1970). An analysis of the experimental analysis of behavior (TEAB). *Journal of the Experimental Analysis of Behavior, 13,* 101–108.

Kantor, J. R., & Smith, N. W. (1975). *The science of psychology: An interbehavioral survey.* Chicago: Principia Press.

Kantrow, R. W. (1937). Studies in infant behavior. IV. An investigation of conditioned feeding responses and concomitant adaptive behavior in young infants. *University of Iowa Studies in Child Welfare, 13* (No. 3), 1–64.

Karn, H. W., & Patton, R. A. (1939). The transfer of double alternation behavior acquired in a temporal maze. *Journal of Comparative Psychology, 28,* 55–61.

Karpicke, J. (1978). Directed approach responses and positive conditioned suppression in the rat. *Animal Learning and Behavior, 6,* 216–224.

Karpicke, J., Christoph, G., Peterson, G., & Hearst, E. (1977). Signal location and positive versus negative conditioned suppression in the rat. *Journal of Experimental Psychology: Animal Behavior Processes, 3,* 105–118.

Kelleher, R. T. (1966). Chaining and conditioned reinforcement: In W. K. Honig (Ed.), *Operant behavior: Areas of research and application* (pp. 160–212). New York: Appleton-Century-Crofts.

Keller, F. S., & Schoenfeld, W. N. (1950). *Principles of psychology: A systematic text in the science of behavior.* New York: Appleton-Century-Crofts.

Kelly, E. L. (1955). Consistency of the adult personality. *American Psychologist, 10,* 659–681.

Kendrick, D. F., Rilling, M., & Stonebraker, T. B. (1981). Stimulus control of delayed matching in pigeons: Directed forgetting. *Journal of the Experimental Analysis of Behavior, 36,* 241–251.

Killeen, P. (1975). On the temporal control of behavior. *Psychological Review, 82,* 89–115.

Kimble, G. A. (1961). *Hilgard and Marquis' Conditioning and learning* (Rev. ed.). New York: Appleton-Century-Crofts.

Kupalov, P. S. (1969). The formation of conditioned place reflexes: In M. Cole & I. Maltzman (Eds.), *A handbook of contemporary Soviet psychology* (pp. 735–762). New York: Basic Books.

Lane, H. (1961). Operant control of vocalizing in the chicken. *Journal of the Experimental Analysis of Behavior, 4,* 171–177.

Lashley, K. S. (1917). The accuracy of movement in the absence of excitation from the moving organ. *American Journal of Physiology, 43,* 169–194.

Lashley, K. S. (1951). The problem of serial order in behavior. In L. A. Jeffress (Ed.), *Cerebral mechanisms in behavior* (pp. 112–136). New York: Hafner.

Loeb, J. (1912). *The mechanistic conception of life.* Chicago: University of Chicago Press.

Lyon, D. O. (1982). Concurrent behavior: Are the interpretations mutually exclusive? *The Behavior Analyst, 5,* 175–187.

Maatsch, J. L. (1954). Reinforcement and extinction phenomena. *Psychological Review, 61,* 111–118.

Mackintosh, N. J. (1974). *The psychology of animal learning.* New York: Academic Press.

Mahoney, M. J. (1977). Reflections on the cognitive-learning trend in psychotherapy. *American Psychologist, 32,* 5–13.

Maki, W. S., & Hegvik, D. K. (1980). Directed forgetting in pigeons. *Animal Learning and Behavior, 8,* 567–574.

Mandler, G. (1962). From association to structure. *Psychological Review, 69,* 415–427.

Marr, M. J. (1979). Second-order schedules and the generation of unitary response sequences. In M. D. Zeiler & P. Harzem (Eds.), *Advances in analysis of behavior* (Vol 1, pp. 223–260). New York: Wiley.

Melvin, K. B. (1971). Vicious circle behavior. In H. D. Kimmel (Ed.), *Experimental psychopathology: Recent research and theory* (pp. 95–115). New York: Academic Press.

Migler, B., & Millenson, J. R. (1969). Analysis of response rates during stimulus generalization. *Journal of the Experimental Analysis of Behavior, 12,* 81–87.

Millenson, J. R., & de Villiers, P. A. (1972). Motivational properties of conditioned suppression. *Learning and Motivation, 3,* 125–137.

Millenson, J. R., & Hurwitz, H. M. B. (1961). Some temporal and sequential properties of behavior during conditioning and extinction. *Journal of the Experimental Analysis of Behavior, 4,* 97–106.

Miller, G. A. (1956). The magical number seven, plus or minus two: Some limits on our capacity for processing information. *Psychological Review, 63,* 81–97.

Miller, G. A., & Frick, F. C. (1949). Statistical behavioristics and sequences of responses. *Psychological Review, 56,* 311–324.

Miller, G. A., Galanter, E., & Pribram, K. H. (1960). *Plans and the structure of behavior.* New York: Holt, Rinehart & Winston.

Miller, N. E. (1951). Learnable drives and rewards. In S. S. Stevens (Ed.), *Handbook of experimental psychology* (pp. 435–472). New York: Wiley.

Miller, N. E., & Stevenson, S. S. (1936). Agitated behavior of rats during experimental extinction and a curve of spontaneous recovery. *Journal of Comparative Psychology, 21,* 205–231.

Morse, W. H. (1966). Intermittent reinforcement: In W. K. Honig (Ed.), *Operant behavior: Areas of research and application* (pp. 52–108). New York: Appleton-Century-Crofts.

110   DELPRATO

Morse, W. H., & Kelleher, R. T. (1977). Determinants of reinforcement and punishment. In W. K. Honig & J. E. R. Staddon (Eds.), *Handbook of operant behavior* (pp. 174–200). Englewood Cliffs, NJ: Prentice-Hall.

Mowrer, O. H. (1939). A stimulus-response analysis of anxiety and its role as a reinforcing agent. *Psychological Review, 46,* 553–565.

Mowrer, O. H. (1947). On the dual role of learning—a reinterpretation of "conditioning" and "problem-solving." *Harvard Educational Review, 17,* 102–148.

Mowrer, O. H., & Jones, H. M. (1945). Habit strength as a function of the pattern of reinforcement. *Journal of Experimental Psychology, 35,* 293–311.

Nevin, J. A. (1969). Interval reinforcement of choice behavior in discrete trials. *Journal of the Experimental Analysis of Behavior, 12,* 875–885.

Nevin, J. A. (1979). Overall matching versus momentary maximizing: Nevin (1969) revisited. *Journal of Experimental Psychology: Animal Behavior Processes, 5,* 300–306.

Nevin, J. A. (1982). Some persistent issues in the study of matching and maximizing. In M. L. Commons, R. J. Herrnstein, & H. Rachlin (Eds.), *Quantitative analyses of behavior: Matching and maximizing accounts* (pp. 153–165). Cambridge, MA: Ballinger.

Parrott, L. (1983). Systematic foundations for the concept of "private events": A critique. In N. W. Smith, P. T. Mountjoy, & D. H. Ruben (Eds.), *Reassessment in psychology: The interbehavioral alternative* (pp. 251–268). Washington, DC: University Press of America.

Pavlov, I. P. (1927). *Conditioned reflexes* (G. V. Anrep, Trans.). London: Oxford University Press.

Pliskoff, S. S., & Green, D. (1972). Effects on concurrent performance of a stimulus correlated with reinforcer availability. *Journal of the Experimental Analysis of Behavior, 17,* 221–227.

Premack, D. (1959). Toward empirical behavior laws: I. Positive reinforcement. *Psychological Review, 66,* 219–233.

Rachlin, H. (1973). Contrast and matching. *Psychological Review, 80,* 217–234.

Rachlin, H., & Baum, W. M. (1969). Response rate as a function of amount of reinforcement for a signalled concurrent response. *Journal of the Experimental Analysis of Behavior, 12,* 11–16.

Ray, R. D. (1977). Psychology experiments as interbehavioral systems: A case study from the Soviet Union. *Psychological Record, 27,* 279–306.

Ray, R. D., & Brown, D. A. (1975). A systems approach to behavior. *Psychological Record, 25,* 459–478.

Ray, R. D., & Brown, D. A. (1976). The behavioral specificity of stimulation: A systems approach to procedural distinctions of classical and instrumental conditioning. *Pavlovian Journal of Biological Science, 11,* 3–23.

Ray, R. D., Upson, J. D., & Henderson, B. J. (1977). A systems approach to behavior III: Organismic pace and complexity in time-space fields. *Psychological Record, 27,* 649–682.

Razran, G. H. S. (1939). The nature of the extinctive process. *Psychological Review, 46,* 264–297.

Reynolds, G. S. (1961). Behavioral contrast. *Journal of the Experimental Analysis of Behavior, 4,* 57–71.

Rilling, M., Kendrick, D. F., & Stonebraker, T. B. (in press). Stimulus control of forgetting: A behavioral analysis. In M. L. Commons, A. R. Wagner, & R. J. Herrnstein (Eds.), *Quantitative studies in operant behavior: Acquisition.* Cambridge, MA: Ballinger.

Ritter, W. E. (1919). *The unity of the organism* (Vol. 2). Boston: Gorham Press.

Russell, B. (1953). On the notion of cause, with applications to the free-will problem: In H. Feigl & M. Brodbeck (Eds.), *Readings in the philosophy of science* (pp. 387–407). New York: Appleton-Century-Crofts.

Russell, E. S. (1945). *The directiveness of organic activities.* Cambridge: Cambridge University Press.

Schafer, R. (1975). Psychoanalysis without psychodynamics. *International Journal of Psycho-Analysis, 56,* 41–55.

Schafer, R. (1976). *A new language for psychoanalysis.* New Haven: Yale University Press.

Schafer, R. (1978). *Language and insight*. New Haven: Yale University Press.

Schlosberg, H., & Katz, A. (1943). Double alternation lever-pressing in the white rat. *American Journal of Psychology, 56,* 274–282.

Schoenfeld, W. N. (1978). "Reinforcement" in behavior theory. *Pavlovian Journal of Biological Science, 13,* 135–144.

Schoenfeld, W. N., & Farmer, J. (1970). Reinforcement schedules and the "behavior stream." In W. N. Schoenfeld (Ed.), *The theory of reinforcement schedules* (pp. 215–245). New York: Appleton-Century-Crofts.

Schwartz, B. (1980). Development of complex stereotyped behavior in pigeons. *Journal of the Experimental Analysis of Behavior, 33,* 153–166.

Segal, E. F., & Bandt, W. M. (1966). Influence of collateral water drinking on bar pressing under complex reinforcement contingencies. *Psychonomic Science, 4,* 377–378.

Sherman, J. A. (1965). Use of reinforcement and imitation to reinstate verbal behavior in mute psychotics. *Journal of Abnormal Psychology, 70,* 155–164.

Sherrington, C. (1906). *The integrative action of the nervous system*. New Haven: Yale University Press.

Shettleworth, S. J. (1975). Reinforcement and the organization of behavior in golden hamsters: Hunger, environment, and food reinforcement. *Journal of Experimental Psychology: Animal Behavior Processes, 104,* 56–87.

Shettleworth, S. J. (1978). Reinforcement and the organization of behavior in golden hamsters: Pavlovian conditioning with food and shock unconditioned stimuli. *Journal of Experimental Psychology: Animal Behavior Processes, 4,* 152–169.

Shimp, C. P. (1966). Probabilistically reinforced choice behavior in pigeons. *Journal of the Experimental Analysis of Behavior, 9,* 443–455.

Shimp, C. P. (1969). Optimal behavior in free-operant experiments. *Psychological Review, 76,* 97–112.

Shimp, C. P. (1973). Sequential dependencies in free-responding. *Journal of the Experimental Analysis of Behavior, 19,* 491–497.

Shimp, C. P. (1975). Perspectives on the behavioral unit: Choice behavior in animals. In W. K. Estes (Ed.), *Handbook of learning and cognitive processes* (Vol. 2, pp. 225–268). Hillsdale, NJ: Lawrence Erlbaum Associates.

Shimp, C. P. (1976). Organization in memory and behavior. *Journal of the Experimental Analysis of Behavior, 26,* 113–130.

Shimp, C. P. (1978). Memory, temporal discrimination, and structure in behavior. In G. H. Bower (Ed.), *The psychology of learning and motivation* (Vol. 12, pp. 39–76). New York: Academic Press.

Shimp, C. P. (1979). The local organization of behavior: Method and theory. In M. D. Zeiler & P. Harzem (Eds.), *Advances in analysis of behavior* (Vol. 1, pp. 261–298). New York: Wiley.

Shimp, C. P. (1981). Local structure of steady-state operant behavior: In C. M. Bradshaw, E. Szabadi, & C. F. Lowe (Eds.), *Quantification of steady-state operant behavior* (pp. 189–203). Amsterdam: Elsevier/North-Holland Biomedical Press.

Shimp, C. P. (1982). Reinforcement and the local organization of behavior: In M. L. Commons, R. J. Herrnstein, & H. Rachlin (Eds.), *Quantitative analyses of behavior: Matching and maximizing accounts* (pp. 111–130). Cambridge, MA: Ballinger.

Sidman, M. (1960). *Tactics of scientific research*. New York: Basic Books.

Silberberg, A., Hamilton, B., Ziriax, J. M., & Casey, J. (1978). The structure of choice. *Journal of Experimental Psychology: Animal Behavior Processes, 4,* 368–398.

Silberberg, A., & Ziriax, J. M. (1982). The interchangeover time as a molecular dependent variable in concurrent schedules. In M. L. Commons, R. J. Herrnstein, & H. Rachlin (Eds.), *Quantitative analyses of behavior: Matching and maximizing accounts* (pp. 131–151). Cambridge, MA: Ballinger.

Skinner, B. F. (1934). The extinction of chained reflexes. *Proceedings of the National Academy of Sciences, 20,* 234–237.

Skinner, B. F. (1938). *The behavior of organisms.* New York: D. Appleton-Century.

Skinner, B. F. (1953). *Science and human behavior.* New York: Macmillan.

Skinner, B. F., & Morse, W. H. (1957). Concurrent activity under fixed-interval reinforcement. *Journal of Comparative and Physiological Psychology, 50,* 279–281.

Small, W. S. (1900). An experimental study of the mental processes of the rat. *American Journal of Psychology, 11,* 133–165.

Smith, N. W. (1983). Sensing is perceiving: An alternative to the doctrine of the double world. In N. W. Smith, P. T. Mountjoy, & D. H. Ruben (Eds.), *Reassessment in psychology: The interbehavioral alternative* (pp. 161–211). Washington, DC: University Press of America.

Smith, S. S., & Guthrie, E. R. (1921). *General psychology in terms of behavior.* New York: D. Appleton.

Spence, K. W. (1951). Theoretical interpretations of learning. In S. S. Stevens (Ed.), *Handbook of experimental psychology* (pp. 690–729). New York: Wiley.

Spence, K. W. (1960). *Behavior theory and learning.* Englewood Cliffs, NJ: Prentice-Hall.

Staddon, J. E. R. (1977). Schedule-induced behavior. In W. K. Honig & J. E. R. Staddon (Eds.), *Handbook of operant behavior* (pp. 125–152). Englewood Cliffs, NJ: Prentice-Hall.

Staddon, J. E. R., & Ayres, S. L. (1975). Sequential and temporal properties of behavior induced by a schedule of periodic food delivery. *Behaviour, 54,* 26–49.

Staddon, J. E. R., & Simmelhag, V. L. (1971). The "superstition" experiment: A reexamination of its implications for the principles of adaptive behavior. *Psychological Review, 78,* 3–43.

Stonebraker, T. B., & Rilling, M. (1981). Control of delayed matching-to-sample performance using directed forgetting techniques. *Animal Learning and Behavior, 9,* 196–201.

Taub, E., & Berman, A. J. (1968). Movement and learning in the absence of sensory feedback. In S. J. Freedman (Ed.), *The neuropsychology of spatially oriented behavior* (pp. 173–192). Homewood, IL: Dorsey.

Timberlake, W. (1982). The emperor's clothes: Assumptions of the matching theory. In M. L. Commons, R. J. Herrnstein, & H. Rachlin (Eds.), *Quantitative analyses of behavior: Matching and maximizing accounts* (pp. 549–568). Cambridge, MA: Ballinger.

Timberlake, W., & Grant, D. L. (1975). Autoshaping in rats to the presentation of another rat predicting food. *Science, 190,* 690–692.

Tolman, E. C. (1932). *Purposive behavior in animals and men.* New York: Appleton-Century-Crofts.

Tulving, E. (1962). Subjective organization in free recall of "unrelated" words. *Psychological Review, 69,* 344–354.

Tulving, E. (1964). Intratrial and intertrial retention: Notes toward a theory of free recall verbal learning. *Psychological Review, 71,* 219–237.

Vogel, R., & Annau, Z. (1973). An operant discrimination task allowing variability of reinforced response patterning. *Journal of the Experimental Analysis of Behavior, 10,* 1–6.

Wasserman, E. A. (1977). Conditioning of within-trial patterns of key pecking in pigeons. *Journal of the Experimental Analysis of Behavior, 28,* 213–220.

Watson, J. B. (1907). Kinaesthetic and organic sensations: Their role in the reactions of the white rat to the maze. *Psychological Monographs, 8,* (2, Whole No. 33).

Watson, J. B. (1914). *Behavior; an introduction to comparative psychology.* New York: Holt.

Watson, J. B. (1924). *Psychology from the standpoint of a behaviorist* (Rev. ed.). Philadelphia: J. B. Lippincott.

Wayner, M. J., & Greenberg, I. (1972). Effects of septal lesions on palatability modulation of schedule-induced polydipsia. *Physiology and Behavior, 9,* 663–665.

Weiss, B. (1970). The fine structure of operant behavior during transition states. In W. N. Schoenfeld (Ed.), *The theory of reinforcement schedules* (pp. 277–311). New York: Appleton-Century-Crofts.

Weiss, B. (1981). Microproperties of operant behavior as an aspect of toxicity. In C. M. Bradshaw, E. Szabadi, & C. F. Lowe (Eds.), *Quantification of steady-state operant behavior* (pp. 249–265). Amsterdam: Elsevier/North-Holland Biomedical Press.

Weiss, B., Coleman, P. D., & Green, R. F. (1955). A stochastic model for time-ordered dependencies in continuous scale repetitive judgments. *Journal of Experimental Psychology, 50,* 237–244.

Weiss, B., Laties, V. G., Siegel, L., & Goldstein, D. (1966). A computer analysis of serial interactions in spaced responding. *Journal of the Experimental Analysis of Behavior, 9,* 619–626.

Wendt, G. R. (1936). An interpretation of inhibition of conditioned reflexes as competition between reaction systems. *Psychological Review, 43,* 258–281.

Wertheim, G. A. (1965). Some sequential aspects of IRTs emitted during Sidman-avoidance behavior in the white rat. *Journal of the Experimental Analysis of Behavior, 8,* 9–15.

Wickelgren, W. A. (1976). Memory storage dynamics. In W. K. Estes (Ed.), *Handbook of learning and cognitive processes* (Vol. 4, pp. 321–361). Hillsdale, NJ: Lawrence Erlbaum Associates.

Wickens, D. D. (1940). Conditioned response data and the holistic point of view. *Psychological Review, 47,* 155–168.

Williams, D. R. (1968). The structure of response rate. *Journal of the Experimental Analysis of Behavior, 11,* 251–258.

Wilson, M. P., & Keller, F. S. (1953). On the selective reinforcement of spaced responses. *Journal of Comparative and Physiological Psychology, 46,* 190–193.

Wong, P. T. P. (1971). Coerced approach to shock, punishment of competing responses, and resistance to extinction in the rat. *Journal of Comparative and Physiological Psychology, 76,* 275–281.

Wong, P. T. P. (1979). A behavioral field approach to general activity: Sex differences and food deprivation in the rat. *Animal Learning and Behavior, 7,* 111–118.

Zeiler, M. D. (1970). Other behavior: Consequences of reinforcing not responding. *Journal of Psychology, 74,* 149–155.

Zeiler, M. D. (1977). Schedules of reinforcement: The controlling variables. In W. K. Honig & J. E. R. Staddon (Eds.), *Handbook of operant behavior* (pp. 201–232). Englewood Cliffs, NJ: Prentice-Hall.

Zener, K. (1937). The significance of behavior accompanying conditioned salivary secretion for theories of the conditioned response. *American Journal of Psychology, 50,* 384–403.

Zener, K., & McCurdy, H. G. (1939). Analysis of motivational factors in conditioned behavior: I. The differential effect of changes in hunger upon conditioned, unconditioned, and spontaneous salivary secretion. *Journal of Psychology, 8,* 321–350.

4 Language as Behavior: Functional Mediation Versus Morphological Description

Emilio Ribes
National University of Mexico at Iztacala

The field of *linguistic* or *verbal* behavior as approached by behavior analysis has shown a limited experimental development if compared with the traditional strong areas of animal and applied research. This has much to do with the insufficiency of the current dominant theoretical framework derived from operant conditioning principles, and mainly represented by Skinner's *Verbal Behavior* (1957).[1] Contrary to common practices in the experimental analysis of behavior, verbal behavior—as equivalent to language—has been the subject not of empirical scrutiny, but of hermeneutic exercises (Michael, 1980; Salzinger, 1982). This trend might comply with various reasons, outstanding among them the difficulty of isolating independent behavioral segments according to the classificatory scheme proposed by Skinner, and the inadequacy of the concept of reinforcement to cope with phenomena not describable—and not reducible—to punctate, repetitive, molecular events in time (Ribes, 1983).

Because any progress to be achieved in the experimental analysis of language as behavior requires a conceptual redefinition of the problem, I first examine the criteria necessary to identify the various functional levels in which language as

---

[1] U. T. Place (1981a, 1981b, 1982) has recently published an interesting series of papers dealing with the general issue of Skinner's *Verbal Behavior* as an analysis of intentional behavior alternative to intensional terms. In these articles he correctly points out some of the limitations in Skinner's treatment of language, and suggests some ways to improve it. Nevertheless, I think that *Verbal Behavior* has two serious handicaps. First, there are numerous and deep logical inconsistencies in the treatment of the issues involved, sometimes in overt contradiction with operant principles. Secondly, there is a conceptual limitation born of the reflex paradigm on which behavior theory as conditioning theory is built up. Paradigmatic restrictions of conditioning theory do not allow for a thorough and nonreductionistic study of human behavior (see Ribes, in press).

behavior may be organized, and second, an alternative conceptual scheme to that provided by conditioning theory.

A DEFINITION OF LANGUAGE AS BEHAVIOR

Language may be approached from several perspectives, each stressing a particular dimension or property. This conceptual diversity in the analysis of language leads, in fact, to the delimitation of different empirical and theoretical problems. Thus, the description of these distinctive topics under the common label *language* has rather confused the field and prompted categorical mistakes. Therefore, I first try to distinguish language as behavior from all other aspects embraced by the same term.

Language may be understood in five different ways: (a) as action; (b) as behavior, or interaction; (c) as description; (d) as product; (e) as a set of rules.

Language as action has been the traditional province of biology and phonetics (and in terms of its sound effects, with acoustics). Language is identified with articulated vocal activity, and with the neural processes and structures participating in its regulation and emission. Language is thus described in terms of biological behavior or action. The morphology of the organism's activity is the criterion defining the boundary of language.

Language as behavior, or better said, as interbehavior, is the subject matter of psychology and must fulfill two conditions. First, it must consist of a conventional reactional set acquired by an individual through the interaction with the members of a particular social group. Second, as a specific kind of interbehavior, distinctive of vocal (or other) actions and rules describing them, language must consist in substitution of contingencies, either in particular situations (referential language) or in relation to transituational conditions in the form of interactions with language itself (nonreferential language). Language as interbehavior deals, therefore, with the processes regulating particular interactions of an individual, involving conventional reactional sets and substitutional contingencies.

Language as description is part of the realm of logic and semantics. Linguistic actions or interactions as paradigmatic *expressions* are taken as the description of special situations, events, or intentions. Logic as the analysis of proper expressions in ordinary or formal language studies the rules of interpretation of categories embedded in linguistic actions that "contain" descriptions of actions, states, purposes, or intentions, either in terms of practical rules of talking, or in terms of certain rules of causal statements regarding the contents of description. Semantics, on the other hand, looks for correspondence and rules of interpretation between the content of language and states, intentions, and events assumed to be related with language as their expression. In both cases, the interest does not rest upon the particular action as such, but rather rests in the action as an inferential index of "contents" related to events, states, intentions, and rules of mental expression, that is, "meanings".

Language as product is the field of interest of disciplines as diverse as sociolinguistics, philology, literature, formal linguistics, and aesthetics. In these cases the products of linguistic interactions of individuals and groups are analyses according to "styles," that is, according to social or individual patterning of conventions identified in the objectified products of language: texts, tapes, codex, transcriptions, and so on. Styles of writing, talking, reading, communicating, symbolizing, and creating language conventions are analyzed from the vestigial products of language practices or from the recording of current ones. Individual circumstances are not considered. Rather, the identification of, conformity to, and creation of styles are the main objectives under study.

Finally, language may consist in a set of rules. Logic and grammar, as well as special formal languages such as those of mathematics and cybernetics, comprise abstractions of possible relations among conventional linguistic products, abstractions that work as rules for predicting, analyzing, and describing particular conditions that are instances of those rules. These disciplines are, thus, related with the rules (or abstracted descriptions) of actions as descriptions or objects themselves.

The distinctions previously formulated are not merely a formal exercise. They mean that language is not some "thing," but an abstraction about concrete relations involving conventional behavior, as event or as product. In each of the several fields enumerated, different levels of abstraction are taken into account and, therefore, involve distinctive empirical and theoretical subject matters. Their overlapping, because of the common use of the same term, *language,* leads to confusion of categories and problems. Each of these domains is legitimate in its own right and no reduction is needed to study any of them, resorting to concepts and descriptions originating in the other disciplines. From a conceptual point of view, language as interaction or interbehavior has no logic, grammar, biological structure, or content. Language as interbehavior has its own problems, methods, and categories: those of psychology. To pose as problems for psychology those originating in grammar, neurology, or logic is tantamount to assuming that the events studied by those disciplines, as abstracted relations, are the very same to the extent that a single *word* is used in the ordinary language descriptions of their subject matters.

This naive nominalism, instead of distinguishing among different fields of event relations involving conventional reactive sets, confounds them into a single one, reducing and intermixing uncontrastable categorical systems and their *data language.* This is not to say that the various disciplines are unrelated. On the contrary, they seem to complement each other, excepting those cases, such as the field called philosophy of mind, that exclude by definition the study of language as intentional psychological actions from a scientific perspective. Therefore, a behavioral analysis of "language" as contingency-substitutional interaction does not preclude the study of other aspects such as social style, logical structure, grammatical rules, morphological properties, and so on. Nevertheless, a behavioral approach to language is or must be independent of the problems implicated by categorical descriptions specific to those other disciplines dealing with some set of relations involving also conventional systems, but foreign to the analysis of the behaving circumstances of an individual while interacting under substitutional contingencies.

Because of this, instead of discussing the convenience of terms such as verbal behavior, speech, language, or some other, to deal with the psychological problems involved in the interactions under substitutional contingencies, I put aside the ordinary term language, and use instead *contingency-substitutional behavior*.

LANGUAGE AS CONTINGENCY MEDIATION: SUBSTITUTION AND DETACHMENT

Behavior—or interbehavior as Kantor (1959)[2] has proposed—is, in essence, an interactive process. As such, it consists of a complex system of interdependent relations between the individual organisms and the objects, events, and other organisms in the environment. Psychological behavior (interactive) as distinct from biological behavior (reactive) is, therefore, inseparable from the environmental events with which it relates. In this sense, behavior as interrelation is distinguishable only in terms of the functional organization of the mutual dependencies between the actions of the organism and the events and objects in the environment. In order to provide a theoretical framework for the genesis of contingency-substitutional behavior, I revisit some reformulations previously developed about the concepts of contingency and behavior field (Ribes, 1982a; Ribes & López, in press).

The concept of contingency as born from the conditioning paradigm has been used in two ways. First, it has been used to describe the temporal proximity of responses and subsequent stimuli as secured by the dependency of the stimulus on the "operant" response (Skinner, 1948). Nevertheless, this temporal proximity is by no means essential to the contingency itself, since there can be delayed stimuli contingent on a response. Second, *contingency* has been used to describe the future effects of a stimulus on the frequency of a response preceding it in time (Skinner, 1938). Schoenfeld, Cole, Lang, and Mankoff (1973) have pointed out, however, that contingency (including its ancillary categories of reinforcement and punishment) actually means that the temporal distribution of stimuli is determined by the temporal distribution of responses. The subsequent quantitative effect on responding occasioned by the stimulus distribution is an

----

[2]In order to become familiarized with some of the technical terms being employed, which are based on J. R. Kantor's writings, the reader may review his *Principles of Psychology* (1924, 1926) and *Psychological Linguistics* (1977).

index of the reciprocal dependencies taking place in behavior interactions. With respect to the conditioning procedure as a whole, the experimental operations define one-sided contingency relations, for instance, the delivery of the "reinforcer" conditional (or contingent) on the occurrence of a predetermined response, or the occurrence of a stimulus (the UCS or the reinforcer) conditional on the presentation of a previous one (as in classical conditioning or in discriminated fixed time [FT]schedules). Effects of the ongoing operation indicate functional properties built into the procedures as two-sided or reciprocal contingencies. Thus, the actual properties of conditional stimuli, discriminative stimuli, and operant responses are contingent on the very same formal contingency relating them with the unconditional stimulus or the reinforcer.

Considered in this way, any contingency relation involves a reciprocal dependency, an interdependency, either between stimuli or between stimuli and responses. The process of behavioral development consists in a progressive change in the structure or organization of contingencies, in terms of differential participation of individual behavior in structuring such contingency fields. What kinds of contingency fields may be identified and how are they to be described in terms of the individual interaction? Because the conception of contingency just outlined does not allow for a causal, mechanical description of relations, new ways to look at interactive processes are needed. The search for mediated relations may result in a conceptual improvement compared to the formulation of causal statements (Marr, 1982).

How is mediation to be understood? In traditional theorizing in psychology, mediation has been used in two ways, both framed under the assumptions of a causal analysis: (a) as a conceptual tool helping to fill up temporal and spatial gaps in the causal relations between events (e.g., chaining); or (b) as the inference of an unobservable causal event between stimulus operations and responses. Mediation here is conceived as an alternative to causal analysis. Mediation describes complex, interdependent, synchronic relations. There is no single factor "causing" the relation. There are factors setting conditions for the interaction and factors interrelated among them. The search for mediated relations consists in the identification of critical factors allowing for different kinds of organization of such interactions. To identify a mediator in a contingency field does not mean that this factor is the cause of the behavioral effects observed. Instead, it is conceived as a necessary event in order to build up a multiple reciprocal contingency, but in no way as sufficient to account for such a relation in which it participates as an element. Explanation is thus considered as the formulation of criteria to classify different mediational processes, and the empirical identification of parameters and setting conditions that allow such contingency fields to be organized.

Two features characterize mediational relations as behavior to be considered "verbal" or "linguistic": functional detachment of reactional systems, and contingency substitution.

Reactional systems consist of the functional arrangement of biological responses according to the demands imposed by the physicochemical properties of objects and events acting upon the organism. Reactional systems, from a behavioral viewpoint, are not equated with the morphophysiological organization of the organism's response systems, because, for instance, in talking, hearing oneself is part of the same reactional set, as happens also with visual and motor responses in any kind of coordinated movement. Behavior evolves as the expansion and differentiation of response functions with regard to the physicochemical properties of the environment that relate to them. This process evolves as the segmentation of ever larger functional interactive units of stimulus and response, compared to those being biologically effective in the newborn organism. Thus, responding is initially linked to very specific dimensions and parameters of stimulation, and it is through the history of individual interaction that the response systems become functional to objects and events that are not biologically "programmed" to relate in such a manner with the individual. Classical conditioning provides an example of functional detachment of the glandular responses. Salivation is a biochemical response to the physicochemical conditions produced by dry powdered food, but becomes a functional response to a bell sound only through the contingent association of the bell sound and food introduction in the mouth. This occurrence of the salivary response to the bell is a functional detachment of its original biologically restricted relation to specific physicochemical "eliciting" stimulus properties. Thus, response detachment implies an increased stimulus range to relate with, as well as a progressive differentiation of such a response expansion.

Psychological behavior, to use Kantor's term, is by definition biological behavior functionally detached from the specific physicochemical conditions that relate to its invariant occurrence. The evolution of the individual's behavior is a progressive process of detachment of reactional systems, first relative to specific energetic parameters, and afterward, in regard to situational circumstances and specific dimensions of objects or events. Substitutional contingencies are the developmental outcomes of detaching response systems from situational conditions themselves, as is detailed later.

Humans, in contrast to animals, not only live in groups, but also are regulated in their collective living by contingencies that have been created through the history of the human species, contingencies specific to particular cultures and societies. The defining property of these contingencies is their conventional character. Language, as a social practice, evolves *as* and *from* convention, and individuals participate in such a social practice through the acquisition and exercise of the conventional reactional systems involved in "language." Conventional reactional systems, in contrast to purely biological response sets, do not have any necessary relation or correspondence with physicochemical properties of objects or events, or with the contingencies specific to particular situations. Strictly biological responses, as well as those behaviors detached as a consequence of direct experience or interaction, are functionally constrained either to the energetic dimensions of events or to the particular circumstances to which they are situationally bound. Nonconventional responding is, therefore, situationally bound behavior. It is attached to the here-and-now observable properties of objects and events to which it has become related because of past or current contingencies. Thus, the individual organism is unable to respond to events' properties and contingencies not present in time or space, or not available to sensory reactivity.

On the contrary, conventional responding, although acquired and exercised by the individual in particular situations, does not keep any necessary morphological correspondence with the events and/or the circumstances prevailing in such situations. Additionally, to the extent that conventional responding by the individual is shared as a component of a social practice, it becomes potentially detachable from the particular situational history of any individual. Thus, although conventional reactive sets are developed and interacted with, always as elements of situational contingencies, their social, arbitrary character allows them not to depend, as response, on any property of such situations. Nonconventional responses have severe limitations in order to be emitted independently of specific energetic modalities or particular correspondences with objects and events, e.g., seeing, hearing, and classes of movements. In contrast, conventional responses—mainly gestural, phonetic, and graphic—do not depend on time, space, or observed presence of any particular physicochemical property.

As is stressed later, the detachability of conventional responding does not mean that this potentiality becomes actualized because of the mere fact of its arbitrary morphology. This feature allows for specific forms of detachability, but a history of interactions promoting substitutional mediation patterns is necessary. Otherwise, conventional responding is restricted to the same modes of functionality as nonconventional reactivity. This is not surprising at all if it is considered that human social environment is completely conventional as a relation system and, thus, operative through linguistic interactions involving texts, writing, talking, listening, and complex arrangements of symbols. Because the human environment is, from the very beginning, linguistic by nature, in the absence of explicit contingencies demanding substitutional interactions, conventional responding in the individual may not result in any functional detachment from situational conditions.

What are the characteristics of response detachment that define substitutional mediation? Substitutional mediation implies that the interaction in which the individual is involved is not under the contingencies built in the situational relations of current events and objects.

This particular kind of interaction has two outstanding functional features. First, to the extent that the interaction involves at least two distinctive conventional responses, individuals participating in such a relation respond to each other and to the events in terms that are not restricted to current contingencies as represented by the physicochemical situational dependencies. The current interaction is expanded because of contingencies introduced by conventional responding, which are not only added to situational circumstances, but transform them as substitutional relations. Second, these substitutional relations may consist of relations regarding a particular event or object, but detached from the temporal, spatial, and apparent properties of such an event—*referential substitution*—or as relations regarding conventional response-produced events, without attachment to any particular physicochemical events—*nonreferential substitution*. In both cases, interactions are regulated by contingencies depending on the conventional responses involved as relation. Such an arrangement allows for the detachment of nonconventional and conventional reactivity regarding any particular physicochemical property or dimension in the current situation. I come back to this issue later.

THE ACQUISITION OF CONVENTIONAL REACTIONAL SYSTEM: THE GROWTH OF LANGUAGE

In the analysis of language development, the acquisition of conventional morphology and style of responding has been confounded with emergence of substitutional interactions based on the availability of such systems. Four aspects must be distinguished:

(a) The acquisition of phonetic and graphic morphologies;
(b) The acquisition of stylistic units of spoken and written conventional behavior;
(c) The functional development of such morphologies and stylistic units in relation to events, actions, objects, texts, and heard speech; and
(d) The transition from situational conventional responding to substitutional interactions.

The last point is treated in a separate section. I first examine the various aspects of behavior morphology and function acquisition related to the first three points, because I believe that the understanding of "language" as behavior requires a developmental analysis. Otherwise, no bridge is established between the early acquisition of conventional phonetic responses and the emergence of substitutional processes involved in complex linguistic and symbolic exchanges.

(a) The Acquisition of Phonetic and Graphic Morphologies

As I previously stressed, substitutional behavior develops to the extent that responding has an arbitrary functional correspondence with the physicochemical dimensions of objects and events in the environment. Because of this, any analysis of the evolution of complex human behavior must begin with the problems related to the acquisition of conventional responding.

Conventional responding is built on potential movements and phonetic emissions of the newborn. As is evident, graphic behavior develops much later than vocal behavior, perhaps in part because of the arbitrariness of the former regarding any form of spontaneous activity. The acquisition of vocal behavior, and the gestural and facial components socially associated, work as a multiple process of breaking up, differentiating, and chunking of the unstructured but wide spectrum phonetic activity of the individual. Nevertheless, this process is not random, but becomes, from its very beginning, deeply intermingled with events associated with and consisting of behavior and actions of people. As Osgood (1953) pointed out, articulated language is the outcome not of a process of expansion of sounds, but, on the contrary, of restriction of the physical dimensions of available potential vocal activity.

I do not think there is a single descriptive mode of analyzing such an acquisition process, but because the newborn is, behaviorally speaking, poorly differentiated and coordinated as a responsive individual, it is likely that, in the beginnings, chunking and breaking-up may work through what we have called an interruption process (Ribes & López, in press), similar to the concept of reinforcement espoused by Guthrie (1935). Afterward, as a consequence of the establishment of differential reactivity to acoustic stimuli in the form of a primitive "listening" repertoire, shaping and imitation may play an important role (Bijou & Baer, 1965). I stress that the acquisition of initial morphology must, by no means, be conceived in terms of punctate, molecular units of vocal responding. In fact, as some recent findings show (Moerk, 1980; Rondal, 1978), vocal units may even consist of what later is described by linguists as phrases.

(b) The Acquisition of Stylistic Units

Linguists (Chomsky, 1957; McNeill, 1971) have insisted in the structural patterning of language as an argument against a behavioral account of "grammatical" speech. Grammar, as a property of individual speech, has been thought either to be learned as complex nonassociative algorithmic rules, or to be released by exposure to practical conventions. In both conceptions, it is assumed that there is an implicit generative and/or transformational grammar working through individual speech, and therefore, that mature linguistic development must correspond to some sort of rule-governed process by which individuals conform their speech to those categories described by grammarians and linguists when analyzing ideal natural languages. But the fact that the social practice of speech may be described in terms of rules and conventions (which always trail actual practices) does not demand the assumption that individuals, when speaking, are following those rules, or that even more radically, they have a tacit knowledge of grammar before speaking.

Social practices as convention may be described and formally expressed as rules, but practices as such are not rules nor events regulated by those rules. Because of this, categories accounting for such social conventions as individual actions cannot be identical to those describing the formalized products of those actions as corresponding to ideal patterns. To impose such categories as those of grammar on individual or social speech is tantamount to the formulation of pseudoproblems by category mistakes (Ryle, 1949). The patterning of social and individual speech (or writing) has to be dealt with on a specific level of analysis, under the premise that grammar is not a psychological problem.

How can one account for speech patterning in individuals and social groups without resorting to ideal convention descriptions? If it is accepted that in speaking, individuals do not exercise rules and that they consequently do not require previous knowledge of those rules in order to speak and/or to acquire articulated oral language, then, as practical observation shows, it is no surprise that most people speaking correctly are unable to express the rules that grammatically describe their speech. Conventions, if not described as rules, may be alternatively depicted as modes or styles. *Modes* refer to interindividual invariances in behavior; grammar, as related to the abstraction of the practices in speaking and writing, can be better examined as styles of behavior. Sociolinguistics and philology are devoted to the genesis and description of particular social practices in speaking and writing. Psychology should deal with the process through which individuals acquire the morphological and functional dimensions of such conventional repertoires.

Some years ago, in studies of the acquisition of "generative" grammatical behavior in children, some clues regarding conventional patterning of speech were identified. Needless to say, our experiments were designed to show the effectiveness of reinforcement variables in the establishment and generalization of grammaticality in children, assuming that the overall issue was conceptually legitimate. Because of this, the data I discuss are not the outcome of procedure logically designed to look for an alternative to "grammaticality" or reinforcement induction processes.

Having observed in various studies (Botero, Cantú, García, & Ribes, 1977a; Botero, Cantú, García, & Ribes, 1977b; Ribes, García, Botero, & Cantú, 1977) that there was an increasing tendency to respond with the correct grammatical particle during baseline periods using prompting-choice procedures, we carried out several experiments to look for straightforward effects of prompts on acquisition. The first reported study (Ribes & Cantú, 1978a) on article gender (masculine "el" and feminine "la" in Spanish) showed clear-cut effects of improved performance with directly trained and untrained article-noun combinations, as may be observed in Fig. 4.1. These "acquisition" effects were produced by the single procedure of prompting a choice of gender alternatives regarding a noun.

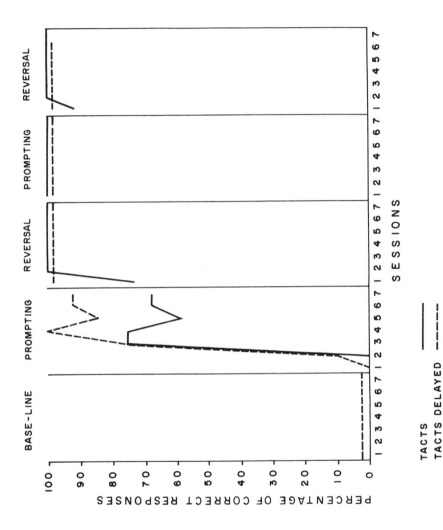

FIG. 4.1.   Percentage correct tacting responses of children using article-gender to noun correspondences under a nonreinforced prompting procedure.

125

No reinforcement or feedback procedures were used. Other unpublished studies replicated these effects with article number (e.g., singular "la" and plural "las") and the correct "use" of active-passive verb voices. The finding of "generative" effects without the use of reinforcement or any consequence seems to indicate acquisition of linguistic behavior style in the form of listening and observing behavior, and therefore may contradict the common assumption about the nonverbal character of listening behavior (Skinner, 1957). The results also raise doubts regarding the need to use reinforcement for current responding to yield new response morphology-style acquisition. The appeal to reinforcement history in the past with 2-year-old children is a weak logical argument, especially when studies aimed at demonstrating the power of reinforcement variables are founded on the rationale of a difference between the baseline and experimental periods.

A second group of studies, with what could be called an interpolation design (following Ferster & Skinner's, 1957, notation of interpolated schedules), were addressed to the exploration of minimal stylistic units. The first reported experiment (Ribes & Cantú, 1978b) showed that socially "reinforcing" the gender of articles associated with correct nongender suffixes produced an increase in article-noun gender relations that had been tested previously, and in a new set of test items as well (see Fig. 4.2). These findings were also replicated with article number and active-passive verb voice. The likelihood that syntactical relations may be directly learned as stylistic minimal units opens a stimulating field of research about the acquisition of conventional patterns of speech and writing.

In summary, and without going into details about the particular response-fragments that might be involved, it could be asserted that normative conventional speech and writing may be acquired, not as the recomposition of punctate units represented in phonemes, syntagms, and words, but as the outcome of a complex process including learning to be a listener and/or reader, and the reactivity to and the emission of minimal stylistic units, represented by pattern invariances in social speech. This assumption implies that grammar is not a problem to be dealt with in relation to individual linguistic development, and that conventional responding is acquired, not only in terms of small fractions of behavior, but also as larger units, and the process is not restricted to speaking, but also necessarily includes listening, reading, and writing.

(c) Functional Development of Conventional Reactional Systems

Two warnings should be advanced before entering into the general issue under the present heading. First, conventional responding, although consisting in gestural, phonetic, and graphic arbitrary actions, is not emitted in isolation from other nonconventional behaviors. Therefore, it is not possible to analyze the functional development of conventional responding independently of other non-

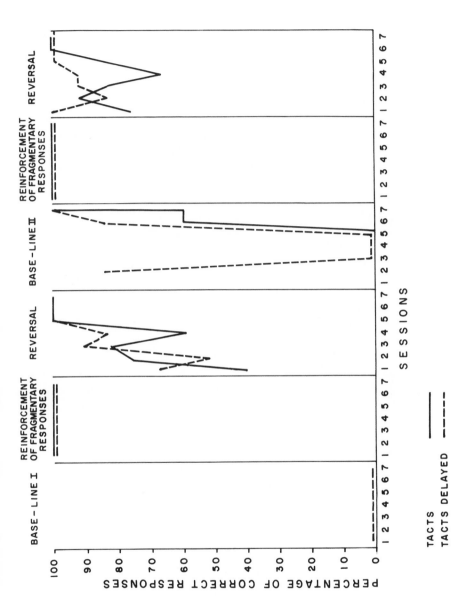

FIG. 4.2. Percentage correct tacting responses of children using article-gender to noun correspondences after the reinforcement of article-gender to noun suffix correspondences.

127

conventional responses and environmental circumstances. It would be a fruitless strategy to study linguistic evolution in the individual looking only at phonological patterns separated from the rest of "nonverbal" behaviors. Because conventional morphology evolves from biological responding as affected by the influence of an environment consisting in conventional products and behaviors of other people, it is too arbitrary to assume that language, as conventional behavior, is autonomous in origin and hence distinctive from any other human action, including morphological nonconventional actions. Because of this, I would claim that all human behavior, to the extent that it interacts from its very beginnings with a conventional environment, is functionally speaking conventional behavior. This radical statement, nevertheless, should be taken with caution, because as previously mentioned, differential detachability should be expected from behaviors with conventional morphology in comparison to those linked to biological situational responding. Second, because I examine the functional development of conventional reactivity in terms of evolutive stages, it is important to set forth two basic premises. One premise is that stages refer not to chronological periods, but to functional sequences, that is, to the availability of specific kinds of interactive repertoires as necessary conditions for the evolution of more complex forms in the organization of behavior. The other premise is that functional stages are not linearly related in time, but on the contrary may coexist and even emerge simultaneously for diverse kinds of morphological competences.

As mentioned in the preceding section, conventional behavior develops without the availability of a conventional phonetic response system. In fact, conventional behavior evolves in the form of nonconventional responses to stimulus segments involving physicochemical dimensions of objects and events, under the functional regulation of conventional properties as actions or action effects. Conventional stimuli and contingencies interlocked with objects, events, and purely physicochemical contingencies set the necessary circumstances for the progressive evolution of language as behavior. I may point to several tentative developmental momentos, which are by no means exhaustive:

1. Differential orientation to speech stimuli and direct behavioral contacts;
2. Interruption of phonetic "spontaneous" activity and shaping of normative sound patterning;
3. Differential reactivity to speech stimuli as related to objects and events;
4. Responsive and spontaneous articulated speech to speech stimuli, actions, and objects;
5. Brief conventional reactivity to larger speech stimulus units (stylistic listening patterning) and extended conventional responding to situational nonconventional contingencies;
6. Emission of conventional responses producing changes in the situational contingencies, either as actions (including speech production) or as events and object relations;

7. Diversification of situational contingency changes through extended reactive conventional units (complex style development);

8. Initial responding to and through conventional graphic response-produced stimuli;

9. Differential responding to event properties and situational contingencies conditional on functional regulation by conventional stimuli;

10. Development of functional equivalences among events, conventional graphic stimuli, and speech stimuli, in relation to nonconventional and conventional graphic and spoken responding;

11. Production of changes in situational contingencies through conventional responses affecting behavioral interactions with current events and objects;

12. Complex conventional mediation of response-produced stimulus changes under situational contingencies; and

13. Differential conventional and nonconventional responding to nonapparent or present events mediated by the conventional response of others.

These various functional stages in the development of conventional behavior are actually prelinguistic, according to our concept of language as contingency substitutional behavior. They may be classified into three general kinds of interaction:

1. Responding by the individual is differential to and dependent on contingencies as represented by the relations between events in the environment, but is not functional to change or to produce new conditional interactions with regard to those relations;

2. Responding by the individual is necessary for relations of events to occur and therefore is instrumental in mediating contingency relations to which the individual is functionally reactive; and

3. The contingency mediating activity of the individual is conditional on relations between events, which differentiate in time and space the relevant physical dimensions that are to be functional for such a mediation.

In these three general functional stages, the individual interacts with situational contingencies, restricted by the parameters of time, space, and observable properties. Contingency substitutional behavior emerges, as I show, only when the individual detaches the interactive relations involved in contingencies from those here-and-now observed dimensions of objects, events, and individuals so included. This may be possible when two conditions are met:

1. When individuals develop behavioral aptitudes as those pointed out in the preceding paragraphs, that is, in which active contingency mediation is conditional on changing singular properties of events in terms of event relations; and

2. When behavior morphology is functionally detachable from specific physical dimensions involved in situational contingencies, condition *only* allowed by
conventional morphologies. This is especially important because I believe that
conventional morphology in responding, under regulation by the same contingency process, is more easily detachable, and hence more plastic to changing
conditions, than biological, situationally bound responses. This may be the difference between highly evolved primates and human infants.

Data informing about this process must be obtained, at least partially, from
longitudinal studies in which the observational unit is the adult-child interaction.
My colleagues L. Antonio Pineda, Jorge Pérez, Assol Cortés and I are carrying
out a longitudinal study of mother-child interaction with several dyads. Data
have been collected since early ages (3- or 4-month-old children) and will continue until the children become 4 or 5 years old. Because we conceive language
development as the evolution of conventional and nonconventional responding
into contingency substitutional behaviors, our observations are not limited to oral
speech actions. Following Moerk's pioneer work (1974), we are looking at
interactions, but because language (or prelinguistic) behavior is not reducible to
conventional morphologies, gestural, graphic, and motor nonconventional behaviors are also taken into account as components of early "linguistic" development. Although our research is at an initial stage, I may advance some characteristics about the data categorization and relations being looked for.

Conventional language is being analyzed in terms of vocal and gestural morphologies in a first level. Formal properties, including grammatical particles
(verbs, adjectives, articles, etc.) are also examined in a second level. Finally, a
third level looks at the stylistic patterns involved in various kinds of talking, e.g.,
asking, ordering. These structural dimensions of conventional behavior are observed simultaneously with vocal and motor nonconventional responses, both in
mother and child. Nevertheless, from the continuous recording of the whole
interaction being observed, we examine particular relations between the child,
the mother, and the environment according to criteria as those describing the
developmental momentos mentioned previously.

Some interesting questions arise from these analyses. What are the relations
between phonetic and gestural response differentiation? Is there a systematic
effect of the size of the phonetic repertoire in relation to the appearance of the
various grammatical particles? Do the features of the child's repertoire correspond to isomorphic dimensions in the interaction with the mother? Is stylistic
development conditional on morphological and formal differentiation and variation? Does functional development of conventional responding depend on the
stylistic sophistication of speech? Are behavioral functions correlated with the
formal content of "language"? Are different morphological conventional competences asymmetrical in their emergence?

THE TRANSITION TO SUBSTITUTIONAL
INTERACTIONS

Substitutional behavior, as previously clarified, does not refer to a simple representational (standing-for) process as the term might suggest. By *substitutional behavior* I mean forms of interaction in which an individual mediates contingencies, through conventional responding, that are not given in the situation as straight physicochemical relations. Consequently, the mediation process normally involves two individuals, the mediator (referor) and the mediated (referee), although in some conditions this interaction may be developed in a single individual playing both functional roles. Substitutional behavior as truly "linguistic" behavior, may be organized into two distinctive functional processes. In one, contingency mediation is substitutional always regarding an event (or referent, to use Kantor's, 1977, term), although contingencies thus transformed might be completely autonomous and different from those prevailing in the current situation. The other process deals with mediation between purely conventional behavior or conventional behavior products, and thus with contingencies independent of particular events. The former process deals with communication and interactive language among people, as studied by linguists and social and clinical psychologists, as well as those researchers interested in language as an interpersonal process. The latter process deals with the traditional field of thinking, problem solving, conceptual, and symbolic behaviors. Although both are essential for the understanding of language as behavior, I restrict myself, for the most part, to the analysis of referential substitution. However, and in close connection with the most sophisticated functions in referential substitution, I point to some important features of nonreferential substitution.

In *referential substitution* three basic interactive elements may be identified: the referent (or situational events and stimuli), the referor (or the conventional mediator), and the referee (or the conventionally mediated). Although in some circumstances these elements may correspond to the object-speaker-listener relationship in traditional analysis, they do not necessarily do so. The relation may be given in the form of a text, a reader, and a listener, or in the form of a text, a writer, and a reader, and so forth. An additional feature is crucial for understanding the difference of substitutional reference regarding traditional descriptions of "communication" and so on. This feature bears on the issue of the kind of contingency relation involved in referential substitution. Differently from any other contingency mediation (excepting nonreferential substitution), situational interdependencies are not conditional on the physicochemical dimensions of events or relations of events. Rather, contingencies based on the events being referred to are substituted for (as transformed contingencies) by those arising from three basic interactions: (a) the referor's conventional responding to the referent; (b) the referee's conventional responding to the referor; and (c) the referee's conventional responding to the referent as mediated by the referor. Hence, although there is an event that is functional in the interaction, the contingency involved transforms the properties of that event in terms of the conventional responses given to it by both the referor and the referee, as well as by the conventional responses and stimuli referred to the event between both individuals. Because of this, what has been called tacting (Skinner, 1957) does not fit with the concept of referential substitution as explicated here. Tacting would be an instance of simpler contextual interactions, and would exclude any relation in which verbal stimuli might be tacted.

What are the additional conditions introduced by substitutional contingencies as conventional mediation? Four basic conditions may be identified. First, conventional responding by both individuals allows for functional detachment regarding time in which referred events occur. Second, by the same token, there is a detachment in relation to the place where events occur. Third, even when referred events might be present and act upon the referor and referee, conventional responding is reactive to properties and dimensions not apparent to a nonconventional observer, e.g., fragility and wisdom. Finally, the mediational characteristics of the referor's responding take into account not only the event properties and contingencies arising from the referred event, but also those coming from the conventional and nonconventional responses and response-produced stimuli by the referee. It is obvious that the kind of interaction described here involves a process much more complex than those stated as linear relations by communicational, semantic, or the discriminated operant formulations.

Referential substitution must evolve from three necessary conditions:

1. The specific forms of detachment fostered by conventional stimuli and responding that allow for functional shifts to varying physicochemical properties and dimensions in objects and events (the last momentos of functional development previously enumerated);

2. The aptitude to be mediated by conventional responses of another individual in relation to contingencies of and among physical and social events not present in the situation, or not directly observable or apparent. This would be equivalent to talking about the individual acting as a listener or reader under transformed physical and social conditions; and

3. The explicit training of the individual to act as a mediator for another individual regarding events and properties not present as ready available current contingencies.

Because this last condition involves the acquisition of the functional aptitude to substitute contingencies, I must stress that referential substitution does not evolve as a single-stage process, but rather as a multi-stage ability to interact in terms of different relations among the referent, the referor, and the referee. I examine a tentative look at this issue.

Although including a set of complex and diverse interdependencies incorporated in any substitutional interaction, referential substitution may be analyzed with regard to three basic elements and their interrelations: the referent, the referor, and the referee. The referee and the referor are always individuals, but the referent may be an object, an action, an event, or also an individual, taken both as conventional or nonconventional stimuli. Four general stages of substitution may be identified (both in development and as a process), in terms of the roles played by the referor and the referee when they become also referent and referor. Even when the mediating process relies heavily on the conventional actions of the referor, the behavior of the referee is also critical. Why so? Because the referee's behavior is the functional consequence (or supplementation in our terms: Ribes & López, in press) to the mediating action itself. The referee, in initial stages of acquisition of substitutional referring, must be conceived as the social regulator of legitimate mediations.

Substitutional mediations, of course, must conform themselves to the functional correspondences authorized by the linguistic community, in such a way that referential behaviors *do* relate events and individuals into socially meaningful contingencies. I now describe a very simple situation involving two individuals, A and B, as well as an event C that might be an object, an action, another individual, and so forth. Let us also simplify the basic relation as a referent (*ENT*), referor (*OR*), referee (*EE*) sequence. Given these premises, four kinds of referential substitution may arise in terms of the role (as *ENT, EE,* and *OR*) assumed by individuals A and B:

(1) C (ENT) ↔ A (QR) ↔ B (EE)

(2) B (ENT) ↔ A (OR) ↔ B (EE)

(3) A (ENT) ↔ A (OR) ↔ B (EE)

A
(4) B (ENT) ↔ A (OR) ↔ A (EE)
C

The four cases provide for differential regulation of substitutional contingencies, ranging from the most "objective" condition (1), in which the referee is an individual other than the referor and hence may have an independent contact with the referent, to the most "subjective" condition (4), in which the referor, the referee, and eventually the referent are the same individual.

In the first case, I believe that conditions are provided for the development of individual A as a referor. A has to respond conventionally about an event distinctive to the referee, in relation to which the referee may contrast, if necessary, a different sort of response. Therefore, corrections from other individuals may serve to adjust deviations in the normative correspondence of conventional responding by A, which makes A functional as mediator of nonpresent or nonapparent situational contingencies. In the second case, individual B is both referent and referee of A's conventional response. This condition involves a restriction in the possibility of the referor contrasting the effects of the referent on the referee's behavior. This restriction becomes especially relevant in the establishment of conventional responding relative to conditions that are observable but private to the individual. Not only "correct descriptions" of actions, feelings, and other states are thus promoted (Ryle, 1949), but also a sociocultural frame about the "subjective" events to which anybody might be able to refer is set forth. This is strengthened in the third case in which, to the extent that the referee B may regulate his or her response to the mediation of A as referor of his or her own behavior and characteristics as referent, B may conform this interaction to those sanctioned by social conventions. This is tantamount to saying that B becomes the monitor of A's conventional responses to his or her own nonconventional and conventional extrasituational behaviors and relations. Finally, in the fourth case, no social recognition is possible about some conventional correspondence conformity because the individual A is both referor and referee of the interaction. Obviously, the most severe restriction applies when, besides, the individual is also the referent. Excepting this last instance, in the rest of these cases there is always the possibility of an additional independent observer and the contrastability of reference as written behavior.

The development of referential substitution just outlined not only stresses the need for public criteria (the referee's supplementation and interaction with the referent) for the establishment of this kind of mediation, but also deals with two additional issues.

One issue is that referential substitution evolves toward circumstances in which detachability increases. This process is completely achieved as autonomous from social immediate regulation when the individual is both referor and referee. This restriction—additional to the fact that conventional responding itself may be nonobservable to others, even when referred to some particular events (as occur with writing, "silent" speech, and reading)—accounts for the necessary conditions that give rise to nonreferential substitution as complex symbolic behaviors. Conceptual problem solving and other "higher" processes are based on the capability of the individual to respond conventionally as mediator of new relations to his or her own or others' conventional behavior.

Second, it is worth mentioning that my analysis is consistent with that of Vygotsky regarding speech development. Vygotsky (1962, Russian original 1934), criticizing Piaget's conception of language evolving from egocentric speech (1926, French original 1923), emphasized the social nature of language as conventional behavior, and thus, its precedence to any form of egotistic modality of speech and to origin of thinking as inner speech. Obviously, important implications about private events derive from this conception (Ribes, 1982b), incompatible with Skinner's analysis of the issue (1945, 1957).

NONREFERENTIAL SUBSTITUTION AND THINKING AS CONVENTIONAL BEHAVIOR

I cannot end the treatment of the general problem of language as behavior without pointing to two aspects of conventional interactions, related to traditional conceptions of thinking and symbolic processes.

I shall not focus on the problem of a definition of thinking and symbolic behaviors; but some conceptual delimitations may prove relevant to our analysis. I believe, in agreement with Vygotsky, that language converges with pre-linguistic problem-solving repertoires in the emergence of strictly linguistic thinking processes. Selector interactions are nonconventional behaviors in which a response becomes detached from any singular object or stimulus as a functional event. These selector interactions are the precondition, with referential substitution, for the development of nonreferential substitution. Although not all thinking processes are linguistic, and not all language is identical to thinking, if thinking is understood as responding to continuously varying boundaries of stimulus classes, then it should be clear that thinking in terms of conventional responses is possible after referential substitution has evolved.

As previously stated, nonreferential substitution means that the individual interacts conventionally with his or her own conventional behavior or behavior-produced stimuli. This interaction between behavior, behavior-stimuli, and objectified behavior-products breaks away from any relation with particular objects or events. To the extent that the interaction is not necessarily linked to situational events, it becomes functionally trans-situational. This allows the individual, paradoxically, to expand the range of functional interactions with events, since conventional responding is not biologically bound to them. Nevertheless, in order for this to happen, two conditions must be met.

First, conventional responding should have a history of referential substitution activity. Otherwise, conventional events would be empirically empty. Second, these conventional response sets must be, in some degree, functionally related to one another. This relation is achieved, using Quine's (1960) term, through a process of translation. By translation I mean the possibility of setting correspondences among conventional reactional systems in terms of their referenciality, or the formal rules that define their functional properties and relations as constructed contingency fields.

Nonreferential substitution then would be a process of translation of conventional reactive sets in order to integrate responses or complete response systems (as those of formal languages) that may not bear any referential or situational relationship as functional interactive units. Translation should be understood, hence, not as a simple associative mechanism, but rather as a multivocal process of mediation of independent separate conventional response sets by conventional actions. Three aspects become crucial in this context: First, the intrareactive rules which allow for relations within a conventional set; second, the interreactive correspondences of two (direct) or more (mediated) response sets, in terms of their morphology and operational rules (syntax); and third, the extraconventional correspondence of response sets with situational contingencies and events, that is, their referential interactive history. This approach stresses the need to take into account the organizational structure of particular and general conventional systems (including formal and natural languages), to the extent that their structure involves contingency systems setting restrictions on relations within or between conventional systems.

Provided that conventional reactive systems may be conceived as having (Rr) or not having (Rf) a referential interactive history, several suggestive forms of nonreferential substitution emerge. These forms of mediation or levels of functional organization of conventional response systems must be understood as involving sets of different morphological characteristics and extension. So, it may happen that within a natural language we may find different groups of conventional response systems. Assuming that mediation may be done by an Rr or an Rf, six types of nonreferential substitution might take place. The responses within parentheses are the mediated sets:

$$(1) \ Rr \ (Rr \leftrightarrow Rr),$$
$$(2) \ Rr \ (Rr \leftrightarrow Rf),$$
$$(3) \ Rr \ (Rf \leftrightarrow Rf),$$
$$(4) \ Rf \ (Rr \leftrightarrow Rr),$$
$$(5) \ Rf \ (Rr \leftrightarrow Rf),$$
$$(6) \ Rf \ (Rf \leftrightarrow Rf).$$

The first three instances exemplify mediation by responses with referential history of relations between referential responses (as problem solving in ordinary language), between referential and nonreferential responses (as when numerical or geometrical systems are related to things through ordinary language descriptions), and between nonreferential responses (as when two formal languages as those of computers are related through ordinary language). The last three instances exemplify mediation by nonreferential responses of relations between two sets of referential responses (as when through a mathematical description two sets of descriptive categories of different empirical domains are related), between referential and nonreferential response sets (as when a formal language—e.g., algebra—relates or establishes new correspondences of events as ordinarily described with special logic conventions), and between two nonreferential response sets (as when two grammars are related by a mathematical system or two music genres are related mathematically).

I believe that conceiving language as a multiple-stage mediational contingency process will allow for fruitful research issues and closer relations with our colleagues studying the structural properties of language.

REFERENCES

Bijou, S. W., & Baer, D. M. (1965). *Child development II: The universal stage of infancy*. New York: Appleton-Century-Crofts.

Botero, M., Cantú, E., García, V., & Ribes, E. (1977a). Estudio experimental sobre el uso generativo del número del artículo en niños prescolares. In *Análisis de la Conducta: Investigación y Aplicaciones. Memorias del Segundo Congreso Mexicano* (pp. 165–181). México: Trillas.

Botero, M., Cantú, E., García, V., & Ribes, E. (1977b). El uso generativo del artículo en niños prescolares y su relación con la generalización del estímulo y la respuesta. In *Análisis de la Conducta: Investigación y Aplicaciones. Memorias del Segundo Congreso Mexicano* (pp. 199–212). México: Trillas.

Chomsky, N. (1957). *Syntactic structures*. Der Hagen: Mouton.

Ferster, C. B., & Skinner, B. F. (1957). *Schedules of reinforcement*. New York: Appleton-Century-Crofts.

Guthrie, E. R. (1935). *The psychology of learning*. New York: Harper & Row.

Kantor, J. R. (1924–26). *Principles of Psychology*. New York: Alfred A. Knopf.

Kantor, J. R. (1959). *Interbehavioral psychology*. Chicago: Principia Press.

Kantor, J. R. (1977). *Psychological linguistics*. Chicago: Principia Press.

Marr, J. (1982). Determinism. *The Behavior Analyst, 5*, 205–207.

McNeill, D. (1971). The capacity for the ontogenesis of grammar. In D. Slobin (Ed.), *The ontogenesis of grammar* (pp. 17–40). New York: Academic Press.

Michael, J. (1980). Untitled presentation. *Behaviorism, 8*, 161–163.

Moerk, E. L. (1974). Changes in verbal child-mother interactions with increasing language skills of the child. *Journal of Psycholinguistic Research, 3*, 101–116.

Moerk, E. L. (1980). Relationships between parental input frequencies and children's language acquisition: A reanalysis of Brown's data. *Journal of Child's Language, 7*, 105–118.

Osgood, C. E. (1953). *Method and theory in experimental psychology*. Oxford: Oxford University Press.

Piaget, J. (1926). *The language and thought of the child*. New York: Harcourt, Brace.

Place, U. T. (1981a). Skinner's Verbal Behavior I: Why we need it. *Behaviorism, 9*, 1–24.

Place, U. T. (1981b). Skinner's Verbal Behavior II: What is wrong with it. *Behaviorism, 9*, 131–152.

Place, U. T. (1982). Skinner's Verbal Behavior III: How to improve Parts I and II. *Behaviorism, 10*, 1–20.

Quine, W. V. O. (1960). *Word and object*. New York: Wiley.

Ribes, E. (1982a). *Language and symbolic behaviors as contingency substitutional processes*. Paper read at the First Biannual Symposium on the Science of Behavior. National University of México-Iztacala, México City, February 8–10.

Ribes, E. (1982b). Los eventos privados ¿Un problema para la teoría de la Conducta? *Mexican Journal of Behavior Analysis, 8,* 11–29.

Ribes, E. (1983). Has behavior analysis actually dealt with language? In N. Smith, P. Mountjoy, & D. Ruben (Eds.), *Reassessment in psychology: The interbehavioral alternative* (pp. 233–250). Washington, DC: University Press of America.

Ribes, E. (in press). Human behavior as operant behavior: An empirical or conceptual issue? In C. F. Lowe, M. Richelle, D. E. Blackman, & C. M. Bradshaw (Eds.), *Behaviour analysis and contemporary psychology.* Hillsdale, NJ: Lawrence Erlbaum Associates.

Ribes, E., García, V., Botero, M., & Cantú, E. (1977). Generalización de los efectos del reforzamiento en el comportamiento "sintáctico" de niños escolares. *Mexican Journal of Behavior Analysis, 3,* 169–180.

Ribes, E., & Cantú, E. (1978a). Efectos de la instigación en el "uso" generativo de partículas gramaticales: ¿Adquisición o mantenimiento? *Mexican Journal of Behavior Analysis, 4,* 59–66.

Ribes, E., & Cantú, E. (1978b). Efectos del reforzamiento de respuestas fragmentarias en el "uso" del género del artículo en niños prescolares. *Mexican Journal of Behavior Analysis, 4,* 29–40.

Ribes, E., & López, F. (in press). *Teoría de la Conducta: Un análisis de campo y paramétrico.* México: Trillas.

Rondal, J. A. (1978). Maternal speech to normal and Down's Syndrome children matched for mean length of utterance. In C. Meyers (Ed.), *Quality of life in severely and profoundly mentally retarded people: Research foundations for improvement,* Monograph No. 3, pp. 193–265. Washington, DC: American Association on Mental Deficiency.

Ryle, G. (1949). *The concept of mind.* New York: Barnes & Noble.

Salzinger, K. (1982). *The maintenance of verbal behavior.* Paper read at the First Biannual Symposium on the Science of Behavior. National University of Mexico-Iztacala, México City, February 8–10.

Schoenfeld, W. N., Cole, B. K., Lang, J., & Mankoff, R. (1973). "Contingency" in behavior theory. In F. J. McGuigan & D. B. Lumsden (Eds.), *Contemporary approaches to conditioning and learning* (pp. 151–172). New York: Winston.

Skinner, B. F. (1938). *The behavior of organisms.* New York: Appleton-Century-Crofts.

Skinner, B. F. (1945). The operational analysis of psychological terms. *Psychological Review, 52,* 270–277.

Skinner, B. F. (1948). "Superstition" in the pigeon. *The Journal of Experimental Psychology, 38,* 168–172.

Skinner, B. F. (1957). *Verbal behavior.* New York: Appleton-Century-Crofts.

Vygotsky, L. (1962). *Thought and language.* Cambridge: MIT Press & Wiley.

5 Categorizing and Concept Learning

Lyle Grant
Athabasca University

The present chapter is concerned with the topics of conceptual behavior and categorization, the process by which people use common terms to describe different objects or events that are members of a given class or category. The purpose of this chapter is to demonstrate the applicability of behavior analysis concepts to the understanding of these processes, which are often considered distinctively cognitive subject matters. Definitions of conceptual discrimination and categorization are initially presented followed by a discussion of the pragmatic importance of these processes. The history of research in conceptual discrimination and categorization is briefly described and evaluated, as are current trends in cognitive psychology and instructional psychology. Finally, certain disadvantages of categorization processes in promoting self-deception and illusion are described.

STIMULUS DISCRIMINATION, CONCEPTUAL DISCRIMINATION, AND CATEGORIZATION

Under a standard stimulus discrimination procedure, responses to an individual stimulus (an S+) are reinforced whereas responses to other stimuli (S−'s) are not. This results in a high rate of responding to the S+ (i.e., the discriminative stimulus), and a low rate of responding to the S−'s. A conceptual discrimination also follows this pattern, with the exception that a class of stimuli is employed as the S+ and nonmembers of that stimulus class are used as the S−'s. Classes of stimuli and events are composed of instances that are similar to each other in

139

some respects (e.g., all are blue, or all have wheels) but also differ from one another in some respects (e.g., different shades of blue, different sizes of wheels). The ways in which the members of a stimulus class are similar to one another are called the *critical properties* or *critical features*. The ways in which the individual members of the stimulus class differ from one another are called the *variable properties* or *variable features*. Critical properties must be present in an instance in order for it to be a concept instance, whereas variable features may or may not be present in a concept instance.[1]

As a result of conceptual discrimination training, responding is likely to occur when new members of the stimulus class are presented and responding is less likely to occur to novel nonmembers of the stimulus class. It is necessary to use new stimuli (i.e., stimuli not used during training) to test for conceptual discrimination in order to ensure that responding is under the control of the critical properties of the stimulus class rather than under the control of particular stimuli used during training.

Conceptual discrimination may occur with or without the critical properties of the stimulus class controlling a verbal response (a "tact" in Skinner's [1957] classificatory system).[2] For example, a child who has had an unpleasant experience with a dog might subsequently run from all dogs. The properties held in common by dogs would be controlling the behavior of running and thus this would qualify as an instance of conceptual discrimination whether or not the child could also tact dogs as such. However, we are more apt to say that the child can categorize a dog when he or she can successfully tact dogs than we would when the child can only run from them. This use of categorize appears to be coextensive with recent cognitive definitions of the term. For example, Anglin (1977) identifies categorization in the following way: "When we use a word to refer to an object, whether consciously or unconsciously, we categorize that object together with others to which we have applied and could apply the same term" (p. 1). Categorization is occasionally used to describe sorting tasks in which tacting is not necessarily required. However, in the present paper categorizing will be said to occur when the same tact occurs to different members of a class of stimuli. Category discrimination, then, may be viewed as a special case

---

[1]Another type of property is a *discritical* property, which must *not* be possessed by a concept instance. For example, if the illustration contains the discritical property *has read a novel*, then the illustration is a noninstance of *bird*. Discritical properties appear to be important in inducing correct responding to some concept noninstances in many day-to-day cases of categorizing.

[2]A tact is a relation in which a nonverbal stimulus or circumstance acts as a discriminative stimulus for a verbal response. In this chapter, "category tact" is sometimes used to describe cases in which the critical properties of verbal material (e.g., prose descriptions of instances and noninstances of reinforcement) are observed to act as S+'s for a verbal response. In these instances "category tact" is justified only to the extent that the critical nonverbal properties "referred to" by the prose have also been established as S+'s for a tact. This presumption seems importantly justified in many instances of skilled reading, though transfer of the observed relation to the tact may not always take place.

of conceptual discrimination in which some feature or combination of features acts as a discriminative stimulus for a tact.

THE IMPORTANCE OF CATEGORIZATION

Part of the reason why categorization is so important stems from the more general importance of conceptual discrimination. When responding comes under the control of a stimulus property, the organism can respond to that property in any stimulus configuration in which it appears. The organism is thus often able to successfully respond to novel situations as long as those situations contain properties that have been previously established as discriminative stimuli. In contrast, a world in which each newly encountered stimulus was wholly novel would be rather intractable. For example, each new tree, toothbrush, and sentence would require complete relearning.

Categorization itself is of enormous practical importance in our daily lives. Whether students succeed or fail depends importantly upon how effectively they are able to discriminate classes of stimuli from one another and tact such stimuli appropriately. Our systems of law and government are concerned with making distinctions among different types of categories, as in determining how to classify instances of punishable and nonpunishable behavior. In the sciences, taxonomic classificatory schemes have long been recognized as indispensable. Systems of psychology and philosophy are similarly concerned with labeling various classes of events, making distinctions between different types of categories, and establishing relationships among categories. Thus, advancing our knowledge of the behavioral processes involved in categorization raises the prospect that psychologists and philosophers can deal with the categories of their subject matters more effectively.

Another reason why categorization is so important involves our ability to manipulate concept words, words we use to "refer" to categories. Much of creative thought involves the manipulation of concept words to construct alternative courses of action or thought. In pondering over "consider" and "suppose" sorts of statements, we are rearranging previously acquired category tacts to refer to specific combinations of stimulus features that do not currently exist, but that may be extremely useful to bring about. For example, the inventor manipulates concept words to construct a potential alternative reality in which some device performs some function better than existing ones. Within cognitive psychology, this sort of manipulation is a mental activity. However, for the behaviorist, this activity consists of the occurrence of two or more verbal operants (i.e., tacts) that were previously acquired and maintained under the control of different stimulus conditions, but now come to occur in the same context. For example, suppose an inventor conceives of a combination knife and ball-point pen. The tacts "knife" and "pen" were initially acquired and strengthened in the presence of instances of two distinct stimulus classes. The compound tact "knife-pen" represents a new tact in which properties of different stimuli control the response. Compound tacts of this sort occur because the inventor's characteristic reinforcement is explicitly contingent upon production of new combinations of stimulus properties and an initial step in this process is to tact such novel combinations. (The specifics of this process of creative tacting represent an exercise in problem solving in which, for example, the inventor can make use of self-prompts and self-probes in order to set the occasion for occurrence of recombinant tacts. See Skinner (1968, 1969) for analyses of problem solving in terms of the construction of stimulus conditions so as to facilitate solutions.) Visionary political and social thinkers have engaged in a similar process to imagine worlds in which people live cooperatively and harmoniously as a result of some new arrangement of environmental properties. Essentially, by bringing concept words under the stimulus control of corresponding stimulus properties, the individual is no longer constrained to respond to those properties in the specific combinations in which they have previously been encountered. This point is returned to at the conclusion of this paper in a discussion of the desirable and harmful effects of the manipulation of concept words.

Categorization also appears to be an important elemental process involved in certain areas of current psychological research and theory, areas other than that discussed under the rubric of categorization itself. For example, attribution theory is concerned with how people categorize other people on the basis of factors like apparent controlling variables, sex role appropriateness of an individual's actions, and the consistency of aspects of a person's behavior. Work in judgment under uncertainty has often dealt with how people categorize the probability of future events. Studies of semantic memory are concerned with the processes by which people respond to category names and relationships between category names. Applied work with students has been oriented toward discovering the circumstances under which categories are learned.

HISTORICAL TRENDS IN THE STUDY OF CATEGORIZATION

Beginning with Hull's (1920) initial experiment in concept formation, experimental psychologists appear to have been fascinated with concept learning and categorization as research topics (see Bourne, 1966, and Clark, 1971, for reviews). Although it would seem that this research interest would flow from the great practical importance of these processes in daily affairs, experimental psychologists in the area have had a collective penchant for studying conceptual behavior and categorization in ways that are not particularly relevant to the way these processes transpire in natural, and especially classroom, settings. For example, a great deal of research has been devoted to studying the learning of concepts defined in terms of rather exotic relationships among critical features despite the paucity of any such natural concepts. Markle and Tiemann (1974) note that part of this problem stems from the use of artificial concepts with clearly defined features and the use of procedures that require the subject to state the concept definition (i.e., tact the critical features in property-by-property fashion) after exposure to concept instances and noninstances:

> There is a vast literature of research on the learning of concepts. As is often true of psychological experimentation, the laboratory findings in concept attainment have been derived from a dominant research design of dubious relevance to the real world of instruction. The historical model is the research of Bruner, Goodnow, and Austin (1956). In this classic design, the individual learner is confronted with a thoroughly rational universe of pictured items in matrix form, containing all possible combinations of a very limited number of values of a limited number of attributes—each picture may have the attribute, color, with a value of red or green or blue. On the basis of one given example, the learner plays a game with the psychologist, selecting other specimens from the array and presumably thereby testing his hypotheses until he discovers the rule for class inclusion. Stating the rule, a rule such as "all members of the class are both blue and triangle," indicates mastery of the concept. While slight variations exist in experimental design, a great deal is known about what facilitates and what hinders attaining concepts under these conditions. (p. 312)

In his extensive survey of research in concept learning before 1971, Clark also calls attention to the disparities between the experimental paradigms in concept learning research and concept learning as it occurs in the classroom. In his influential paper, Carroll (1964) also makes this point.

Since the late 1960s and early 1970s, interest in conceptual and categorization processes has taken two more promising directions. First, cognitive psychologists have become concerned with the structure of natural-language categories. One line of current thinking here is that an understanding of the nature of knowledge is best accomplished through the study of the categories people use in day-to-day life rather than by studying artificial concepts unrelated to those we use. Second, instructional and other applied psychologists have embarked on their own programs of research that are specifically oriented toward improving concept teaching practices. Selected current directions in each area are briefly considered.

CURRENT DIRECTIONS IN COGNITIVE WORK IN CATEGORIZATION

Cognitive psychologists have made both conceptual and empirical strides in furthering our understanding of categorization. Many of these advances have been tied to a reconsideration of the notion that natural-language concepts are structured, defined, and identified by critical features, as described earlier. According to what Smith and Medin (1981) have described as the "classical view" of conceptual processes, concepts are composed of critical or defining features that people use to categorize concept instances and noninstances. This classical view of conceptual discrimination is adequate for describing responding to artifical laboratory concepts composed of clearly defined critical and variable features, but has proved less useful in describing the contingencies in natural-language concepts, which do not fit the neat patterns of the artificial concepts. Three specific instances of this are seen in the study of *typicality effects,* the study of concepts defined in terms of a *family resemblance* among members of the conceptual stimulus class, and in the emergence of the notion of *cue validity.*

People tend to tact some concept instances as being "more typical" or "better examples" than other concept instances and they do so with considerable consistency from person to person (e.g., Ashcraft, 1978; McCloskey & Glucksberg, 1978; Rips, Shoben, & Smith, 1973; Rosch, 1973). For example, people rate *apple* as a highly typical instance of *fruit* and rate *olive* and *pumpkin* as atypical instances. People rate *ocean liner* as a typical instance of *ship* and rate *canoe* as an atypical instance (McCloskey & Glucksberg, 1978). In addition, people tend to more rapidly decide that typical concept instances are concept instances than they decide that atypical instances are concept instances (Smith, Shoben, & Rips, 1974).

Typicality effects demonstrate that not all instances of a concept have equal status in terms of the strength of responses to those instances. From a behavioral perspective, this serves to remind us that conceptual stimulus classes consist of individual members which differ from one another in the extent they serve as discriminative stimuli for a category (or abstract) tact. In addition, typicality effects suggest, as do other data (see Smith & Medin, 1981, for a review), that variable features act as discriminative stimuli for category tacts. For example, both spiders and dogs have all the critical features of *animal,* but spiders are rated as animal instances much more slowly than dogs are. This suggests that the variable features of the two types of animals are controlling the strength of the category tact. In this connection, it is interesting to note that Skinner (1957) acknowledged this aspect of categorization long before it became of current interest within cognitive psychology: "The verbal response *chair* is as abstract as *red.* It is not controlled by any single stimulus. Most of the properties of a single chair which evoke a response on any given occasion—the size, color, material, mode of construction, and so on—are irrelevant" (pp. 110–111).

Another manifestation of the cognitive psychologist's interest in natural-language concepts has been the realization that some categories are not defined in terms of critical features at all, but in terms of some "critical mass" or "critical sum" of properties, some of which are more heavily weighted than others in the extent to which they act as discriminative stimuli for category tacts. Consider, for example, the category of *poetry*. If words at the ends of lines in a text passage rhyme we would probably be more apt to identify the text as "poetry" than if they did not, and the same may be said for the use of rhythm, the stanza format of the text material, the use of devices such as alliteration, assonance, or metaphor, as well as other more ethereal and abstruse characteristics. No one of these properties of text material can be described as a critical feature of poetry, but when instances of text passages contain more and more of these features, people are increasingly apt to identify these passages as "poetry." Some of these properties would undoubtedly have more bearing on the classification than others, which is to say that the presence of any given feature would be associated with a probability that the instance would be classified as an instance of poetry. For example, the format of the text material might be more important than the use of metaphor.

Poetry is but one example of a stimulus class defined in terms of a *family resemblance* among various properties that determine class membership. Rosch and Mervis (1975), who initiated the study of these sorts of concepts, describe the notion in the following way: "A family resemblance relationship consists of a set of items of the form AB, BC, CD, DE. That is, each item has at least one, and probably several, elements in common with one or more other items, but no, or few, elements are common to all items" (p. 575).

The recognition that natural-language categories cannot be readily described by possessing critical features left something of a void in the description of such categories. If every concept instance does not possess critical properties, then how are the constituent properties of natural-language concepts to be described? One general approach to this question is to consider stimulus properties as being probabilistically related to conceptual stimulus class membership. One specific means of conceiving of the degree to which a given property is probabilistically related to stimulus class membership is in terms of *cue validity* (Rosch & Mervis, 1975; Rosch, Mervis, Gray, Johnson, & Boyes-Braem, 1976). Cue validity is the conditional probability that a stimulus is a concept instance given that the stimulus possesses a particular property. Cue validity is determined on the basis of both (a) the degree to which the property occurs in concept instances and (b) the degree to which the property does not occur in concept noninstances. For example, "feathered" has a high cue validity for the concept of bird because virtually every instance of bird possesses feathers and because most noninstances of birds lack feathers (though there are exceptions such as dancers in Las Vegas). "Flies" has a lower cue validity for the concept of bird both because some birds do not fly and because stimuli other than birds (noninstances of birds) do fly. "Has mass" has an even lower cue validity because so many noninstances of bird have mass even though all instances of bird have mass.

Cue validity is a useful concept because it highlights the fact that the degree to which a discriminative stimulus property controls behavior is a function not only of the relative presence of that property in concept instances, but also of the relative absence of that property in concept noninstances. Although the notion of cue validity is conceptually appealing, in practice it is difficult to calculate cue validities for the properties of natural-language concepts (Murphy, 1982). For example, although we know that most birds fly, it is difficult to quantify the degree to which instances of birds possess the property of flight. Further, it would be even more difficult to calculate the extent to which noninstances of birds possess the property of flight.

Another promising development within cognitive psychology has been the emergence of the "exemplar view" of categorization (Smith & Medin, 1981). Although there are variations upon this general theoretical perspective, the exemplar view tends to emphasize that conceptual knowledge is rooted in actual instances and noninstances of concepts rather than in abstract mental representations. Evidence for the exemplar view is based upon studies of categorical decision making in which people are enjoined to examine their own tacting practices. In such studies, people often tend to base their decisions on discrete instances they can recall rather than abstract representations of the conceptual class as a whole. For example, in judging the statement "All insects are flies" as true or false, subjects will (a) recall instances of insects-they-have-known (e.g., by visualizing them) and (b) observe if they do or do not characteristically tact those insects as "flies" (e.g., Glass & Holyoak, 1975). A statement like "all insects are flies" is rejected rapidly, apparently because the subject need only recall one specific counterexample to judge the statement false. Similarly, people will quickly judge the assertion "The diameter of a large pizza is 42 inches" false by recalling a single instance of a large pizza they have encountered and observing that its diameter was much less than 42 inches (Walker, 1975). In contrast, people are relatively slow to judge statements like "All birds have feathers" as true, apparently because the subject engages in recall of multiple exemplars of birds in an unsuccessful effort to recall one without feathers.

From a behavioral perspective, the emergence of the exemplar view is a highly desirable development (or at least a closer approximation to a more desirable terminal repertoire) insofar as it begins to cast attention upon the contingencies involving the behaver's past interactions with category instances and noninstances in the environment as a determinant of current behavior. Further, the exemplar view begins to move away from the view that categorical knowledge involves abstract mental representations, core meanings, and other distinctly mentalistic explanations.

CURRENT DIRECTIONS IN CONCEPT AND CATEGORY TEACHING

As the Markle and Tiemann quotation presented earlier testifies, contemporary instructional psychologists began to have serious doubts about the direction of previous research in conceptual and category discrimination. Although in cognitive psychology this same sense of dissatisfaction was expressed with an increasing concern with natural-language concepts as they are used in day-to-day affairs, in instructional psychology the concern became one of how best to teach the sort of concepts that are typically taught in the classroom. As in the parallel case in cognitive psychology, in the area of concept teaching the new approach has included both conceptual-logical and empirical-experimental advancements. The major conceptual-logical innovation has been the method of *concept analysis,* whereas experimental investigations have suggested more effective means of teaching concepts.

Concept Analysis

Concept analysis is a process in which conceptual stimulus classes are explicitly defined in terms of their critical and variable features in such a way that instances and noninstances can be constructed for instructional or evaluative purposes (Becker, 1974; Becker, Engelmann, & Thomas, 1975; Engelmann, 1969; Markle & Tiemann, 1970; Roid & Haladyna, 1982). An example of a concept analysis of the concept of reinforcement is presented in Table 5.1.

As illustrated, reinforcement is defined in terms of three critical properties: (a) a stimulus being contingent upon a response; (b) an increased rate of the response; and (c) the increase in the rate of the response being due to the response-consequence contingency (Catania, 1979). In addition, the concept of reinforcement is also deemed to have several variable features, including the type of animal whose behavior is being reinforced and the size of the response unit. Note that these listed variable properties are not an exhaustive compilation of all possible variable features. For example, one could go on specifying all kinds of variable features of reinforcement including the color of the reinforcer, the sex of

TABLE 5.1
Concept Analysis of the Concept of Reinforcement

Properties	Critical	Variable
1. Stimulus contingent upon response	X	
2. Increase in response rate	X	
3. Increase in response rate due to the stimulus being contingent upon the response	X	
4. Type of animal		X
5. Magnitude of increase in response rate		X
6. Type of stimulus (auditory, tactile, visual, gustatory, or olfactory)		X
7. Size of response unit (large or small)		X
8. Observability of the response		X
9. Pleasurableness-painfulness of the stimulus		X

the behaver, the intermittency of the response-consequence relation, and so forth. In practice, the listing of the variable features of a stimulus class in a concept analysis will only include those variable properties that are commonly correlated with the critical properties of the concept and thereby have high cue validities for that concept. For example, in teaching the concept of reinforcement one would probably not be too concerned with whether the organism involved was clothed or unclothed, since this variable feature of reinforcement would not be apt to be improperly established as a discriminative stimulus for classifying instances and noninstances of reinforcement. In contrast, one would be more concerned here with whether the organism involved has "good feelings" with regard to some consequent stimulus, because these good feelings are a variable property of reinforcement that are commonly correlated with the critical properties of the concept. Many beginning students come to inappropriately discriminate instances and noninstances of reinforcement on the basis of these affective factors and must be taught not to do so. As such, attention must be given to this variable feature at the concept analysis stage of concept teaching.

Once a concept has been subject to a property-by-property concept analysis, it is then possible to construct instances and noninstances of the concept for use in teaching and evaluation. The general principle that should guide the derivation of examples is to construct instances that (a) include all the critical features and (b) both include and exclude the variable features. In deriving noninstances, the general principle should be to construct "close-in" noninstances in which all the critical features except one are present. In addition, the presence of the variable features should be varied across noninstances (Becker, 1974; Becker, Engelmann, & Thomas, 1975; Markle & Tiemann, 1970). Specific methods of implementing these principles are discussed later.

Concept analysis is of great value in that it permits students to be presented with a set of instances and noninstances of concepts that allow the student to discriminate what the concept is and is not. However, a more fundamental, and as yet largely untapped, benefit of concept analysis is its role in clarifying the content of a body of knowledge for subject matter experts (Grant & Spencer, 1983). Often, authors and experts in a subject matter are themselves unclear about the critical and variable features of a concept. Concept analysis is of great value here in inducing the expert to define terms clearly and determine if the concepts being taught have substance. In addition to avoiding ambiguity, concept analysis is also useful in making theoretical disagreements among subject matter experts concrete and explicit. For example, Table 5.2 presents a concept analysis of *radical behaviorism* (Day, 1983; Skinner, 1961) along with four sample teaching instances and noninstances. As Todd and Morris (1983) have noted, radical behaviorism is poorly understood within psychology.

More broadly, concept analysis and instances/noninstances derivation may be of considerable benefit in psychology and philosophy to define terms clearly and avoid the pitfalls of vague generalities and empty abstractionisms. Essentially,

	TABLE 5.2		
	Concept: Radical Behaviorism		
	Properties	*Critical*	*Variable*
1. Commitment to experimental methods as a means of dealing effectively with behavior		X	
2. Commitment to a functional analysis of scientific verbal behavior as a means of understanding and improving upon those practices		X	
3. Commitment to a functional analysis of private events and their relationship to observable events		X	
4. The way the position is lableled by writers			X
5. To whom the position is ascribed by writers			X

For each of the following illustrations, specify whether or not the viewpoint is an instance of radical behaviorism. Provide a rationale for your answers in terms of the presence and absence of the critical properties of radical behaviorism.

1. "The radical *behaviorists* led first by John B. Watson (1913) and later by B. F. Skinner (1938) argued that science must investigate public, observable events. The behaviorist concluded that because mental events such as thoughts and images and consciousness cannot be observed directly, they have no place in the science of psychology."* Assume that these behaviorists had a commitment to the experimental method as a means of uncovering important facts about behavior, including scientific verbal behavior.

Analysis: This is not an instance of radical behaviorism since this position avoids the study of the way in which private events are involved in psychological functioning. This is an instance of Watsonian or metaphysical behaviorism, which avoids discussions of private events.

2. "Verbal behavior which is 'descriptive of images' must be accounted for in any adequate science of behavior. The difficulties are the same for both the behaviorist and subjectivist. If the private events are free, a scientific description is impossible in either case. If laws can be discovered then a lawful description of verbal behavior can be achieved, with or without references to images."† Assume that this behaviorist has a commitment to experimental methods as a means of studying behavior.

Analysis: This is an instance of radical behaviorism since it indicates: (a) commitment to the functional analysis of private events (i.e., images) and their relationship to observable (verbal) behavior; (b) a commitment to experimental methodology; and (c) a commitment to the functional analysis of scientific verbal behavior.

3. (Behaviorists) "required that the meaning of a term be fixed by an operational definition—some test whereby the correctness of the ascription of a term was to be decided. The meaning of a term *was* the operations which specified its correct use."** Assume these behaviorists had a commitment to the experimental method and to the study of private events.

Analysis: This is not an instance of radical behaviorism since this position lacks a commitment to the functional analysis of verbal behavior as a means of understanding the "meaning" of terms. This is an instance of one form of methodological behaviorism, which

(continued)

TABLE 5.2 (*Continued*)

has a commitment to defining psychological terms using operational definitions but lacks a larger commitment to functionally analyzing the variables responsible for the scientist's use of terms.

4. "To be consistent the psychologist must deal with his own verbal practices by developing an empirical science of verbal behavior. He cannot, unfortunately, join the logician in defining a definition, for example as a 'rule for the use of a term' (Feigl); he must turn instead to the contingencies of reinforcement which account for the functional relations between a term, as a verbal response, and a given stimulus. This is the 'operational basis' for his use of terms; and it is not logic but science."§ Assume this behaviorist has a commitment to experimental methods and to the study of private events.

Analysis: This is an instance of radical behaviorism since there is (a) a commitment to the functional analysis of verbal behavior as a means of understanding the use of scientific terms; (b) a commitent to experimental methods; and (c) a commitment to the study of private events.

Answers appear on page 162 of this chapter.

when one is made to define one's terms in a manner in which concrete instances and noninstances are (or are easily) derived, it is difficult to be imprecise, even when it is convenient to do so.

The use of concept analysis in dealing with scientific terms is also consistent with the radical-behavioral emphasis upon a functional analysis of scientific verbal behavior as an alternative to operationism (this contrast is exemplified in Table 5.2, items 3 and 4). Concept analysis induces the scientist to specify the variables responsible for his or her use of terms through critical-property analyses and instances and noninstances of the concept. This in turn encourages improvement of the scientist's self-knowledge of the contingencies relevant to his or her use of scientific terms. Research focusing on the conditions responsible for the acquisition and maintenance of psychological category tacts (e.g., through concept programming) may be regarded as exercises in "the empirical science of verbal behavior" (Skinner, 1961, p. 281) applied to the functional analysis of scientific usages. The data supporting concept analysis and programming indicate that these techniques have much to offer now in improving scientific verbal behavior by more precisely specifying the stimuli and conditions responsible for it. Another useful direction in research would be a functional analysis of the variables responsible for the expert's specification of critical properties of scientific category tacts and the attendant derivation of category instances and noninstances. These two activities are often construed as distinctly logical processes not amenable to functional analysis. As Engelmann and Carnine (1982) put it:

> The position adopted in the present work is that there is nothing wrong with behaviorism as far as it goes. It simply does not go far enough in permitting us to

deal theoretically with stimuli. The guidelines that we use for analyzing stimuli are logical. When we say that they are logical, we use the term in a very broad sense. If something is not possible either through "induction" or "deduction," we will consider impossible and will further assume that a learner could not learn it. (p. 366)

The behaviorism characterized here, however, is of the methodological sort, since radical behaviorism advocates a program of functionally analyzing the way we respond verbally to (and thereby deal theoretically with) stimuli. The guidelines that we use for analyzing stimuli are not logical in some sense that prohibits a functional account of them. The guidelines are rules for tacting (e.g., as "critical," "variable" or "probabilistic") the stimulus properties relevant to teaching a concept. These rules are specifications of behavior (e.g., identify a property as "critical"), the conditions under which the behavior is to occur (when the property is possessed by all instances of a conceptual class) and the consequences of the behavior (being able to derive appropriate instances and noninstances for teaching the concept). The processes by which these rules govern and fail to govern the behavior of following them are behavioral insofar as it may be usefully described in terms of the contingencies responsible for acquisition and maintenance of behavior with respect to the rule. In deference to the accomplishments of Engelmann and Carnine, it should be noted that their sophistication in analyzing stimuli has advanced beyond the immediate reach of a functional analysis, but in this respect there is nothing wrong, in principle, with behaviorism.

One aspect of concept analysis that is ostensibly at odds with recent work in cognitive psychology is the continuing emphasis upon the notions of critical and variable (or irrelevant) properties. As described earlier, the appropriateness of the notion of critical or defining features has been questioned in recent cognitive work with natural-language concepts, many of which appear not to be defined in terms of a given set of critical features. This poses no difficulties for many concepts, especially in the sciences, in which concepts continue to be usefully definable in terms of critical features. For example, in behavior analysis writers of concept programs have indeed been successful in defining behavioral concepts in terms of their critical and variable features and in deriving instances and noninstances from such concept analyses (Miller, 1980; Peterson, 1978; Reese & Woolfenden, 1973).

Nonetheless, it is often extraordinarily important to teach natural-language concepts that lack clearly definable critical properties and therefore have ambiguous instances and noninstances. One approach to the problem is to teach each of the component features that are probabilistically related to conceptual class inclusion and to specify the probabilistic relationships involved. For example, in teaching *poetry* it is possible to (a) analyze each of the critical features of the component properties (i.e., stanza format, rhyme, rhythm, alliteration, assonance, metaphor, etc.); (b) specify the probabilistic nature of the component properties as itself a critical feature of *poetry;* (c) specify the relative importance each property has in controlling the category tact "poetry" as another feature of the concept; and (d) derive unambiguous instances and noninstances. Engelmann and Carnine (1982) make this final suggestion:

> Above all, remember that nouns have uncertain boundaries. Do not become em-
> broiled over those examples that are questionable. If an example is not clearly
> negative or not clearly positive, do not use it. The communication with the learner
> is designed to convey what convention has already been established, not to create
> classification conventions or precise boundaries where none exist. (p. 67)

(See Englemann and Carnine [1982, pp. 55–67] for a discussion of issues and procedures involved in teaching natural-language concepts.)

Conditions Responsible for Effective Concept Teaching

In addition to the procedural advance of concept analysis, workers in the field of concept teaching have also empirically validated the effectiveness of a number of methods of concept and category instruction. These variables have included the use of definitions, contexts, synonyms, and instances and noninstances.

A concept definition is a rule that specifies the features of a stimulus or circumstance that determine its inclusion in a particular stimulus class. For example, the definition of *alacrity* is "cheerful promptness." The definitional rule here specifies that the critical features of alacrity are those of cheerful promptness. A concept definition is arrived at quite naturally as a result of concept analysis, since a definition involves no more than a property-by-property specification of the critical features of a concept.

A great deal of research in concept teaching has provided strong support for the use of definitions (Anderson & Kulhavy, 1972; Feldman & Klausmeier, 1974; Johnson & Stratton, 1966; Keenan & Grant, 1979; Miller & Weaver, 1976). These studies have shown that definitions are relatively easy to present to the learner, require relatively little time to acquire, and once learned, they often allow the learner to accurately discriminate novel instances and noninstances. Further, definitional concept learning also often transfers to other tasks such as identifying the correct use of the concept word in sentences and identifying synonyms of the concept word (e.g., Johnson & Stratton, 1966).

Concept definitions appear to be useful in concept teaching because they take advantage of the learner's previously established repertoires of behavior. From a behavioral perspective, learning concepts through definitions may be considered a case of rule-governed behavior in which the conceptual rule specifies the stimulus features to which the learner is to respond. For example, acquisition of the concept of alacrity by learning a definition is only possible if the student has previously acquired the tacts "cheerful" and "promptness" under the control of the appropriate stimulus features. In one sense, learning concepts from definitions does not involve true concept learning since the student's responding was previously under the stimulus control of the relevant stimulus properties. What is involved in such learning is, at best, bringing behavior under the stimulus control of some new combination of previously discriminated features, such as those specified by "cheerful" and "promptness." Several experiments have indicated that concept learning through definitions is sometimes not complete. Often the student requires interaction with actual concept instances and noninstances (e.g., Keenan & Grant, 1979; Miller & Weaver, 1976).

Learning categories by reading the category word in a sentence context, or by being given a synonym, also takes advantage of the learner's existing behavioral repertoire. For example, reading the word *alacrity* in a prose context composed of words in one's existing vocabulary may make it possible to tentatively define alacrity by coming under the stimulus control of the other words and phrases. The individual described as behaving with alacrity, for example, might also be described as smiling, telling jokes, being on time, and being ready and willing to deal with the tasks at hand. At the very least, these contextual stimuli would allow the learner to determine what alacrity is not (i.e., correctly respond to noninstances of the category). Crist and Petrone (1977) and Crist (1981) found that studying the use of words in single-sentence contexts was more valuable than studying the definitions of the words. Context cues, however, can often be misleading in informing the reader of the appropriate stimuli and circumstances that are to control category tacts. For example, *flaunt* means "to show off" (Simon, 1980) but it often appears in instances in which the flaunting individual is showing off in a defiant way. *Flout*, though, means to "to defy," and often occurs in contexts in which defiance occurs in an ostentatious and flaunty way. The context instances in which "flaunt" appears are often accompanied by variable features of *flaunt* that are also critical features of *flout*, and vice versa.

Construction of instances and noninstances is exceedingly important in category teaching. In evaluating conceptual mastery, having students respond to novel instances and noninstances is the only way to ensure that student behavior is indeed under the control of the critical features of the category. For the process of concept teaching itself, use of instances and noninstances is necessary in cases in which the student cannot learn the concept merely by learning a definition, learning a previously acquired synonym, or by making use of contextual cues.

The basic formula in constructing instances and noninstances is to include a wide range of the same variable properties in both instances and noninstances, to use instances with all the critical properties present, and to employ noninstances with only a single missing critical property. Inclusion of the same variable properties in instances and noninstances ensures that variable properties are not established as discriminative stimuli for classifying instances and noninstances. Use of noninstances that have only a single missing critical property is important because it ensures that the students make the conceptual discriminations on the basis of each critical property. "Noninstances" and "nonexamples" in the concept teaching literature generally refer to these "close-in" noninstances that are lacking only a single critical property.

A series of experiments conducted by Robert Tennyson and his colleagues (Tennyson, 1973; Tennyson, Steve, & Boutwell, 1975; Tennyson, Woolley, & Merrill, 1972; for a review see Tennyson & Park, 1980) have explored some specific means of arranging instances and noninstances. In particular, they have demonstrated the benefit of constructing *matched* pairs of instances and noninstances and *divergent* matched pairs of instances and noninstances. An instance/noninstance pair are said to be matched when their variable features are as similar as possible and when they differ only in the presence of a single critical property. For instance, the following instance/noninstance matched pair are concerned with teaching the concept of reinforcement:

Example:
Arthur was a normal student in his biology class. He usually got B's and C's on his tests without studying a great deal. One weekend he had nothing else to do so he opened his books and studied the entire weekend. Later he found he got 100% on the test and, as a result, began to study every weekend for his tests.

Nonexamples:
Arthur was a normal student in his biology class. He usually got B's and C's on his tests without studying a great deal. One weekend he had nothing else to do so he opened his books and studied the entire weekend. Later, he found he got 100% on the test and, as a result, was extremely pleased with his effort.

The instance illustrates reinforcement because the consequence followed the response and functioned to make the response more probable. The noninstance contains all the essential features of the instance except that there is no mention of an increase in the frequency of studying. In Table 5.2, items 1 and 2, and items 3 and 4 are matched noninstance/instance pairs of *radical behaviorism*.

Matched instance/noninstance pairs appear to be useful because they exemplify how the presence or absence of a single critical property determines conceptual class inclusion. Because all the other aspects of the illustration remain constant from instance to noninstance, the student is prompted to attend to the individual critical feature that is varied.

Use of matched instance/noninstance pairs is an excellent way to establish critical features as discriminative stimuli. However, single matched instance/noninstance pairs cannot illustrate the range of variation permitted within the conceptual stimulus class. Therefore, the learner's classificatory responding will not necessarily generalize to other instances of the stimulus class. In order to produce this within-class generalization, *divergent* instance/noninstance pairs may be used. A matched instance/noninstance pair is said to be divergent from another matched instance/noninstance pair when their variable features differ widely. For instance, the following matched pair is divergent from the pair presented previously:

Example:
Dr. Norton was experimenting with one of his white rats. He placed the rat on the floor of an experimental chamber that had a grid through which shocks could be administered. The shock went on every minute for 5 seconds and shock would cease only if the rat pressed a lever in the chamber. As a result of this procedure, the rat began pressing the lever within one second from the time the shock came on.

Nonexample:
Dr. Norton was experimenting with one of his white rats. He placed the rat on the floor of an experimental chamber which had a grid through which shocks could be administered. The shock went on every minute for 5 seconds, no matter what the rat did. As a result of this procedure, the rat began pressing the lever within one second from the time the shock came on.

The instance illustrates reinforcement because shock termination was contingent on a lever press, a feature that is absent in the noninstance, in which shocks were terminated independently of responding. This pair is divergent from the previous pair because the variable features differ from pair to pair. For example, the first pair involved a student in an educational environment where an improved grade served as a reinforcer, whereas the second pair involved an animal in a laboratory situation in which the stimulus change from shock to no shock functioned as a reinforcer. Divergent pairs, as defined, do not stipulate that the same critical property be matched across such pairs, though doing so may be useful. Using preschoolers as subjects, Carnine (1980) found that only minimally divergent pairs should be encountered in early training. He suggests that minimizing initial divergency is particularly helpful for younger learners.

Other work in learning categories has concerned the order of interaction with instances and noninstances, and prompting and feedback methods. Tennyson et al. (1972) and Tennyson (1973) found that having the students encounter easy instance/noninstance items first and then progress to increasingly more difficult items was valuable. One means of making items easy or difficult is through the inclusion or exclusion of prompts. For example, in Miller's (1980) concept program, the initial items in a unit were made easy by coupling them with prompts that directed the student's attention to the critical properties of the items.

As students progressed through the items, the prompts were gradually withdrawn or faded, because the goal was to induce the students to respond correctly to (difficult) illustrations without using prompts.

It has also been established that instances and noninstances used in category teaching should be identified to the learner as such (Grant, McAvoy, & Keenan, 1982; Keenan & Grant, 1979). Further, students should also be informed of *why* each instance and noninstance qualifies as such in terms of the presence and absence of the critical features of the concept (Grant et al., 1982; Ross & Carnine, 1982; Tennyson et al., 1975). Tennyson et al. (1975) labeled this type of information *analysis statements*. In both immediate and retention testing, Grant et al. found that including analysis statements in concept programs improved student performance in explaining the rationale for categorizing an illustration as an instance or noninstance of a psychological concept. However, analysis statements improved classification of noninstances only during retention (final exam) testing, indicating that analysis statements are especially helpful in maintaining previously acquired category tacts. Analysis statements appear to be effective because they specify the tacting relations between the important words in a concept definition and concept instances and the absence of these relations in noninstances. By using analysis statements to teach these relationships, we are essentially teaching the "meaning" of the words in the concept definition.

Concepts, Categories, and Mentalism

Earlier it was stressed that concept and category learning have considerable benefits over the acquisition of specific responses to particular stimuli. In concept acquisition, the learner comes to be able to respond successfully to novel environmental stimuli and circumstances. In addition, as the learner acquires more and more tacts under the control of properties of the environment, it becomes possible to combine tacts and thereby construct and imagine combinations of properties of stimuli and events that are not to be found in the natural environment. For example, most of us would probably have no great difficulty in imagining what a six-headed, fire-breathing lion with sharp bony spikes protruding from its body would look like even though we have never encountered one.

As discussed earlier, the ability to imagine and construct novel combinations of stimuli properties is extremely valuable. All literary works of fiction, for example, depend on the writer's ability to stimulate the reader by arranging words that specify various nonexistent combinations of stimulus properties. (Science fiction and fantasy often differ from more conventional fiction only in the unusualness of the sets of properties the writer specifies rather than in the actual existence of the property combinations described.) Further, the greatest social and technological achievements of our species have resulted from our ability to conceive of combinations of properties and events that do not exist, and then to engage in the behaviors that create instances of those hitherto nonexistent combinations of stimulus properties. Our highest aspirations can be analyzed within this pattern of manipulating tacts as a means of conceptualizing as-yet-unrealized states of affairs.

In general, we see that the manipulation of property tacts to specify nonexistent combinations of properties has its uses. But this process can have a very dark side as well. One way in which it runs amok is when we react to the nonexistent combination of properties that has been "created" by category tacts in the same way as we would do the actual or real events we encounter in day-to-day life. Human history is replete with examples of disasters that stem from failures to distinguish between categories synthetically constructed by combining property tacts and those based on actual interactions with confrontable events and circumstances. Consider the persecution of people who are conceived of as being possessed by demons and evil spirits. Here categories (demons and evil spirits) are created by manipulating individual tacts that do correspond to confrontable properties of the environment. We might consider an evil spirit as a category created by combining several tacts. "Evil," is a tact acquired and maintained with respect to harm-producing events. "Spirit" is itself a combination of the tacts "noncorporeal" ("non," or "without," a tact under the control of the absence of some stimulus or condition; "corporeal," or "body," a tact under the control of the physical properties of an organism) and "being," a tact under the control of properties associated with existence). The individual tacts involved here are acquired by speakers as separate responses to different stimulus contexts. Yet, the recombinant tact "evil spirit" is not one acquired with respect to a single stimulus situation but is a tact consisting of component tacts that were acquired and maintained with respect to properties that occur separately in our environment. Although the stimulus properties tacted do not occur conjointly in nature, the separate verbal operants (i.e., tacts) can. The resulting synthetic category tact is harmless if reacted to as such, but when people have reacted to what they believe are evil spirits manifesting themselves in the form of other people, persecution and violence have often ensued. Similarly, the paranoid's problem results from his or her ability to conceptualize and categorize a confluence of stimulus properties that do not have actual instantiations.

The problem of purely verbal synthetic concepts (e.g., absolutes, universals) permeates virtually every aspect of our institutional, cultural, and social life (Kantor, 1981). Consider the seemingly innocuous and mundane concept of "should" when used in the context of "you should have done such and such"— as an admonishment or reproof for having failed to pursue some course of action. Yet, the concept of "should" in this context specifies a nonexistent state of affairs, a course of action composed of a combination of behavioral properties that have been invented though the manipulation of words—the confrontable fact at hand is that what "should" have been done was *not*. The disadvantage of coming under the stimulus control of "should" statements is that behavior becomes invested in a nonexistent fiction. The resultant behavior of blaming, defending, and harming others is all under the stimulus control of a set of properties that do not exist. An alternative, less wasteful course is to confine our attention to what conditions do exist and how we wish to change these conditions if behavior change is considered desirable.

Even certain aspects of the language of conceptual learning detract attention from the fact that concepts have their basis in discriminative responding to confrontable instances and noninstances of stimuli and events. For example, properties of the environment are sometimes spoken of as being "represented in concept instances." However, a stimulus property has no existence other than by its occurrences in instances of a stimulus class. A stimulus property is not an entity that may be represented in concept instances but a common characteristic of those instances.

Much of the important controversy between cognitive and behavioral psychologies relates to whether it is useful to construct synthetic recombinant category tacts to describe behavior or to confine ourselves to category tacts of relation between naturally occurring combinations of stimulus properties and behavior. For example, in cognitive psychology mental "sensory filter" mechanisms have been used to account for selective attending. A "filter" is a category tact acquired with respect to various sorts of devices that prevent exit of certain substances while allowing other substances to pass unimpeded (e.g., the air, gas, and oil filters on a car, furnace filters, coffee filters, etc.). "Sensory" is a tact acquired and maintained with respect to the relation between stimuli (primarily external) and attentive responding with respect to those stimuli. The synthetic recombinant tact "sensory filter" thus refers to the critical properties of a filter as it pertains to the relations between stimuli and attentional responding. The concept of a sensory filter arose out of research in *dichotic listening* tasks in which the subject listens to two different messages (e.g., connected discourse) each presented in a different ear at the same time. One message is *shadowed* or repeated aloud by the subject. Initially it was thought that unshadowed messages were not responded to at all because the filter did its work at the early point of stimulus input, but exceptions to this view came to light. For example, if one's name is presented to the not-to-be-shadowed ear, it is recognized (Moray, 1959). Also, if connected discourse is first presented to the to-be-shadowed ear, then suddenly switched to the not-to-be-shadowed ear, subjects will at least temporarily continue to shadow the material even though it is being presented in the wrong ear (Treisman, 1960). These and other data led to the development of theories in which the sensory filter was said to screen out messages after they had been initially responded to in some minimal way. Ultimately, however, both the early and late positionings of the filter came to be regarded as undesirable insofar as (a) each stressed that there are severe limits on the amount of stimuli that can be attended to, limits not verified by the data; and (b) each was inadequate in accounting for the flexible nature of selective attention (Howard, 1983; Wessells, 1982). This recognition led to the development of capacity theories of selective attention which emphasize that many *automatic* processes can occur simultaneously, but relatively few *controlled* processes can do so. This distinction between automatic and controlled processes is similar to the behavioral distinction between contingency-shaped and rule-governed behavior (Skinner, 1969).

The synthetic category tact "sensory filter" had misleading effects on the behavior of researchers and theorists who came under the control of it, effects now recognized within cognitive psychology. In contrast, the behaviorist, who shuns such synthetic inner categories to account for behavior, would not have been misled. For example, in accounting for attending to one's own name in the unshadowed ear, it is possible to appeal to a history of relatively powerful differential consequences in effect for attending and failing to attend to one's own name. Similarly, in accounting for the Treisman switchover effect, we might speculate that most people have a history of reinforcement for persistent attending to connected discourse and a history of punishment for ceasing to attend to an as-yet-uncompleted message. The point here is not whether these two accounts are correct, but merely that the categories tacted (antecedent stimuli, responses, and differential consequences) all refer to naturally occurring events plausibly confronted by the subjects who came to selectively attend in the ways that they did. Though filter theories are no longer popular, cognitive psychology continues to make use of many other synthetic-recombinant category tacts. There is some hope, however, that the behavior of cognitivists will be modified by the undesirable consequences of coming under the control of recombinant property categories. For example, Neisser's (1976) comments regarding filter theories have a certain naturalistic flavor:

> When perception is treated as something we do rather than as something thrust upon us, no internal mechanisms of selection are required at all. . . . Organisms are active: they do some things and leave others undone. To pick one apple from a tree you need not filter out all the others; you just don't pick them. A theory of apple picking would have much to explain (How do you decide which one you want? Guide your hand to it? Grasp it?) but it would not have to specify a mechanism to keep unwanted apples out of your mouth. (pp. 84–85)

In summary, although conceptual behavior and categorization are the psychological basis of our greatest achievements, they are also the basis of much self-deception, illusion, and autistic retreats from the natural characteristics of the environment to a false world of synthetic concepts. Some measure of protection against the harmful effects of such concepts inheres in the recognition that concepts and categories are not entities in themselves but pertain to relations between our behavior and the properties of the environment with which we interact.

SUMMARY

The present chapter has considered several selected issues in the areas of conceptual discrimination and categorization from a behavioral perspective. In general, these areas of research and theory have experienced a renaissance in recent years in both cognitive psychology and instructional psychology. Genuine advancements have been made as seen in improvements in our understanding of the structure of categories and in more effective means of concept teaching. However, it is suggested that continuing failures in our understanding of the nature of these processes have contributed to undesirable practices in various areas of human endeavor.

ACKNOWLEDGMENT

Portions of this material were previously published by Athabasca University as a part of a course in the psychology of learning. Part of this chapter was prepared while the author was on sabbatical leave at the department of psychology, University of Helsinki, Helsinki, Finland.

REFERENCES

Anderson, R. C., & Kulhavy, R. W. (1972). Learning concepts from definitions. *American Educational Research Journal, 9,* 385–390.

Anglin, J. M. (1977). *Word, object, and conceptual development.* New York: Norton.

Ashcraft, M. H. (1978). Property norms for typical and atypical items from 17 categories: A description and discussion. *Memory and Cognition, 6,* 227–232.

Becker, W. C. (1974). Teaching concepts and operations, or how to make kids smart. In R. Ulrich, T. Stachnik, & J. Mabry (Eds.), *Control of human behavior: Vol. 3. Behavior modification in education* (pp. 299–312). Glenview, IL: Scott, Foresman.

Becker, W. C., Engelmann, S., & Thomas, D. R. (1975). *Teaching 2: Cognitive learning and instruction.* Chicago: Science Research Associates.

Bourne, L. E., Jr. (1966). *Human conceptual behavior.* Boston: Allyn & Bacon.

Carroll, J. B. (1964). Words, meanings, and concepts. *Harvard Educational Review, 34,* 178–202.

Carnine, D. (1980). Three procedures for presenting minimally different positive and negative instances. *Journal of Educational Psychology, 72,* 452–456.

Catania, A. C. (1979). *Learning.* Englewood Cliffs, NJ: Prentice-Hall.

Clark, D. C. (1971). Teaching concepts in the classroom: A set of teaching prescriptions derived from experimental research. *Journal of Educational Psychology, 62,* 253–278.

Crist, R. L. (1981). Learning concepts from contexts and definitions: A single subject replication. *Journal of Reading Behavior, 13,* 271–277.

Crist, R. L., & Petrone, J. M. (1977). Learning concepts from contexts and definitions. *Journal of Reading Behavior, 9,* 301–303.

Day, W. (1983). On the different between radical and methodological behaviorism. *Behaviorism, 11,* 89–102.

Engelmann, S. (1969). *Conceptual learning.* San Rafael, CA: Dimensions.

Engelmann, S., & Carnine, D. (1982). *Theory of instruction: Principles and applications.* New York: Irvington.

Feldman, K. V., & Klausmeier, H. J. (1974). The effects of two kinds of definitions on concept attainment of fourth and eighth grade students. *Journal of Educational Research, 67,* 219–223.

Glass, A. L., & Holyoak, K. J. (1975). Alternative conceptions of semantic memory. *Cognition, 3,* 313–339.

Grant, L., McAvoy, R., & Keenan, J. B. (1982). Prompting and feedback variables in concept programming. *Teaching of Psychology, 9,* 173–177.
Grant, L., & Spencer, R. E. (1983). The psychology of concept learning and teaching. *Alberta Psychology, 12,* 7–8.
Howard, D. V. (1983). *Cognitive psychology.* New York: Macmillan.
Hull, C. L. (1920). Quantitative aspects of the evolution of concepts: An experimental study. *Psychological Monographs, 28,* (No. 123).
Johnson, D. M., & Stratton, R. P. (1966). Evaluation of five methods of teaching concepts. *Journal of Educational Psychology, 57,* 48–53.
Kantor, J. R. (1981). *Interbehavioral philosophy.* Chicago: Principia Press.
Keenan, J. B., & Grant, L. (1979). *The effects of definitions, examples and nonexamples, and feedback on student conceptual responding.* Paper presented at the fifth annual convention of the Association for Behavior Analysis, Dearborn, Michigan.
Markle, S. M., & Tiemann, P. W. (1970). *Really understanding concepts.* Champaign, IL: Stipes.
Markle, S. M., & Tiemann, P. W. (1974). Some principles of instructional design at higher cognitive levels. In R. Ulrich, T. Stachnik, & J. Mabry (Eds.), *Control of human behavior: Vol. 3. Behavior modification in education* (pp. 312–323). Glenview, IL: Scott, Foresman.
McCloskey, M. E., & Glucksberg, S. (1978). Natural categories: Well defined or fuzzy sets? *Memory and Cognition, 6,* 462–472.
Miller, L. K. (1980). *Principles of everyday behavior analysis* (2nd ed.). Monterey, CA: Brooks/Cole.
Miller, L. K., & Weaver, F. H. (1976). A behavioral technology for producing concept formation in university students. *Journal of Applied Behavior Analysis, 9,* 289–300.
Moray, N. (1959). Attention in dichotic listening: Affective cues and the influence of instructions. *Quarterly Journal of Experimental Psychology, 11,* 56–60.
Murphy, G. L. (1982). Cue validity and levels of categorization. *Psychological Bulletin, 91,* 174–177.
Neisser, U. (1976). *Cognition and reality.* San Francisco: Freeman.
Peterson, N. (1978). *An introduction to verbal behavior.* Grand Rapids, MI: Behavior Associates.
Reese, D. G., & Woolfenden, R. M. (1973). *Behavior analysis of everyday life: A program for the generalization of behavioral concepts.* Kalamazoo, MI: Behaviordelia.
Rips, L. J., Shoben, E. J., & Smith, E. E. (1973). Semantic distance and verification of semantic relations. *Journal of Verbal Learning and Verbal Behavior, 12,* 1–20.
Roid, G. H., & Haladyna, T. M. (1982). *A technology for test-item writing.* New York: Academic Press.
Rosch, E. (1973). On the internal structure of perceptual and semantic categories. In T. E. Moore (Ed.) *Cognitive development and the acquisition of language* (pp. 111–144) New York: Academic Press.
Rosch, E., & Mervis, C. B. (1975). Family resemblances: Studies in the internal structure of categories. *Cognitive Psychology, 7,* 573–605.
Rosch, E., Mervis, C. B., Gray, W., Johnson, D., & Boyes-Braem, P. (1976). Basic objects in natural categories. *Cognitive Psychology, 8,* 382–439.
Ross, D., & Carnine, D. (1982). Analytic assistance: Effects of example selection, subjects' age and syntactic complexity. *Journal of Educational Research, 75,* 294–298.
Simon, J. (1980). *Paradigms lost: Reflections on literacy and its decline.* New York: Clarkson N. Potter.
Skinner, B. F. (1957). *Verbal behavior.* New York: Appleton-Century-Crofts.
Skinner, B. F. (1961). The operational analysis of psychological terms. In *Cumulative record,* enlarged edition (pp. 272–276). New York: Appleton-Century-Crofts.
Skinner, B. F. (1968). *The technology of teaching.* New York: Appleton-Century-Crofts.
Skinner, B. F. (1969). *Contingencies of reinforcement: A theoretical analysis.* New York: Appleton-Century-Crofts.

Smith, E. E., & Medin, D. L. (1981). *Categories and concepts*. Cambridge, MA: Harvard University Press.

Smith, E. E., Shoben, E. J., & Rips, L. J. (1974). Structure and process in semantic memory: A featural model for semantic decisions. *Psychological Review, 81,* 214–241.

Strike, K. A. (1974). On the expressive potential of behaviorist language. *American Educational Research Journal, 11,* 103–120.

Tennyson, R. D. (1973). Effect of negative instances on concept acquisition using a verbal-learning task. *Journal of Educational Psychology, 64,* 247–260.

Tennyson, R. D., & Park, O. (1980). The teaching of concepts: A review of the instructional design research literature. *Review of Educational Research, 50,* 55–70.

Tennyson, R. D., Steve, M. W., & Boutwell, R. C. (1975). Instance sequence and analysis of instance attribute representation in concept acquisition. *Journal of Educational Psychology, 67,* 821–827.

Tennyson, R. D., Woolley, P. R., and Merrill, M. D. (1972). Exemplar and nonexemplar variables which produce correct concept classification behavior and specified classification errors. *Journal of Educational Psychology, 63,* 144–152.

Todd, J. T., & Morris, E. K. (1983). Misconception and miseducation: Presentations of radical behaviorism in psychology textbooks. *The Behavior Analyst, 6,* 153–160.

Treisman, A. M. (1960). Contextual cues in selective listening. *Quarterly Journal of Experimental Psychology, 12,* 242–248.

Walker, J. H. (1975). Real-world variability, reasonableness judgments, and memory representations for concepts. *Journal of Verbal Learning and Verbal Behavior, 14,* 241–252.

Wessells, M. G. (1982). *Cognitive psychology*. New York: Harper & Row.

Following are the answers to the exercises in Table 5.2

*Howard, 1983, p. 5.
†Skinner, 1961, p. 280.
**Strike, 1974, p. 105.
§Skinner, 1961, p. 281.

6

Social Relations and Social Behavior

Cloyd Hyten
Rosalind Burns
West Virginia University

As the field of Behavior Analysis has grown in size and developed in content and sophistication, new areas of psychological phenomena have been addressed. The study of social behavior is one such area that shows signs of becoming an important future direction in the field. To date, behavior analysts have generated a relatively small but promising body of basic and applied social research. The analyses of social behavior put forth by Keller and Schoenfeld (1950) and Skinner (1953) provided the theoretical framework for much of the later empirical and conceptual analyses of such social phenomena as imitation (Baer, Peterson, & Sherman, 1967; Whitehurst, 1978), sharing (Barton & Ascione, 1979; Hake, Vukelich, & Olvera, 1975), altruism (Weiner, 1977), cooperation (Hake & Olvera, 1978; Marwell & Schmitt, 1975), trust (Matthews & Shimoff, 1979; Schmid & Hake, 1983), competition (Hake, Olvera, & Bell, 1975; Lindsley, 1966), prosocial interactions (Detrich & Stokes, 1984; Strain, Shores, & Timm, 1977), and social stimulus control (Hake, Donaldson, & Hyten, 1983; Millard, 1979).

As Hake (1982) pointed out, there are several reasons why behavior analysts should continue to explore the realm of social behavior. Social behavior is a very common form of behavior and its analysis will add considerable breadth to the science of behavior. Social behavior is also a most complex form of behavior and its analysis is likely to yield benefits in terms of conceptual expansion and the development of innovative research techniques. These outcomes are essential to the growth of Behavior Analysis as a discipline, but if social research is to be useful in achieving these outcomes it must be based on a valid conceptual foundation. The theoretical analysis of social behavior has significant implica-

163

tions for the formulation of research questions and the interpretation of research findings in both basic and applied settings.

At this point in the development of Social Behavior Analysis we think it is appropriate to examine its conceptual foundations, especially concerning the definition of social behavior. Even a casual review of behavior analytic work in the social area reveals that there is inconsistency in the way social behavior is defined. What is the basis for distinguishing social behavior, social stimuli, and social control from their nonsocial counterparts? The purpose of this chapter is to discuss the definition of social behavior and analyze key concepts and terms frequently used in behavior analytic treatments of social behavior. In so doing, we propose a conceptual analysis of social interaction which addresses the issues that are basic to the analysis of any social behavior.

BEHAVIOR ANALYTIC ASSUMPTIONS

Before the definitions of social behavior are discussed, it is helpful to examine the philosophical assumptions that have guided behavioral social research and theory. The primary assumption underlying most behavioral work in the social area is that social behavior is governed by the same processes that govern nonsocial behavior (e.g., control by consequences), and is thus explainable by the same principles of behavior derived from nonsocial research (Keller & Schoenfeld, 1950, p. 360; Skinner, 1953, p. 298). Social behavior is not seen as a "special" form of behavior requiring a unique conceptual system to account for it. This is a very practical assumption to make when an analysis from one domain is extended to another, particularly in the early stages of such an extension.

This assumption has been a cornerstone of behavior analytic extrapolation. To be sure, humans are a social species, and the majority of the stimuli controlling human behavior are socially mediated. If the primary assumption is invalid, then our accounts of human social behavior that are based on nonsocial research are invalid, or at best incomplete. This is, in fact, what some traditional social psychologists have argued for years (see Asch, 1959, for a discussion of this issue). The view that something unique emerges in social interactions that cannot be explained by nonsocial principles, referred to as the *social emergent* position, has also been offered by behavioral researchers (e.g., Lindsley, 1966). Proponents of this position argue that social behavior deserves separate treatment and separate principles to account for it.

Unfortunately, both philosophical positions are frequently misconstrued or distorted in their presentation. The social emergent position is often taken to imply that there is a fundamental discontinuity between individual behavior and social behavior; therefore, social behavior warrants special treatment because laws of individual behavior are irrelevant at the social level. Such arguments are typically presented by advocates of mentalism, as when special psychic forces (e.g., the group mind) are invoked to explain the behavior of people in groups. The primary assumption described earlier often degenerates into a purely reductionistic position, with advocates arguing that if social behavior does not warrant special principles then it is not necessary to bother investigating it. According to this view, social interactions can be accounted for by what we currently know from years of nonsocial research. Both of these positions are a hindrance to Social Behavior Analysis.

Let us construct more valid assumptions. From a behavior analytic view, what is "special" about social interactions is their degree of complexity, diversity, and variability. Thus, social behavior merits treatment as a subject matter not because it is fundamentally different from individual behavior, but because it offers the best opportunity to study behavior with these characteristics. We cannot know what variables influence these characteristics merely by inferring or generalizing from nonsocial research that was not designed to examine these issues. To put it simply, the best place to develop an account of social interaction is with the study of social interaction (Weingarten & Mechner, 1966).

One function of the original primary assumption was to encourage behavioral scientists to approach the study of social behavior in the same manner as they have approached the study of nonsocial behavior. Because it has been a largely successful approach, this is a reasonable scientific attitude to take. However, behavior analysts must not cling too stoically to existing methodologies or current formulations of principles. The analysis of new and complex phenomena invariably leads to the development of new methodologies and experimental paradigms. The application of existing principles to these phenomena often leads to the refinement or expansion of these principles, or to the development of new but related principles (e.g., the establishing operation; see Michael, 1982). Whether or not new principles will be needed in the analysis of social behavior cannot be foreseen; this can only be determined by extensive conceptual and empirical contact with the subject matter (Parrott, 1983). The development of new methodologies or modified principles should not be seen as a threat to the integrity of a science. Such growth is a necessary process in any field, and it should be viewed as healthy scientific behavior.

BEHAVIOR ANALYTIC DEFINITIONS

Behavior analysts have also been guided in social research by their explicit or implicit definitions of social behavior. Although it is not necessary to state a formal definition of a subject matter before investigating it, conceptual analyses in some form always influence the behavior of the scientist. We do not mean to imply that the behavior of scientists is always rule-governed, only that empirical activity reflects the influence of conceptual analysis on the part either of the scientist or of others in his or her scientific community. At the very least, an empirical analysis of a phenomenon reflects a conceptual position. Thus, because some conceptual analysis or position is being taken with respect to a subject matter, it is best to acknowledge it explicitly and subject it to closer scrutiny.

Keller and Schoenfeld

Among the explicit definitions of social behavior, perhaps the most influential definition is that of Keller and Schoenfeld (1950). Their book, *Principles of Psychology,* was an early and detailed presentation of state-of-the-art Behavior Analysis widely read by behaviorists of the 1950s. Among the many topics discussed was the analysis of social behavior, which they defined as "behavior for which the reinforcing or discriminative stimuli are, or have been mediated by the behavior of another organism" (pp. 257–258). In other words, in a social situation the behavior of one organism is under the control of another organism's behavior; it will behave differentially depending on how the other organism behaves. This is the earliest and most representative behavior analytic definition of social behavior.

Such a definition has several advantages. First, it is completely behavioral; it does not rely on other systems such as inferred mental events or metaphysical constructions. This, of course, is the hallmark of a behavior analytic definition of any psychological phenomenon. Second, the definition provides limits on the category of social behavior by requiring that there exist a functional relation between the behavior of two or more organisms. Thus, the mere presence or proximity of two organisms is not a sufficient condition for social behavior. The organisms must be interacting in some way for the behavior to be defined as social. Keller and Schoenfeld further refined this definition to include situations in which an organism may be interacting with a product of another organism's behavior (p. 352), although they did not elaborate this point. Thus, two organisms may be involved in a functional relation even though they are not responding directly to each other.

Skinner

Oddly enough, Skinner (1953, pp. 297–312) contradicts the requirement for a functional relation between the behavior of interacting organisms when he defines social behavior as the behavior of two or more organisms with respect to one another "or in concert with respect to a common environment" (p. 297). Obviously, such a statement is intended to include group phenomena such as the behavior of organisms in flocks, mobs, or audiences. Behavior in these situations can be included in a social behavior analysis, but not on the structural basis of mere conglomeration or proximity of organisms. We must side with Keller and Schoenfeld and insist that a functional relation between the behavior of organisms is the essential criterion for social behavior. Hence, if two people cry out, "Oh no!" in response to seeing an auto accident and their behavior happens to be synchronized, it is not meaningfully considered social behavior because there has been no influence of one upon the other. In other group circumstances, however, such synchronized behavior is at least partially controlled by the behavior of coactors (as in the case of rowdy football fans cheering their team on); thus a functional relation does exist and the behaviors can be defined as social.

Keller and Schoenfeld's definition of *social behavior* may be abbreviated to behavior under the control of another organism's behavior. It is clear that a functional relation exists between the behavior of those two organisms. However, the definition has a major drawback: It focuses on the behavior of only one of those organisms—the one whose behavior is under the control of the other. What about the organism whose behavior serves as the discriminative or reinforcing stimulus? Should not that behavior be considered social also? If both organisms are involved in a reciprocal social interaction, each providing controlling stimuli for the other, then both organisms are engaging in social behavior according to the Keller and Schoenfeld definition. What if one organism's behavior is under nonsocial control and the other's is under the control of the first organism's behavior? For example, a child watches his parents on a street corner to determine when to cross the street, but the parents are watching the traffic lights. The behavior of the child and the parents is involved in a functional relation, but according to Keller and Schoenfeld, only the child's behavior should be considered social. Such a restriction is problematic.

The Social Relation

It is awkward and misleading to speak of functional relations between organisms in which only one of the participating organism's behavior is considered social. Should we consider being influenced by another organism somehow more social than influencing another organism's behavior? In both cases a functional relation exists between the behavior of two organisms. What else should the label "social" mean? By restricting the label social to behavior under the control of another organism, emphasis is detracted from the behavior of the other organism which exerts that control. Social behavior is the product of interaction and any feature of a definition that diminishes one side of that interaction is likely to produce inadequate or incomplete analyses. There is evidence that this has, in fact, already occurred. In a review of prosocial behavior research, Detrich and Stokes (1984) have cited several studies (e.g., Strain & Timm, 1974) that presented data concerning the performance of a subject with respect to a group of coactors. The emphasis in these studies was on the behavior of the subject without regard for the interaction between that subject and specific coactors; i.e., no dyadic analyses were presented. Such analyses are incomplete because they have analyzed only one half of the interaction. As Detrich and Stokes argued, this makes a thorough analysis of social control impossible. Similar criticisms have been aimed at Skinner's analysis of verbal behavior (Skinner, 1957) for neglecting the listener side of the verbal interaction (e.g., see Parrott, 1984; Ribes, 1983, p. 237).

These problems stem from definitions of interaction that stress the behavior of one of the participating organisms more than that of the other participating organism. The focus of Keller and Schoenfeld's definition is wrongly placed on social behavior instead of social functional relations. This can lead to a misguided emphasis on the analysis of a response isolated from its specific social context, as if there are certain responses that can be classified as social on the basis of their topography alone. What is social is not anything about the behavior per se, but the fact that two or more organisms participate in the occurrence of that behavior. Thus, the emphasis in any definition of social behavior should not be on the behavior of any one of the involved organisms, but on the functional relation existing between the behavior of both of them. This functional relation will be termed a *social relation*. A social relation exists when there is systematic covariation between the behavior of two or more organisms, for which the controlling stimuli are mediated by the organisms involved.

The concept of the social relation is intended to prevent incomplete empirical or conceptual analyses of social phenomena by emphasizing the interactive nature of social behavior. Social relations always exist with respect to a specific set of involved organisms; they cannot be defined in terms of the actions of only one organism. Therefore, it is inappropriate to ask a question such as, "Is drinking a can of Coke social behavior?" This can only be answered by another question, "With respect to whom?" If there is a functional relation between the person's drinking the Coke and another person's behavior, then and only then can the behaviors involved be labeled social. There is nothing inherently social or nonsocial about any response. Furthermore, social relations are always defined with respect to a given response class or classes. Relation, as used here, is not meant to refer to some kind of all-encompassing relationship between organisms; it is specific to the behavior or behaviors of interest. There are a number of additional points in the definition of a social relation that need to be elaborated.

Source and Reactor Roles. The behavior of any one organism in a social relation can be characterized in terms of its role in that relation. The behavior can serve as a controlling stimulus for the behavior of another organism (a source role), or it can be emitted under the control of another organism's behavior (a reactor role). A given response can, of course, serve both roles in social relations with a reciprocal nature (e.g., conversation). Source and reactor roles may be seen as analogous to the speaker and listener roles elaborated in *Verbal Behavior* (Skinner, 1957). Although they refer to the role behavior occupies in a social relation, they may be used to label the participants as source organism or reactor organism for convenience' sake where it is prudent.

Behavior serving a source or reactor role in a social relation may properly be considered social behavior. This stands in contrast with Keller and Schoenfeld's definition of social behavior; it restricted the term *social behavior* to behavior in the reactor role. The concept of the social relation emphasizes equally the behavior of each participating organism. This avoids the awkwardness inherent in describing a social interaction as social for only one of the involved organisms. It is hoped that it will also encourage social researchers to do more complete, interactive analyses of their subject matter.

The Issue of Awareness.   Social relations are functional relations; they are defined by the control exerted by and impinging upon participating organisms. As such, it is not necessary that the participating organisms "know" or be "aware" of the nature of the interaction. Nor is it necessary that one or both organisms "intend" to interact in order for a social relation to exist. It is very tempting to suggest that a situation is not really social unless the organisms know they are interacting with each other, but to do so is to distort the meaning of the word *social*—reducing it to a synonym for awareness. Organisms can and do influence each other's behavior with and without awareness of each other or the nature of their relationship. It is the functional relation that qualifies the interaction as social.

We do not mean to imply that awareness is insignificant in social relations. Awareness, in the sense of verbal behavior descriptive of other behavior and its controlling relations, is certainly characteristic of many human social relations. If and when it occurs, it may substantially alter the kinds of social behavior observed in a social relation. Verbal behavior of this form can increase the complexity of the relation by evoking historical or auxiliary stimulus functions associated with the particular coactor. For example, on learning that your partner in a competitive task is an old enemy, you may adjust your behavior to become more competitive. At some point it may be useful to distinguish these kinds of social relations from others, but the labels *social* and *nonsocial* should not be used to differentiate them.

Unfortunately, many social researchers have implicitly or explicitly used awareness as the major criterion in their definition of social behavior. For example, Hake and Vukelich (1972) described an experimental condition as social only if the subjects could see each other and knew about the social contingency. Conditions in which subjects still influenced each other's behavior but did not know they were interacting with a partner were referred to as nonsocial. Such labeling is confusing; it fails to distinguish between functional relations, awareness, and interpersonal visual contact. It is best to speak of the interactions in both conditions as being social, and then go on to specify those additional characteristics of the social relation that are important to the analysis (such as the interpersonal visual contact).

Keller and Schoenfeld (1950) implied that awareness is a defining criterion for social behavior when they said they would not "include as social the delivery of a pellet by the experimenter to a bar-pressing rat—it may be a social situation for the experimenter, but it is not for the rat" (p. 258). Why not? Clearly a social relation exists: The behavior of the rat influences the behavior of the experimenter in delivering food, which, in turn, reinforces bar-pressing. Presumably, Keller and Schoenfeld's justification is that the experimenter knows he is interacting with the rat, but the rat doesn't know that the experimenter is controlling his food! Whether or not the rat can or does "know" he is participating in a social interaction has no bearing on the fact that there is an interaction occurring. Using awareness as a defining criterion for the distinction between social and nonsocial behavior only confuses two separate issues: the existence of a functional relation, and the influence of behavior described as "being aware" on that functional relation. Furthermore, it has the effect of excluding some legitimate social interactions from study as social phenomena solely on the basis of often ill-defined states of awareness. These problems are avoided by the concept of the social relation.

It is not surprising that Keller and Schoenfeld (1950) discussed basic animal research in exemplifying nonsocial behavior. That this research is usually called nonsocial reflects the fact that the experimental community is not as interested in the experimenter's behavior as it is in the subject's behavior. This is a legitimate focus, but it does not negate the existence of a social relation. One may think of all basic research as being social research, where isolated organisms interact with products of the experimenter's behavior. Perhaps historians of science, looking back at experimental psychology, will be interested in what variables influenced experimenter behavior and focus on the social nature of the research. However, given the present focus, it is not necessary to call all experimental arrangements between experimenters and subjects "social research." A social relation may exist in all of these cases, but unless one is concerned with the interaction between organisms the label "social" should not be used.

In a social relation, the behavior of at least one of the involved organisms is controlled by social stimuli—stimuli that have been mediated by another organism involved in that relation. What are these social stimuli? What are nonsocial stimuli? What is meant by mediated? How do we differentiate social control from nonsocial control? It is to these two topics, social stimuli and social control, that we now turn our analysis.

SOCIAL STIMULI

What is a Social Stimulus?

Keller and Schoenfeld (1950, p. 258) and Skinner (1953, p. 299) describe a social stimulus as a stimulus mediated by an organism. By *mediated* it is meant that some physical object or energy has been emitted, altered, or manipulated in some way by an organism. We must be careful not to neglect the social function of such stimuli. There are two essential ingredients of a *social stimulus:* First, it must be mediated by an organism, and second, it must be reacted to by another organism. Thus, social stimuli are organism-mediated stimuli, but they are always defined with reference to a social relation between source and reactor organisms.

The two defining criteria of a social stimulus serve to differentiate them from nonsocial stimuli. Mediated stimuli that serve no function within a given social relation are considered nonsocial stimuli. As used here, *function* refers to the various eliciting, evoking, reinforcing, and punishing properties of stimuli. Stimuli that have not been mediated by the organisms involved in the social relation may be considered nonsocial also. These stimuli may be objects or events that have not been mediated by any other organism, or they may have been mediated by some organism outside of the social relation of interest. The latter stimuli are nonsocial with respect to the given social relation, although the same stimuli may be considered social with respect to another social relation. To illustrate, suppose a therapist attempts to increase the social interactions of a shy child by delivering reinforcers whenever the child greets a peer. The consequences are social stimuli in the social relation between therapist and child; they are best considered nonsocial with respect to the interaction between the child and his or her peers. Social stimuli do not exist as entities independent of their respective social relations.

Stimulus Mediation.   At this point, we must clarify what is meant by *mediation,* and discuss the functional consequences of such mediation. When we say that an organism has mediated a stimulus, we mean that the stimulus has been associated with or has interacted with that organism. In a similar fashion, Keller and Schoenfeld (1950) defined mediated stimuli as ''arising from, or in connection with'' the source organism (p. 258). Organisms can mediate stimuli by altering them physically or by altering their stimulus functions. The two kinds of mediation are not mutually exclusive; some physical changes produce functional changes as well. Nevertheless, it is useful to distinguish between social stimuli that are effective components in social relations because they have undergone physical alteration by a source organism, and those that are effective due to some conditioning or transfer process. The nature of the mediation is an important aspect to consider because it may determine certain characteristics of a social stimulus function.

Organisms can physically mediate stimuli by manipulating their presence or location. Mediated stimuli become social stimuli when their functions are brought to bear on a reactor organism. Source organisms can bring reactor organisms into contact with these functions by transporting an object to the reactor organism, or by producing an event in its presence. Organisms can also physically mediate stimuli by altering their form. Extensive changes in the form of a stimulus are particularly likely to result in changes in its function. For example, the mild laughter of a listener may serve to reinforce the behavior of a speaker engaged in conversation; however, should the laughter become excessively loud and uncontrolled it may instead be reacted to as "ridicule" and exert a punishing influence.

Source organisms can also mediate stimuli by interacting with them in ways that merely alter their functions, not their physical characteristics. In the most well-known of these processes, stimulus functions are altered as a result of respondent or operant conditioning. By virtue of their pairing with some conditioned or unconditioned stimulus of a source organism, stimuli acquire respondent social functions for reactor organism behavior. For example, the smell of a perfume or cologne worn by a lover may stimulate a number of conditioned perceptual responses on the part of the lover's partner (even in the absence of the lover). The potency and durability of the respondent functions depend on the contingency or contiguity between the paired stimuli, the intensity of the stimuli, and other factors and parameters too numerous to mention here (for elaboration see Black & Prokasy, 1972; Donahoe & Wessels, 1980, pp. 75–116). Stimuli may also acquire operant functions as a result of their arrangement in an operant contingency involving several organisms. Events that are present when an organism's behavior is reinforced by another may acquire discriminative stimulus properties, for instance. As with respondent social stimuli, operant social stimuli are susceptible to all of the factors that influence their nonsocial counterparts, such as satiation, generalization, or schedule parameters (see Honig & Staddon, 1977).

In humans, stimulus mediation can also occur as a product of verbal interactions. Verbal behavior plays a significant role in many of our social relations. Even though it has no direct physical effect on the environment itself, verbal behavior can establish objects, events, and the behavior of other organisms as controlling social stimuli. The verbal responses of a source organism can serve as "establishing stimuli" (as defined by Michael, 1982) for a reactor organism, altering the reinforcing function of another stimulus and evoking reactor behavior. Verbal responses can also create or alter the effectiveness of discriminative stimuli. The directions given by a local resident to a lost traveller establish certain geographical or physical structures as discriminative stimuli for more effective driving. Particularly striking is the ease and rapidity with which stimulus functions can be altered by verbal mediation (assuming competent speakers and listeners). This enables an amazing range of stimuli to participate more readily in social relations. These mediating functions of verbal behavior are not well understood at present; much more work is required before their role in social relations can be fully explicated.

The research of Sidman and his colleagues on stimulus equivalence (Sidman, Cresson, & Willson-Morris, 1974; Sidman & Tailby, 1982; Sidman et al., 1982) suggests another mechanism by which organisms can mediate the functions of stimuli participating in a social relation. Organisms can indirectly mediate the functions of stimuli by directly altering the function of some member of an equivalent stimulus class to which the other stimuli belong. When the function of one member of an equivalent stimulus class is changed, so are the functions of the other members (Sidman & Tailby, 1982). According to this description, a source organism can simultaneously mediate the functions of many equivalent stimuli by mediating any one of them, producing a number of potential social stimuli with considerable efficiency. Again, as with direct verbal mediation, equivalence relations are not well understood at this point in time. Nevertheless, their role in the development and alteration of social stimuli should not be overlooked.

Space-Time Correspondence. Besides the nature of mediation, another important characteristic of social stimuli is their "space-time correspondence." Organism-mediated stimuli vary in how close they correspond in space and time to the source organism. By the time the mediated stimulus makes contact with the reactor organism it may have suffered some diffusion in space or some delay in time. Space-time correspondence varies along a continuous dimension, ranging from low to high correspondence. Stimuli at the high end of this continuum, such as reflected light, correspond very closely to the location and action of the source organism. Other stimuli, such as odors, may correspond very poorly in space and time to the source organism.

It has been suggested that high-correspondence stimuli may be more naturally salient as social stimuli because of their close relation to the location and, more importantly, the actions of the source organism (Hake et al., 1983). It may be that the behavior of reactor organisms is more readily controlled by high-correspondence stimuli. Simply because a stimulus is low in correspondence to the source organism does not necessarily mean that it will be a less effective social stimulus. However, because they are so removed from the actions of the source organism, low-correspondence stimuli may not exert social functions without special histories of interaction with source and reactor organisms. Although developmentally mature humans often participate in social relations via social stimuli low in space-time correspondence (such as written products), it should be noted that this is not without an extensive history of contact with high-correspondence social stimuli. The earliest, and perhaps most enduring, social stimuli with which we have contact are high-correspondence visual and tactual stimuli mediated by parents and intimate others.

Types of Social Stimuli

Behavior. Social stimuli fall into two broad categories: behavior, and objects or events. Behavior often serves a social stimulus function between organisms. Interactions in which behavior is the controlling stimulus are perhaps the most readily identified as social because the controlling relationships are so obvious to an observer: Some action on the part of one organism directly evokes a response from a second organism. When behavior is identified as the controlling social stimulus, it is typically meant that the interacting organisms are within perceptual range of each other and that, in fact, it is the sight and/or sound of the behaving organism that is the controlling stimulus. Both the visual and the auditory stimuli are products of behavior—not the behavior itself. Reactor organisms usually interact directly with source organisms via some natural product of behavior (such as reflected light or sound waves). *Behavior,* as a social stimulus, refers to those products of behavior that are evanescent and characterized most often by a high degree of space-time correspondence to the source organism.

Social Objects and Events.   Mediated products of behavior include more than the evanescent natural products of action. More permanent behavior-products, as well as mediated existing objects and events, can also serve as social stimuli. These objects and events are effective social stimuli despite the fact that they often have a low degree of space-time correspondence to the source organism. *Social objects* are relatively permanent matter, either produced directly by a source organism (as in synthetic materials) or altered in some way by its behavior, which affect reactor organism behavior. Whereas synthetic products have necessarily been changed physically by an organism, the mediation of existing objects can involve physical alteration or only a change in the stimulus function of the object. *Social events* are transient occurrences other than behavior that are mediated by one organism and reacted to by another.

Social Stimulus Functions.   The three types of social stimuli can exert social control because of previously existing functions or because of acquired functions that are idiosyncratic to the relation between a particular pair of organisms. In the case of behavior as a social stimulus, the existing function of a response may be a natural, reflexive stimulus function, as in the reflexive sucking elicited by a finger in an infant's mouth. The existing function of a response can also be one that has been established by the culture (Kantor, 1982, pp. 246–265). For example, an overburdened sales clerk may halt the onslaught of a horde of shoppers rushing for discounted items by extending an arm straight out with the palm of the hand exposed and perpendicular to the arm in the well-recognized gesture for "stop." In other cases, a behavioral stimulus may have acquired a function peculiar to a particular social relation, as when siblings develop a special "language" to communicate to each other.

Social objects can control reactor behavior through existing functions such as those engendered by the physical properties of the object, or previously established functions endowed by the culture. In such cases, the source organism merely manipulates the presence or location of the object with the effect of bringing the reactor organism under the control of the "natural" function of the object. Social objects can also acquire idiosyncratic functions. Such objects are likely to generate reactor behavior directed toward the source organism. The social object may even evoke responses to it that are similar in form to those evoked by the source organism itself, as when a person smiles at a photograph of a friend. As with social objects, the function of social events may be idiosyncratic to the particular social relation, or merely the existing function of an event which then becomes involved in a social relation. As an example of the former, a financially strapped college student may signal his parents to call him by dialing their phone after 11 p.m. and letting it ring just once. As an example of the latter, a prankster may take advantage of the existing function of a fire alarm bell to force his victims to evacuate a building. In order to be considered social, it is not necessary that an object or event evoke behavior that is normally evoked by another organism (cf. Parrott, 1983). Any organism-mediated object or event that controls some response class of another organism is considered social— regardless of whether that behavior is of an interpersonal form or otherwise.

Our definition of a social stimulus is necessarily broad, so as not to exclude important controlling variables from the analysis of the many factors that influence behavior in social relations. The requirement that social stimuli be organism-mediated and behavior-controlling includes a wide range of mediation as well as diverse reactor responses. Most actions, objects, or events can, at one time or another, participate in a social relation as social stimuli. However, stimuli are defined as social only in the context of the social relations in which they operate; in all cases the distinction between social and nonsocial stimuli depends upon which social relation is being analyzed. In this sense our definition is narrow because it restricts the label social to those stimuli that have been mediated and exert their functions within the confines of a given social relation.

SOCIAL CONTROL

What is Social Control?

All social relations are characterized by the functional relation between the social stimuli of one organism and the behavior of another organism. *Social control* refers to the influence of those stimuli upon reactor behavior. No differential strength is accorded antecedent or consequent stimuli in our analysis; social control refers to the influence of either or both. The social control exerted by the participating organisms is not symmetrical in every social relation. In one case, an organism's behavior may be under the control of another's behavior but not vice versa. In other cases, the control may be completely symmetrical, as in conversational interactions. Social relations may be placed along a continuum representing the symmetry of social control. Those relations at the "low symmetry'' end of this continuum may be referred to as unidirectional social relations, because only one of the participating organisms is exerting social control. Relations that are highly symmetrical may be referred to as bidirectional social relations, because social control is exerted by both organisms.

Analyzing Social Control.   In order to demonstrate that a social relation exists, it is imperative that the researcher analyze the social control operating in the alleged relation. Unfortunately, many basic and applied studies of social interaction have failed to conduct adequate analyses of social control (Detrich & Stokes, 1984; Hake & Vukelich, 1972). This seriously threatens the validity of the research. Unless the social control is isolated, no claim can be made that a social interaction is occurring, and the labeling of stimuli and responses as "social" is unjustified. Next, we examine the strategic considerations that should guide the analysis of social control.

Before social control can be analyzed, it is necessary to specify the target social relation. This involves two steps. First, the organisms that are thought to be participating in the social relation must be identified. It is never sufficient to identify only one subject in a social interaction, even if that subject's behavior is the primary concern. The analysis of social control cannot proceed without the frame of reference provided by the set of all participating organisms. Second, the interaction of interest must be specified. For instance, are we analyzing an altruistic relation, an aggressive relation, or perhaps a competitive interaction? Of course not every social interaction fits neatly into a conventional category. Besides, many conventionally defined categories of social interaction are too broad or too nebulous for behavioral research purposes. In any case, the researcher must take care to define the interaction in terms of the relation between key stimuli and responses. Hake and Olvera (1978) provide an excellent example of this in their analysis of cooperation. For a social relation to be designated as cooperative, the reinforcers for each subject must be in part dependent upon the behavior of the other subject. Furthermore, the behavior of each subject must be controlled by the cooperation contingency and not by some other contingency (such as threats of physical abuse).

Once the target relation has been specified, the nature and degree of social control can be ascertained. The strategy here is to determine which responses of one organism are functionally related to the actions or products of the other organism. In order to argue that the relation is indeed social, the researcher must (at a minimum) rule out the possibility that the behavior of the participating organisms is controlled exclusively by nonsocial stimuli. Various techniques can be used to demonstrate that nonsocial sources are not exerting complete control. In laboratory studies, for example, it is often possible to manipulate the presence of the coactor or its social stimuli, or to control for the influence of nonsocial stimuli. Hyten (1983) used these techniques in the analysis of a social conditional discrimination involving two pigeons matching to sample in adjoining compartments separated by a Plexiglas partition. A leader bird matched to sample in standard fashion with a sample key away from the partition and two match keys next to the partition; to be correct on a trial the follower bird had to peck the same color match key in his compartment as the leader bird had pecked in his compartment. It was possible that accurate matching behavior of the follower was controlled by the nonsocial stimulus of the leader's sample key color. To test for nonsocial control, the leader bird was removed and his sample key was illuminated on successive trials. Follower bird accuracy subsequently decreased to chance levels, indicating that matching accuracy was not, in fact, controlled by nonsocial stimuli.

Merely demonstrating that the relation is social is not adequate if one contends that a specific type of social interaction (e.g., aggression) is being investigated. In order to argue that the existing functional relation is the one specified in the definition of the interaction, the researcher must demonstrate that the appropriate source and reactor behaviors are related. This can also be assessed in a variety of ways. In research where the concern is with the social behavior of a particular subject or client (as in applied studies), trained confederates can be used as interacting partners. The researcher can then determine the effect of specific responses on the subject's behavior (Detrich & Stokes, 1984). In other cases, the researcher may be studying a freely interacting dyad (in the laboratory or in the field), and other tactics will have to be employed.

Where the researchers cannot directly manipulate the behavior of one member of a dyad, a fine-grain analysis of the behavior of both subjects is necessary to elucidate the functional relation. Statistical methods of interaction analysis, such as lag sequential analysis, can be used by social researchers to determine the relation between a particular response class of one organism and the behavior of another (see Gottman & Bakeman, 1979; Sackett, 1978). With these methods, repetitive patterns of interaction can be readily detected, even when there is a considerable time delay or intervening responses between the functionally related responses.[1] The researcher need not employ sophisticated statistical techniques to analyze a social relation in detailed fashion. Consider, for example, the analysis of bidirectional social relations conducted by Hake, Vukelich, and Olvera (1975). The experimental procedure involved pairs of human subjects distributing between them matching-to-sample problems that were worth points and money. Subjects could either give the problem to their partner or take the problem for themselves by moving a problem distribution lever on their apparatus on every trial. Measures of intersubject correspondence (total points of one subject/total points of the other subject) were used to determine if reinforcers were distributed equitably between members of a pair. An increase in correspon-

---

[1]Some of these techniques make use of inferential statistics, and the behavioral researcher may wish to consider the admonitions of Johnston and Pennypacker (1980, pp. 370–374) in deciding whether to adopt them.

dence shows that the behavior of at least one of the persons was under the control of the responses and/or reinforcers of the coactor, a requirement for the definition of cooperation. Correspondence did increase across sessions, but an analysis of the method of problem distribution within sessions revealed that some pairs achieved the equity by letting each other take problems instead of giving problems to each other. Hake et al. used these measures to argue for a functional distinction between two types of social relations: sharing (an increase in taking responses by both subjects leading to equity) and maximal cooperation (an increase in giving responses by both subjects leading to equity).

Types of Social Control

Source organisms control the behavior of reactor organisms via two categories of social stimuli: behavior, and social objects or events. The control exerted by behavioral stimuli may be referred to as *direct control,* and the control exerted by social objects or events referred to as *indirect control.* The terms direct and indirect were chosen to reflect the relationship of the stimuli to the source organism, in order to retain the emphasis on the interaction between source and reactor organisms. Although we do not assume that there are qualitative differences between the effectiveness of direct and indirect control, there are a number of differences in their typical characteristics that warrant elaboration. In the laboratory these characteristics can be altered or eliminated, but in uncontrolled settings they may influence the nature of the social relation considerably.

Direct Control.   We may well expect some practical differences in the direct control exerted by behavioral stimuli as opposed to indirect control by objects of events. Behavior as a stimulus is very complex, even in the most controlled settings. It is typically composed of multiple responses occurring in three-dimensional space as well as patterns of pausing. Responses of the same functional class often exhibit considerable variability in topography and rate (especially outside the lab). Behavior is also characterized by its dynamic flexibility, in that source organisms can often emit a variety of responses in a short period of time according to changing environmental conditions.

The complexity, variability, and flexibility of behavior can make it a very unstable stimulus, as compared to the stability of an inanimate stimulus such as a key light in a pigeon chamber. With a widely fluctuating behavioral stimulus, the social response of the reactor organism is more variable also. If the organisms involved are participating in a bidirectional social relation, the variability "feeds back" on itself and is multiplied. Skinner (1953, pp. 308–309) also noted this tendency of direct bidirectional relations to become progressively unstable. Thus, an important characteristic of direct control is that it often generates variable responding because it is often exerted by a variable stimulus. It is not that behavior as a stimulus is inherently more variable than other stimulus objects or events, but it typically is unless explicitly controlled. Even in laboratory settings, it is much easier for the researcher to control a stimulus light than it is to control a confederate's behavior with the same precision.

Direct control is exerted by stimuli that have a high degree of space-time correspondence to the source organism. Because of the temporal and spatial proximity of the reactor organism to the source organism, changes in source behavior may immediately result in changes in reactor behavior. The mediation of light or sound waves by a behaving source organism is almost instantaneous compared to the delays typically involved in mediating a stimulus object. Thus, delays between the action and reaction of the interacting organisms are minimized in cases of direct control. Furthermore, in proximal interactions, the reactor organism is likely to be in contact with many other stimulus functions of the behaving source organism. The diversity and flexibility of the source organism's behavior make it more likely that the direct control of one response class will be accompanied by the direct control of other response classes.

Indirect Control. Through indirect control, organisms may effectively interact even though they are separated in space and time from each other. Thus, indirect control permits an extension of social relations beyond the restricting confines of inter-organism sensory contact. Social behavior is possible between any organisms that can make any form of direct or indirect contact with each other. The development of writing thousands of years ago and, more recently, the development of advanced communication and transportation technology have led to extensive indirect control in human social relations far surpassing the level of indirect control observed in the social relations of other species. It can even be argued that indirect control is an essential feature of human civilization.

Social objects or events do not usually have the multiple functions or the flexibility that characterize behavior as a social stimulus (Parrott, 1983). Other than natural functions (which are few in number), the number of functions which these stimuli possess depends on the degree of mediation exerted by the source organism. The time and effort required to mediate social objects or events is often appreciably more than that required to mediate a behavioral stimulus, and this may inhibit source organisms from endowing objects or events with multiple functions. Social objects and events are also less flexible than behavior as a stimulus. Behavior is a fluid, continuous process and new responses with new functions can readily be emitted by a source organism in a direct social relation. On the other hand, social objects or social events are often static or discrete; any change in their function requires an additional act of mediation. For these reasons, indirect control is typically less dynamic than direct control; that is, it generates a narrow range of uniform and consistent responding.

The relative permanence of social objects adds another feature to indirect control. It enables a source organism to interact with many reactor organisms across time. One book may become a personal communication between the author and millions of readers, long after it is written. The stability of the social object also permits the reactor side of the social interaction to be revived indefinitely (as long as the object remains intact). A letter from a friend or a lover may continue to evoke emotional responses from the reader each time it is read. Although indirect controlling stimuli usually possess fewer functions than direct controlling stimuli, they are capable of influencing many more organisms and generating repeated episodes of the reactor response over long periods of time.

SUMMARY AND CONCLUSIONS

In this chapter we have presented an analysis of social behavior that stresses the role of each of the organisms participating in the social interaction. The concept of the social relation underscores the fact that social behavior cannot be defined without reference to a set of interacting organisms. Previous behavior analytic definitions have downplayed the social relation by focusing on reactor organisms and reactor behavior. We feel that a complete analysis of social relations cannot be made unless the behavior of both source and reactor organisms is given equal status. For that reason both source and reactor responses are defined as social behavior within the context of a given social relation.

Social stimuli have been defined as organism-mediated stimuli that affect the behavior of another organism. All social stimuli fall into three classes: behavior, social objects, or social events. The inclusion of objects or events as social stimuli considerably expands the range of social relations beyond those that occur when organisms are in face-to-face contact, while retaining the requirement of a functional relation between the behavior of organisms. Several characteristics of social stimuli have been discussed, including the nature of the mediation as well as the correspondence in space and time of the stimulus to its source organism. We have suggested that these characteristics are important in determining the nature of the social relation, but that remains to be verified by empirical activity. There is much room for research here, particularly with the important process of stimulus mediation. Very little is known about the origin and transfer of social stimulus functions beyond what we can suggest from our knowledge of basic respondent and operant conditioning processes. An important area for future social research is the analysis of the role that verbal behavior serves in mediating social objects or events, or as a social stimulus itself. Although these issues may be addressed in basic nonsocial research, we would like to encourage researchers to study them in the context of the social relations in which they naturally participate. There is no need to restrict research to simple nonsocial formats when the issues are more properly addressed in social contexts. The pioneering works of the social researchers mentioned in this chapter have shown this to be not only feasible but productive as well.

Social control is the essential prerequisite for the definition of any social relation. We have stressed the importance of demonstrating social control whenever social behavior is being studied. Many social researchers have been remiss in this respect, and this has threatened the validity of this research. The analysis of social control should not be viewed as a burden by the social researcher. Some researchers may claim to be more interested in the behavior of a subject or client, but to focus on the activity of an organism apart from its controlling variables is to conduct a purely structural analysis. The analysis of social control is no more than the elucidation of the behavior-environment relation, the basic subject matter of all Behavior Analysis. We have discussed two types of social control, direct and indirect, and suggested a number of differences in their characteristics. There is, in fact, some empirical support for this suggestion. Lindsley (1966) found that leadership in a sequenced cooperative task was strongly affected in some pairs by whether or not the partner was visible (direct control) or if only lights correlated with the partner's responses were illuminated (indirect control). These characteristics need to be elaborated empirically; their analysis will aid us in understanding and predicting behavior in a great many social relations.

The study of social relations is a large and potentially fruitful domain for behavior analysts. A handful of behavioral researchers have already begun to address major social phenomena, but much more research lies ahead. If investigation is to continue effectively, it must be based on a valid conceptual foundation. The purpose of this chapter has been to refine such a framework, enabling a more thorough analysis of social interactions. At the heart of our definition is the concept of the social relation, providing the context within which social behavior, social stimuli, and social control may be defined. We have discussed many of the issues central to the analysis of social relations, and clarified the meaning of terms suggested by previous analyses. It is hoped that this will help social researchers to identify their subject matter more clearly, and to avoid spurious criteria for the distinction between social and nonsocial events. Our definition is intended to stimulate a more interactive analysis of social behavior, and thus to prevent one-sided analyses based on topographical characteristics or unspecified sources of social control. A commitment to a more complete, interactive analysis of social relations may necessitate new research focuses (a few of which we have suggested here) and new methodologies. These developments can only foster the growth of Social Behavior Analysis and add to the sophistication of our science.

ACKNOWLEDGMENTS

The impetus for writing this chapter was provided by the late Don Hake, who collaborated with the authors on early versions of the paper. We gratefully acknowledge his substantial contribution to our understanding and interest in the topic. We also wish to thank Linda Parrott and William Buskist for their helpful suggestions and encouragement.

Portions of this chapter were presented at the Association for Behavior Analysis meeting, Milwaukee, Wisconsin, May, 1983.

REFERENCES

Asch, S. E. (1959). A perspective on social psychology. In S. Koch (Ed.), *Psychology: A study of a science* (Vol. 3, pp. 363–384). New York: McGraw-Hill.

Baer, D. M., Peterson, R. F., & Sherman, J. A. (1967). The development of imitation by reinforcing behavioral similarity to a model. *Journal of the Experimental Analysis of Behavior, 10,* 405–416.

Barton, E. J., & Ascione, F. R. (1979). Sharing in preschool children: Facilitation, stimulus generalization, response generalization, and maintenance. *Journal of Applied Behavior Analysis, 12,* 417–430.

Black, A. H., & Prokasy, W. F. (1972). *Classical conditioning II: Current theory and research.* New York: Appleton-Century-Crofts.

Detrich, R., & Stokes, T. F. (1984, May). *You can't judge a book: Topography, function, and prosocial behavior.* Paper presented at meeting of the Association for Behavior Analysis, Nashville.

Donahoe, J. W., & Wessels, M. G. (1980). *Language, learning, and memory.* New York: Harper & Row.

Gottman, J. M., & Bakeman, R. (1979). The sequential analysis of observational data. In M. E. Lamb, S. J. Suomi, & G. R. Stephenson (Eds.), *Social interaction analysis* (pp. 185–206). Madison, WI: University of Wisconsin Press.

Hake, D. F. (1982). The basic-applied continuum and the possible evolution of human operant social and verbal research. *The Behavior Analyst, 39,* 7–23.

Hake, D. F., Donaldson, T., & Hyten, C. (1983). Analysis of discriminative control by social behavioral stimuli. *Journal of the Experimental Analysis of Behavior, 39,* 7–23.

Hake, D. F., & Olvera, D. (1978). Cooperation, competition and related social phenomena. In A. C. Catania & T. A. Brigham (Eds.), *Handbook of applied behavior analysis* (pp. 208–245). New York: Irvington.

Hake, D. F., Olvera, D., & Bell, J. C. (1975). Switching from competition to sharing or cooperation at large response requirements: Competition requires more responding. *Journal of the Experimental Analysis of Behavior, 24,* 243–254.

Hake, D. F., & Vukelich, R. (1972). A classification and review of cooperation procedures. *Journal of the Experimental Analysis of Behavior, 18,* 333–343.

Hake, D. F., Vukelich, R., & Olvera, D. (1975). The measurement of sharing and cooperation as equity effects and some relationships between them. *Journal of the Experimental Analysis of Behavior, 23,* 63–79.

Honig, W. K., & Staddon, J. E. R. (1977). *Handbook of operant behavior.* Englewood Cliffs, NJ: Prentice-Hall.

Hyten, C. (1983). *Social matching to sample: Acquisition and the effects of ratio matching.* Unpublished master's thesis, West Virginia University, Morgantown.

Johnston, J. M., & Pennypacker, H. S. (1980). *Strategies and tactics of human behavioral research.* Hillsdale, NJ: Lawrence Erlbaum Associates.

Kantor, J. R. (1982). *Cultural psychology.* Chicago, IL: Principia Press.

Keller, F. S., & Schoenfeld, W. N. (1950). *Principles of psychology: A systematic text in the science of behavior.* New York: Appleton-Century-Crofts.

Lindsley, O. R. (1966). Experimental analysis of cooperation and competition. In T. Verhave (Ed.), *The experimental analysis of behavior: Selected readings* (pp. 470–501). New York: Appleton-Century-Crofts.

Marwell, G., & Schmitt, D. R. (1975). *Cooperation: An experimental analysis.* New York: Academic Press.

Matthews, B. A., & Shimoff, E. (1979). Expansion of exchange: Monitoring trust levels in ongoing exchange relations. *Journal of Conflict Resolution, 23,* 538–560.

Michael, J. (1982). Distinguishing between discriminative and motivational functions of stimuli. *Journal of the Experimental Analysis of Behavior, 37,* 149–155.

Millard, W. J. (1979). Stimulus properties of conspecific behavior. *Journal of the Experimental Analysis of Behavior, 32,* 283–296.

Parrott, L. J. (1984). Listening and understanding. *The Behavior Analyst, 7,* 29–39.

Parrott, L. J. (1983). Defining social behavior: An exercise in scientific system building. *The Psychological Record, 33,* 533–550.

Ribes, E. (1983). Has Behavior Analysis actually dealt with language? In N. W. Smith, P. T. Mountjoy, & D. H. Ruben (Eds.), *Reassessment in psychology: The interbehavioral alternative* (pp. 233–249). Washington, DC: University Press of America.

Sackett, G. P. (1978). Measurement in observational research. In G. P. Sackett (Ed.), *Observing behavior: Vol. II: Data collection and analysis methods* (pp. 25–43). Baltimore: University Park Press.

Schmid, T. L., & Hake, D. F. (1983). Fast acquisition of cooperation and trust: A two-stage view of trusting. *Journal of the Experimental Analysis of Behavior, 40,* 179–192.

Sidman, M., Cresson, O. J., & Willson-Morris, M. (1974). Acquisition of matching to sample via mediated transfer. *Journal of the Experimental Analysis of Behavior, 22,* 261–273.

Sidman, M., Rauzin, R., Lazar, R., Cunningham, S., Tailby, W., & Carrigan, P. (1982). A search for symmetry in the conditional discrimination of rhesus monkeys, baboons, and children. *Journal of the Experimental Analysis of Behavior, 37,* 5–22.

Sidman, M., & Tailby, W. (1982). Conditional discrimination vs. matching to sample: An expansion of the testing paradigm. *Journal of the Experimental Analysis of Behavior, 37,* 5–22.

Skinner, B. F. (1953). *Science and human behavior.* New York: Macmillan.

Skinner, B. F. (1957). *Verbal behavior.* Englewood Cliffs, NJ: Prentice-Hall.

Strain, P. S., Shores, R. E., & Timm, M. A. (1977). Effects of peer social initiations on the behavior of withdrawn preschool children. *Journal of Applied Behavior Analysis, 10,* 289–298.

Strain, P. S., & Timm, M. A. (1974). An experimental analysis of social interactions between a behaviorally disordered preschool child and her classroom peers, *Journal of Applied Behavior Analysis, 7,* 583–590.

Weiner, H. (1977). An operant analysis of human altruistic responding. *Journal of the Experimental Analysis of Behavior, 27,* 515–528.

Weingarten, R., & Mechner, F. (1966). The contingency as an independent variable of social interaction. In T. Verhave (Ed.), *The experimental analysis of behavior: Selected readings* (pp. 447–459). New York: Appleton-Century-Crofts.

Whitehurst, G. J. (1978). Observational learning. In A. C. Catania & T. A. Brigham (Eds.), *Handbook of applied behavior analysis* (pp. 142–178). New York: Irvington.

7 Behavioral Gerontology

Phyllis N. Williamson
New Mexico State Hospital
Las Vegas, New Mexico

THE CONCEPT OF AGING

The term *aging* has taken on an almost mythical quality in both our society and (even worse) the mental health professions. Although there is no universally agreed-upon age at which one is considered elderly, a rather arbitrary division between middle and old age is typically set at retirement, or 65 years of age. Age would seem to be the most relevant variable that sets the elderly apart from other segments of the population. Unfortunately, when a group of people is so easily differentiated from a larger group it is more likely that certain stereotypes will develop around this subgroup (Wolfensberger, 1972). Such stereotyping has occurred to a number of population groups, one of the most notable being the mentally retarded. Behaviorists were in the forefront dispelling the myths and stereotypes identified with the retarded—e.g., they were untrainable, unproductive, dangerous, and so forth. Many introductory psychology textbooks (e.g., Whaley & Malott, 1971) include a number of demonstrations of the modifiability of the behavior of mentally retarded individuals.

The elderly are also discriminated from the rest of the population based on myths and stereotypes associated with aging. Consequently, age alone is not treated as the only relevant discriminative stimulus; other descriptors are also commonly accepted as relevant to the aged person, e.g., frail or dependent. Descriptors implicitly portrayed by the media include foolish, comical, sarcastic, or ignorant.

Behaviorists have not yet taken the lead in the field of gerontology, as they did with the mentally retarded, in dispelling these myths. In fact, it is primarily the medical profession under the auspices of the medical model that has made the greatest attempts to dispel these stereotypes. From a behaviorist's point of view it is disadvantageous to allow the medical model to lead the way in countering the aging myth because under the medical model, even when gains are made at eliminating stereotyped descriptors of the elderly, the mythical quality of aging remains strong. The aged person becomes confused with the metaphor of aging.

Sarbin and Mancuso (1980) address the tendency to accept metaphors as real entities when a medical model is followed. They argue that by its use the term *schizophrenia* has been successfully transformed from its metaphorical origin to that of a real disease entity. A person is not described as behaving *as if* he or she is schizophrenic [sic] split-brained, but the person actually *has* schizophrenia. This turn of events results from following a particular paradigm, the medical model, and thus qualifies as a myth. As with the powerful and influential myth of "schizophrenia," "aging" is fast becoming a mythical entity itself.

The process of aging does exist, of course. Many developmental psychologists study the course of aging (development, growth, etc.) over the life span. However, aging (the myth) is seen by many as a disease or a mental disorder that is taking on epidemic proportions and that requires serious attention to find a cure.

We cannot cure aging. What behaviorists can do, and are beginning to accomplish, is to re-educate those professionals who come in contact with the aged, clinically or through research, and to restructure the concept of aging.

The intent of this chapter is to clarify the role being played by behavioral gerontology in meeting this need. Several questions are addressed: Has the applied or the basic work in this field been successful at demonstrating the fallacy of the metaphor of aging? Has behavioral gerontology provided an alternative to this metaphor? What more must behaviorists do?

Finally, the economics of perpetuating the mythical quality of aging are quite powerful. The growing numbers of people over the age of 65 (U.S. Department of Commerce, 1979) are producing an upsurge of professionals interested in aging and the aged. Financial resources are swinging in this direction, making the business of aging quite lucrative. If behavioral gerontologists expose the myth of aging, how will this impact the economics of the aging industry?

BEHAVIORAL GERONTOLOGY: ITS BEGINNINGS

It is difficult to identify an actual beginning of behavioral gerontology as a separate research or clinical endeavor. Its beginning is based more on important conceptual papers and research reports than on the actual identification of a specialty area. For the purposes of this discussion there are four contributions that have been major influences on the field. They are discussed according to their conceptual importance rather than their chronological appearance in the literature.

In general, interest in gerontology by behaviorists began to emerge in the late 1960s and has been slowly increasing ever since, although interest is still quite limited (Wisocki & Mosher, 1982). The first major attempt to address indirectly the myth of aging was made by Baer (1970) in a paper entitled "An Age-Irrelevant Concept of Development." He made the important point that development simply refers to varying levels of experiential histories at different points in time. Age is not the crucial variable. People do age and certainly the number of people over age 65 (i.e., the aged) is getting larger. However, this population statistic does not warrant treating the process of age as an entity (the myth). In fact, much of the data indicate that there is more heterogeneity than homogeneity within this population than between the elderly and younger populations (Baltes & Baltes, 1979).

The question may then be asked, why a specialty field called behavioral gerontology? Each specialist will have his or her own answer. It may be to dispel the myth of aging; it may be that the behaviorist prefers this age group (as many seem to prefer working with children); it may be to address special problems such as dementia; or it may be purely economical, e.g., availability of grant money. But it should never be that aging is a special problem in and of itself. Otherwise, it would be hard to explain the approximately 80% of people over 65 who are functioning independently and effectively (Kramer, Taube, & Redick, 1973).

A second major influence was a paper by Lindsley published in 1964. He recommended an expansion of the technique of prosthetic intervention to compensate for deficits frequently seen in the behavior of elderly persons. This paper reminded behaviorists of the interaction between behavior and the environment. Behavior need not be addressed directly; rather, intervention with the environment can lead to competent behavior in an elderly person. As with clients of any age, the clinician must take into account the individual pattern of deficits and then provide a prosthetic environment to compensate for these deficits. Instead of age being the independent variable leading inevitably to a worsening in the behavior of the aging person, the environment is recognized as the important independent variable, which when manipulated results in a functional change in the behavioral repertoire of the individual. Lindsley (1964) would describe this as the individual no longer living "beyond his/her environment."

Cautela wrote two papers, one in 1969 demonstrating the role of conditioning in the development and modification of behaviors of the elderly, preceded by a 1966 paper discussing the utility of behavior therapy with the elderly as well as with other age groups. The importance of Cautela's work was not so much its conceptual base but its demonstration of behavior change with an elderly population. It helped to dispel the stereotype of the aged person as someone who has reached the end of development and whose behavior is intractably set, which was something that had to be demonstrated, incidentally, because Lindsley (1964) had not addressed the issue of changing behavior directly and had perhaps perpetuated the myth of elderly decline by emphasizing multiple deficits developing as one aged.

Finally, Kastenbaum (1968) called attention to the need for empirical testing of whether aging is a biological or a psychological phenomenon. He suggested that describing aging as either a cause or an effect has little value, but that demonstrating the ability of the researcher to control "aged behaviors" in the young or elderly would certainly strengthen the psychological viewpoint and weaken the notion of biological determinism. His emphasis on research validation prodded behaviorists to utilize data rather than theoretical debate to make their point that the behavior of the aged can be explained, predicted, and altered from an environmental and not merely an organismic perspective.

These four contributions have prompted behaviorists to consider the question of age from a different conceptual basis, to apply the technology of behavioral engineering to yet another population, and to attempt behavior change of aged individuals in much the same way as individuals of any other age group. Although there is still relatively little behavioral research in this area, work based on the contributions of Lindsley (1964), Cautela (1966, 1969), Kastenbaum (1968), and Baer (1970) is beginning to address the myth of aging.

BEHAVIORAL GERONTOLOGY: DEVELOPMENTS

The remainder of this chapter deals with recent important developments in the field of behavioral gerontology. It is not a review of everything behaviorists have done, but rather an overview of the highlights of this work with a look toward answering the questions posed at the beginning of this chapter. The material is organized around the three environments in which research has been generated to answer fundamental questions about the predictability and alterability of the behavior of the aged.

Laboratory Environments

Research has been conducted in contrived, laboratory environments to investigate basic questions regarding aged behavior. Some of this work has been purely descriptive, but most of it has had implications for potential clinical intervention with the elderly as well as calling into question the myth of aging. The most significant papers address a traditional issue in gerontology: cognitive decline.

Unfortunately, almost no behavioral research has directly assessed the modifiability of memory disorders in the elderly. Ankus and Quarrington (1972) demonstrated that given appropriate, contingent reinforcers elderly subjects responded to a lever-pressing task according to specific schedule requirements (fixed ratio schedules). They pointed out the lack of utility in testing for memory disorders if the behaviors of their subjects are amenable to conditioning. The risk of emphasizing "memory" as a crucial ingredient of behavior, either problem behaviors or maintenance of appropriate behaviors, lies in the tendency to assume the problem is organic and therefore unconditionable. There is much to debate about the intact organism being a necessary ingredient for conditioning to occur, especially if memory disorders in the elderly are taken to imply an organism that is no longer intact.

Skinner (1957) discusses the loss of verbal behavior over time (memory) as the failure to emit a response under conditions in which it has been extinguished. Under other conditions it is quite possible for a memory-disordered individual to emit the forgotten response. For example, in research currently being conducted by the author, demented patients who are unable to emit the name of their spouse when asked ''What is your wife's (husband's) name?'' are able to select the correct name when given several choices. Traditionally the difference between these methods has been described as the difference between recall or retrieval and recognition, i.e., responses that are dependent on the cue presented. The conceptualization of memory as a question of stimulus control needs to be more fully explored by behaviorists but especially by behavioral gerontologists who deal with the problem of memory as a diagnostic and often prognostic tool. To describe memory deficits of the elderly as retrieval problems sidesteps the issue of stimulus control and, therefore, the modifiability of memory. Reese (1973) is correct in emphasizing the importance of weak organism-environment interactions as a model for explaining memory deficits in the elderly, but behavioral gerontologists must pursue this model in the research laboratory.

Response speed and intelligence measures have received more attention by behaviorists than memory. Patterson and Jackson (1980) provide an excellent review of behavioral research in this area. They emphasize the behaviorist view that maturation alone cannot account for changes in the performance of elderly persons on intelligence tasks. As with memory, stimulus control variables play an important role in such responding and the importance of consequent versus antecedent control is an open area of investigation.

Willis, Blieszner, and Baltes (1981) have demonstrated that when trained in specific problem-solving strategies, elderly subjects improved their performance on similar problem tasks, and that this training effect generalized to nonsimilar problem tasks. Hofland, Willis, and Baltes (1981) also demonstrated that repeated practice on tests of figural relations and induction (common tests of intellectual abilities) resulted in improved test scores. These results suggest that the elderly person's performance on intelligence tests is related to practice and training in problem-solving skills. If the elderly person's environment does not allow for such practice, then it follows that a formal test of cognitive abilities would show a deficit in these areas. But it would be erroneous to assume this is a biological or maturational effect. Labouvie-Vief, Hoyer, Baltes, and Baltes (1974) have pointed out that the so-called decline in intellectual abilities is more likely a weakening of environmental conditions that require the performance of intellectual tasks. Strengthening of these stimulus-response relations in training sessions suggests that such stimulus control could also be reinstated in the elderly person's own environment and thus negate the notion of loss of intellect.

One training strategy that warrants further investigation is the shaping of self-instructions for problem solving (Meichenbaum, 1974). The role that covert verbal behavior plays in the overt behavior of the elderly focuses research questions on the degree of stimulus control exerted by the individual's own behavior versus other stimulus conditions. Behaviorists must pursue these questions further.

Changes in consequent as well as antecedent control occur in the environment of the elderly. Patterson and Jackson (1980) suggest that intellectual skills may not be reinforced in the elderly as they are with younger persons. As a matter of fact, the elderly are more likely reinforced for behaviors that are in opposition to intellectual skills.

Research by Hoyer, Labouvie, and Baltes (1973) compared practice to reinforced practice on a timed paper and pencil test using a group design procedure. They found that contingent reinforcement plus practice resulted in a greater improvement than practice alone (or no practice) but that improvements on generalization tests showed no difference between reinforced and nonreinforced subjects. It may be that feedback is a more crucial variable than contingent reinforcement. In a later study, Bellucci and Hoyer 1975) demonstrated that elderly women could learn to significantly increase their performance on simple tasks and their self-assessment of their performance if noncontingent feedback was provided. However, it is difficult to determine how feedback can be delivered in a truly noncontingent manner. It may be that practice effects also account for the findings. The question of the importance of consequent control over cognitive deficits in the elderly is still an empirical one that behavioral gerontologists have not adequately addressed.

A related area of research that requires further investigation is the identification of effective reinforcing stimuli for elderly populations. Descriptive data indicate that as one ages one's activity level changes so that less time is spent in high-participation activities, e.g., tennis, and more time is spent in low-participation activities, e.g., watching television. Wisocki (1982) identified a wide variety of reinforcing stimuli for an elderly population. The most highly preferred stimuli were ones requiring a minimum of physical activity, such as music, peace and quiet, and theater. If consequent control over behavior of the elderly is a basic research question, then effective controlling stimuli must be more clearly identified. One obvious advantage is that geriatric programs, such as nursing homes, day-care centers, and senior citizens centers, could be planned more effectively and economically.

A final area of research has been addressed by Alan Baron and his colleagues in a number of investigations (Baron & Perone, 1982; Beres & Baron, 1981; Perone & Baron, 1982). This work concerns age differences on laboratory tasks and focuses attention on the possible sources for these differences. Baron and his colleagues have demonstrated that elderly subjects are responsive to contingencies as demonstrated by their learning curves, but more importantly that operant procedures themselves are especially suited for such study. Baron and Perone (1982) cite their work with age differences as indicative of the older subject's sensitivity to assessment rather than a demonstration of behavior deficits per se.

Because operant methodology allows a subject to habituate to the setting, it offers the investigator an opportunity to identify real age differences, if any, rather than reactivity to the methodology.

Research in the laboratory has made its major contributions by chipping away at the myth of aging. Not only do the data support the hypothesis that cognitive decline in the elderly is not solely maturational or biological, but they also offer an alternative explanation, i.e., stimulus control changes. There is still much that must be investigated, particularly in the area of consequent control. For example, what role does practice versus reinforcement or punishment play in cognitive decline or maintenance? The impact of these findings on the economics of the aging myth is still unclear. It may be that deemphasizing biology as an efficient explanation of memory loss will bring into question funding for drug research at least in regard to normal aging (as opposed to, for example, biological research into the effects of cardiovascular disease on memory). More likely, this basic laboratory research will have implications for broadened intervention programs in natural and clinical environments.

Natural Environments

The majority of gerontological research conducted by behaviorists has been done in either institutions or contrived settings. Very little has been done in the natural environment, and much of what has been done has been observational in form. Although there may be some argument about what constitutes a natural environment, this section addresses the behavioral work done in regard to the normal elderly person. That is, what have behaviorists contributed to the prediction and control of the behavior of an older person who is not in need of immediate intervention for what might be considered clinical problems? This work has been carried out in work settings, homes, and nursing homes but has focused more on compensation for behavior deficits than intervention, i.e., changing the behavior itself. For example, an individual who has become incontinent may be given an adult diaper to compensate for the behavior rather than altering the environmental conditions that may contribute to the behavior. Much of the work has been carried out by people who would not call themselves behaviorists but who are interested in environmental engineering.

No one would deny that as an individual matures certain biological and physiological changes occur. Hoyer (1973) has claimed that despite the numerous descriptive studies of what the normal older person does, no one really knows what an older person may be capable of doing if given optimal environmental conditions. Identifying what the average 70-year-old male is currently doing tells us nothing about the environmental conditions, including the societal as well as immediate conditions, that contribute to what he is (or is not) doing.

Much of the research in this area focuses on environmental engineering, family training, rehabilitation, and skill training. Environmental engineering has received the greatest attention. Although there are significant decrements in discriminative sensory abilities associated with increasing age, most elderly people learn to compensate for these decrements quite readily. In fact, these types of deficits become significant problems for a relatively small number of people (Hussian, 1981).

Hussian (1981) suggests that the "inappropriate" behavior of many elderly is at least in part a consequence of reduced sensory input. Lindsley addressed this problem by emphasizing the need for prosthetic environments. Logically, if an individual experiences reduced sensory input, then environmental stimuli that controlled his or her behavior in the past may now have little if any control. Hussian (1981) proposed a need for "supernormal stimulus control"; that is, "behavior-in-context" becomes the target for change rather than the individual behavior.

Hussian's approach points out a critical aspect of intervening with the elderly: the topography of the behavior may not be the appropriate focus for intervention. Rather, the stimulus conditions under which the behavior is (or is not) emitted is the more productive focus. For example, it is common in an institutional setting for a male patient to urinate in a corner of a room or hallway rather than in a urinal. Staff frequently mislabel such a patient uncooperative, confused, or worse, incontinent. Instead of focusing on decreasing the behavior of urinating in the hallway, stimulus conditions that will synthesize the behavior of urinating in the urinal should be developed. Attempts have been made at this by clearly identifying the bathroom, giving verbal prompts, and marking pathways to the bathroom (Marsh, 1980).

In nonclinical settings these considerations are just as important. In the book *The Thirty-Six Hour Day* (Mace & Rabins, 1981), pages are devoted to giving families advice about how to optimally arrange the environment so as to compensate for sensory or cognitive deficits that alter previously effective stimulus-response relations.

Research in nursing home environments has emphasized the importance of furniture arrangement and prompting as the controlling variables for social interaction. The average elderly resident who may have only sensory deficits often becomes isolated in a nursing home if environmental supports are not provided. The results of such isolation are often that the person becomes nonverbal, poor in self-maintenance behavior, and increasingly dependent on nursing care. A more complete review of the research in this area can be found elsewhere (Williamson & Ascione, 1983), but two examples of the effects of environmental manipulation are found in Peterson, Knapp, Rosen, and Pither (1977) and McClannahan and Risley (1975). The former demonstrated that talking increased significantly in a lounge area when chairs were arranged around tables rather than against walls but actually decreased if chairs were arranged in an ellipse. The latter study qualified the effect of spatial manipulations and availability of activities by demonstrating that verbal prompts to participate significantly increased participation more than manipulating the physical characteristics of the environment alone. The work in this area provides evidence that stimulus variables are as important a consideration in the control of the behavior of elderly populations as with other groups.

Further research must address questions such as how the natural fading of historically effective controlling stimuli contributes to the development of mal-adaptive behaviors, and how such effects can be diminished or prevented. Speech and language pathologists know that training a person to respond to new auditory stimuli that is concomitant to the use of a hearing aid is essential. Behavioral gerontologists must also focus on training the elderly, and those around them, to respond to new and/or different stimuli.

One approach to prevention has received only minimal attention. Training in self-management skills was suggested by Hoyer (1973), who pointed out the discrepancy between self-regulated reinforcer delivery and other-regulated rein-forcer delivery as being especially relevant to the elderly. Since Hoyer (1973), only Bellucci and Hoyer (1975) have published research involving self-regulato-ry techniques. This is certainly a major oversight. Skinner (1983) addressed the use of self-management skills to compensate for physiological limitations that occur with increasing age on a personal level. He emphasized the point made earlier that stimulus control is a crucial ingredient to problems of the elderly, and views many problems as being related to difficulty in the accessibility of verbal behavior, and that, although the problem of accessibility may not be solved directly, the conditions under which the desired verbal behavior is emitted can be improved.

Besides providing advice and training to families in methods of compensating for the deficits of elderly family members, there is a growing interest in other family-related issues. It is a myth that families abandon their elderly members. Elderly family members maintain frequent contact with their relatives even if they do not live in the same household (Shanas, 1979). Research is emerging that has to do with communication processes among family members (Niederehe & Fruge, 1983) and attitudes of family members toward one another (Rankin, Linsk, Pinkston, Nelson-Young, & Kean-Hagerty, 1983). More direct interven-tion has been provided by teaching operant techniques with considerable success to family caregivers of impaired elderly family members (Haley, 1983; Rankin et al., 1983).

Behaviorists interested in health care for the elderly have emphasized re-habilitation and exercise. Much of this work falls into the area of self-manage-ment. Medication compliance has received less attention with this age group, which is surprising given the increasing memory problems identified with many elderly. In the area of rehabilitation and health maintenance Hussian (1981) has suggested self-monitoring as a technique to improve communication between the physician and the elderly person regarding physical conditions, e.g., glucose levels. The behavioral gerontologist's role does not end if a biological disorder is identified as the primary etiology for a problem behavior: The behaviorist can provide valuable data about the effectiveness of medical intervention in alleviating behavioral symptoms.

DeVries (1975) has demonstrated that physical training has a sedative effect equivalent to, if not greater than, tranquilizers for the elderly and certainly has fewer potential side effects. Libb and Clements (1969) used a contingency program with elderly individuals in which conditioned reinforcers were delivered for exercising on a stationary bicycle. Their technique was effective in increasing the overall amount of daily exercise. The generalization of exercise benefits has been demonstrated by Powell (1974). Comparing exercise to social activity, he found significant improvement on memory and problem-solving tasks for the former but not for the latter activity. Unfortunately, no naturalistic data are available for nonclinical geriatric populations. It would be interesting to determine the amount of exercise in which the average elderly person engages compared to clinical populations with their concomitant physical and behavioral problems.

Relaxation training and biofeedback techniques have been demonstrated to be effective in conditioning specific behaviors of the elderly. Garrison (1978) reported success in training an elderly man to respond to stressful stimuli with a relaxation rather than an avoidance response. Bellucci and Hoyer (1975) demonstrated the effectiveness of feedback on the performance of simple tasks with elderly women. Additionally, the use of polygraph-feedback (along with verbal praise) to condition the rectosphincteric response of fecally incontinent geriatric men was shown to be effective by Engel, Nickomanesh, and Schuster (1974).

The interaction between behavioral medicine and behavioral gerontology has not been clearly identified. The elderly are considered by many to be an "at risk" population for psychological stress (Abrahams & Patterson, 1978–79), which in any age group increases the risk of physical disorders. It is obvious from the geriatric literature that the coordination of efforts could be a productive endeavor, particularly in the area of prevention.

Another area of research in natural environments has to do with education and skill training. Much of what has already been discussed involves skill training, but because of role changes that occur with advancing age, certain new (not just compensatory) skills must be learned. An older person who remains employed often must utilize new techniques, such as different organizational skills, to compensate for slower response speed or management skills necessary for promotion, to work effectively as well as to counter prejudices against older workers (Neugarten, 1972). Birren & Woodruff (1973) have identified an increase in multiple careers in association with an increase in continuing education. These data imply that behaviorists should be investigating effective educational methods with the older individual, especially in light of the previous discussion regarding changes in sensory abilities. Seimen (1976) has found that self-paced programmed instruction provides an effective and inexpensive method of teaching new information to the elderly—a method that could be used creatively to compensate for an elderly person's auditory or visual deficits as well as the anxiety accompanying the participation in educational programs with younger people.

Besides the employed elder, the retired worker could benefit from a behavioral approach. Social transitions such as retirement, widowhood, and lowered economic conditions warrant planning. Prior to the occurrence of these events individuals should be planning and developing new behavioral repertoires, e.g., use of leisure time and new sources of reinforcement. Behavioral gerontologists are in an excellent position to serve as guides in the achievement of these objectives. They have as yet not taken advantage of this opportunity.

Behaviorists have done very little to demonstrate empirically the applicability of their methodology and philosophy in the natural environment of the elderly. Prevention, remediation, and compensation have all been minimally addressed. Instead, as is seen in the next section, behaviorists have chosen to put most of their efforts into replicating behavior change techniques with elderly clinical populations to the exclusion of investigating the controlling variables for response deficits or maintenance. The function of stimulus control must be broadened as an equally effective technique in synthesizing desired behaviors. What better opportunity to apply this principle than with a population whose behaviors may remain relatively constant while the stimulus control of those behaviors fades?

The research in natural environments has made minimal progress at combating the metaphor of aging. If more substantial data are collected to demonstrate the role of fading stimulus control in the development of aged behaviors, then gains will be made in providing alternative explanations to this myth. An interesting research question to pursue is identifying the necessary conditions to synthesize aged behaviors in young populations.

There is much that behaviorists can do to take advantage of (as well as to add to) the economics of the aging industry—i.e., pursue the intersection of behavioral medicine and behavioral gerontology; provide employment/retirement training; contribute to health maintenance; and improve architectural planning.

Clinical Environments

Behaviorists have contributed most in the area of gerontology to our knowledge of the prediction and control of maladaptive behaviors of elderly who reside in or receive services from clinical programs. Both stimulus control and contingency management issues have been addressed, with the latter receiving the greater amount of research effort. A generalization can be made from this research literature that learning-based intervention can produce beneficial changes for the behavior-disordered elderly.

Skill training and behavior management programs make up the largest group of research studies with this population. Although these terms are often used interchangeably in the literature, they are distinctly different. Skill training refers to teaching an individual a new skill, whereas behavior management programs arrange contingencies so that responses still in an individual's repertoire are emitted under desired conditions. There often appears to be some overlap in these techniques because in skill training reinforcing and punishing stimuli are often incorporated into the procedure to shape new responses. A review of the behavioral geriatric literature (Williamson & Ascione, 1983) indicates that environmental manipulation, antecedent and consequent, is not only effective but probably the most reasonable approach to intervention with the elderly.

Countless behaviors exhibited, or not exhibited, by the elderly remain within their repertoire, but the environmental supports for emitting these behaviors either no longer exist or are much more difficult for the older person to discriminate. Behaviors associated with eating, ambulating, toileting, socializing, verbalizing, bathing, and exercising have been amenable to change in either an increasing or a decreasing direction (Patterson & Jackson, 1980; Williamson & Ascione, 1983). A number of studies have emphasized the impact of behavior management programs on the "dependency cycle" that often develops in residential programs for the elderly (Barton, Baltes, & Orzech, 1980). Baltes and Baltes (1982) summarize experimental and observational studies within an operant paradigm as being substantially supportive of the hypothesis that dependency is acquired and maintained by the social contingencies that surround many of the elderly. Nigl and Jackson (1981) demonstrated the effectiveness of a behavior management program in increasing social responses in the geriatric residents of a nursing home who were diagnosed as pyschotic. Their findings are an important extension of the literature because their subjects were part of a nondemented but elderly clinical population.

Skill training seems called for only in special instances when new behaviors must be brought into the individual's repertoire. Patterson and Jackson (1980) have summarized the literature pertaining to the training of social skills. Social skills training is much more than merely increasing social participation. Skills taught include social assertion, interpersonal skills, and problem solving. Gallagher and Thompson (1981) have demonstrated the effectiveness of skill training with severely depressed elderly. Important skills taught in their intervention package include observation of one's own behavior, both overt and visceral, discriminating the correlation between behavior and activity, and setting personal goals.

Self-management is a skill that can be taught to an elderly person as a new behavior or, more often, as a skill applied to new circumstances. Gallagher and Thompson (1981), for example, teach self-monitoring as a skill. As discussed previously, very little has been done in this area with the elderly. Another approach to the problem of self-management has been taken by several investigators. Langer and Rodin (1976) manipulated the rules of a residential program so that one group of residents was encouraged to be taken care of and another group encouraged to take primary responsibility for their own care. Results of this manipulation were interpreted to mean that the more control an elderly person has the better off he or she is as measured by nurses' rating, health, and mortality. A follow-up study suggested these effects were maintained 18 months later (Rodin & Langer, 1977). Providing more personal control is a popular approach with the elderly currently and is based on the "learned helplessness" model. However, I suspect that this line of research will send behavioral gerontologists barking up the wrong tree, and result in neglecting the stimulus control variables in the presence of which adaptive behaviors are emitted or withheld. In support of this contention, Hutchison, Carstensen, and Silberman (1983) make a cogent argument that behavioral effects of "locus of control" studies with the elderly are more likely results of improved resident/staff interactions than enhanced personal control.

Environmental engineering is another form of behavior management and has been discussed previously. It applies to clinical as readily as to normal populations. Hussian (1982) demonstrated that an environmental engineering methodology is effective for the control of wandering, self-stimulation, and inappropriate sexual behavior. Specifically, he manipulated the size, shape, color, and so forth of artificial stimuli to ensure initial response discrimination and then gradually faded these stimuli back to naturally occurring ones.

It is difficult to justify concentrating on only stimulus control or consequent control variables in clinical settings. Usually both must be considered. Rebok and Hoyer (1977) discuss the usefulness of combining contingency management with what they call behavioral ecology. They suggest that the level of analysis and intervention must extend from the individual's behavior in its functional context to its social environmental context. MacDonald, Davidowitz, Gimbel, and Foley (1982) provide an application of this analysis by use of a treatment package. They combined rearrangement of a ward's physical environment with prompting activity and providing contingent reinforcement for activity participation. The major contribution of their work is the demonstration that subgroups of an elderly population may respond differently to different interventions. They found that residents with low base rates responded more to the physical rearrangement and reinforcement contingencies. Thus, if a milieu intervention is to take place in a group residential setting rather than an individually determined program, a combination of stimulus control and consequent control should provide a context for optimal behavior change for the majority of residents.

Clinicians make a major error when they respond automatically to behavior deficits by suggesting that behavior management is necessary, when it may be that the behavior has never been in the person's repertoire or that physical limitations require the introduction of new controlling variables to synthesize the desired behaviors. Conversely, skill training is unnecessary if the antecedent or consequent stimuli that previously maintained a behavior have changed. Programs that go to great lengths to decrease incontinence by using behavior management techniques (e.g., Schnelle et al., 1983) make the same error if the behavioral deficit is due to poor antecedent stimulus control, not consequent control. In fact, it is quite possible that emphasis on the latter technique when the former is more appropriate will worsen the client's behavior by infantilizing him or her. Such infantilizing often results in either anger and subsequent aggression or an exacerbation of dependency.

Staff training is another means of affecting the social/environmental context of an elderly resident's behavior. Surprisingly, there is a dearth of studies in the literature evaluating the parameters that could be examined in staff training programs. Some studies include staff training as part of some other contingency management program, but do not identify the effect of training alone or look at its long-term benefits. Three studies that have attempted to do this have found (a) information about elderly problems alone does not affect resident behavior; (b) information combined with skill training in contingency management or skill training alone does affect resident behavior; and (c) contingency management of staff behavior, through written contracts, affects resident behavior positively (Linsk, Howe, & Pinkston, 1975; Marmol, 1973; Sperbeck & Whitbourne, 1981). The utility of staff training should be further evaluated, especially because of the limited resources available for individual intervention in large residential programs.

One final area that is crucial in clinical settings is assessment. Hussian (1981) has described some modifications in standard assessment that are useful because they compensate for unique characteristics of an elderly population, e.g., decreased speed of response. He also identified a deficit in our assessment technology in that there are few operationally sound measures of elderly compensatory behavior. In addition, few standard behavioral checklists apply to the elderly. Other assessment instruments normed on elderly populations are not typically operationally based, e.g., Senior Apperception Technique, Geriatric Sentence Completion Test. Rosberger and MacLean (1983) attempted to demonstrate the pragmatic use of assessment by measuring base rates of inappropriate behavior and the subsequent effects of intervention. Their approach is important for outcome evaluation, but is still too narrow in its scope to tell us anything about the controlling relations operating on the elderly subject's behavior. In fact, behavioral assessment in general emphasizes topography over controlling relations (Wynne, Brey, Clark, & Williamson, 1983). The geriatric literature is doubly limited by the lack of behavioral assessment tools.

Given the caveat regarding too great a focus on topography, two research groups have made rigorous attempts to develop valid assessment instruments for elderly residential populations. Schnelle and Traughber (1983) developed a cost-effective system of assessment for reliably discriminating different populations and evaluating treatment outcome with large groups of geriatric nursing facility residents. Patterson, Eberly, and Harrell (1983) developed a unique modular approach to assessment, which they claim can provide nomothetic as well as idiographic data. Although Schnelle and Traughber (1983) do not address the issue of controlling relations, some of the items in their inventory approach the issue, for example, the conditions necessary for locomotion to occur.

The traditional assessment of presumed organic deficits is often accepted by behaviorists because of a concern over the question of the intact organism. That is, many behaviorists claim their principles apply only to an intact organism despite the demonstration that organically "caused" deficits are amenable to behavior change, e.g., Rosberger and MacLean (1983). Perhaps this is why there have been no attempts to assess organicity from a truly behavioral perspective. This area of research is currently being addressed by this author and her colleagues.

Behavioral research in clinical settings has contributed to the eventual demise of the metaphor of aging by demonstrating that change in behaviors of the elderly is possible. The alternative focus is on behavior in its context rather than aging or aged behavior. Behavioral research confirms the hypothesis that techniques that have been used effectively with other populations are also effective for intervention with the elderly. From an economic perspective, clinical research has demonstrated cost-effective methods for providing treatment by utilizing existing resources, e.g., staff, to effect improvement in residents' conditions. As the need for supportive group living environments increases with the increase in the size of the elderly population and decrease in the availability of children to care for their parents this will be an important economic consideration. Behaviorists can also contribute to the development of a new occupational field, i.e., behavioral geriatric paraprofessionals. This might, in fact, attract more people to working with the elderly.

Behavioral research with elderly clinical populations must also broaden its conception of stimulus control variables. The current emphasis on topography (i.e., increasing or decreasing observed behaviors) will eventually stagnate the field as it has others (Wynne et al. 1983). The greatest need is in assessment methodology. Investigating the role of controlling relations in maladaptive and organic behaviors will advance the field far beyond the medical model approach and the myth of aging.

BEHAVIORAL GERONTOLOGY: IMPLICATIONS

Behavioral research has clearly demonstrated the plasticity of behaviors in the elderly. Baltes and Baltes (1979) describe plasticity as variability within the same organism. In this sense then, behaviorists have contributed much to dispel the myth of aging—i.e., the metaphor of aging as an entity rather than a description of a developmental period. The elderly as a group are more heterogeneous in their behavior than other, younger, age groups (Baltes & Baltes, 1979). Although behaviorists have been limited in their naturalistic observations of the elderly, behavioral methodology has allowed for the manipulation and demonstration of this intra-individual plasticity.

Perhaps because of the ease with which medical, physiological, and neurological explanations can be applied to problems of the elderly, behaviorists have not yet had a major impact on the treatment of the aged or the concept of aging. On the other hand, behavioral techniques are so easily applied by technicians that they are often seen merely as behavior management tools and not as the extension of a conceptually unique explanation of the etiology of problem behaviors. In many respects behavioral gerontologists are to blame for this limited use of "behaviorism" as only a methodology. Most publications by behaviorists dealing with elderly populations are examples of reinventing the wheel with yet another population, unfortunate only to the extent that behavior principles are probably most useful in explaining (and subsequently being used to synthesize) the behaviors of the normal aged person because of the often compensatory nature of their problems. This stands in contrast to current efforts made to increase appropriate or decrease inappropriate behaviors (topographical intervention) in yet one more subgroup.

A behavioral science should focus on the conditions necessary to synthesize behaviors of interest and not merely "explain" them (Wynne, 1971). In addition, focusing solely on topography limits the productive intervention on controlling relations with this population perhaps more than any other. Organic deterioration stands as the prime example of where behaviorists either draw the line for synthesizing new behaviors, or are satisfied to merely describe how organically caused deficits can be increased. These comments are not meant to belittle contributions already made by behaviorists but to identify other directions that should be taken as well. It is as if behaviorists are not interested in the controlling variables if the organism is not intact.

The prevention of behavior disorders and not just treatment of such disorders is necessary. Behaviorists must do more to identify those conditions that promote behavioral decline among some elderly but not among others. Perhaps a focus on observational research—that is, what are the controlling variables that operate on the normally functioning elderly versus the poorly functioning elderly?—will add to our knowledge of the prevention of specific behavioral decline with age.

As for the economics of the aging myth, the aging industry is a reality and growing quickly. It is hoped that behavioral gerontology will take a foothold before it meets the same blockage posed by another lucrative approach, the mental health industry (Magaro, Gripp, McDowell, & Miller, 1978). Because of its methodology, behavioral research has the potential of affecting the models that deal with questions of aging more than any particular model has of influencing and producing behavioral research. These economic effects have been recognized by other authors interested in the aging industry (Morgan, 1981).

Perhaps some of the issues being raised in this chapter have not yet been clearly addressed for one more reason. As all behaviorists eventually learn, behaviorism is not well understood. This is particularly true in behavioral gerontology. Behavioral techniques are used by non-behaviorists, or by gerontologists not formally trained as behaviorists, or by pseudo-behaviorists; that is, people who think they are behaviorists because of the techniques they use. These professionals fail to recognize behaviorism as a philosophy of behavior (Day, 1975). At the risk of sounding elitist, much that has been done in the name of behavioral gerontology has been done by good researchers and good clinicians who do not accurately discriminate radical or contemporary behaviorism from conceptually different research and clinical approaches. A good example of this misunderstanding can be found in articles, chapters, or books that purport to summarize behavior therapy with the aged. For example, MacDonald & Kerr (1982) describe applied behavior analysis, or radical behaviorism (they incorrectly use the terms interchangeably), as holding that only observable behavior is the meaningful object of study and that private events are irrelevant to the analysis of human behavior. This chapter is not intended as a rebuttal to such descriptions; suffice it to say that they are wrong (see Day, 1969). But it may be precisely this misunderstanding that prevents behaviorists from tackling critical problems of the aged.

If behaviorists relegate problems commonly associated with the elderly such as poor memory, confusion, intellectual deterioration, or sensory impairment to exclusively neurological causes then they miss the opportunity to demonstrate the role of stimulus relations (antecedent or consequent) in the development and maintenance of these problems. Just as radical behaviorism attempts to deal with private events such as thinking and feeling so too can it attempt to explain the deficits often associated with age. Problems in memory may involve a neurological component, but they most certainly involve changes in the level of environmental support available to an elderly person. The supporting stimuli are most likely both overt and covert. Dementia itself might be conceptualized as a category of impaired private events manifested by maladaptive or socially inappropriate observable behaviors (Williamson, Clark, & Wynne, 1984). Both the observable and the private events can and should be dealt with. To this end, behavioral gerontologists must seriously undertake the task of redefining such terms (and behaviors) as dementia, memory disorder, and sensory deficits in terms uniquely characteristic of their philosophy of the science of human behavior.

Perhaps even behavioral gerontology is a misnomer. Perhaps we may be more accurately described as behaviorists interested in special problems of the elderly, i.e., gerontological behaviorists. But then we run the risk of having our field summarized as research aimed at the study of functional relations between events—carried out by elderly researchers! I am prepared to run the risk.

ACKNOWLEDGMENTS

The author acknowledges with appreciation the contributions of discussions with Patricia Brey, C. D. Clark, Charles A. Lyons, and Louis Wynne, to the development of many of the ideas presented in this chapter. Special thanks are due for critical comments provided by Drs. Lyons and Wynne on an earlier draft. I am especially indebted to Dr. Wynne, without whose support and encouragement this chapter would not have been written.

REFERENCES

Abrahams, R. B., & Patterson, R. D. (1978–79). Psychological distress among the community elderly: Prevalence characteristics, and implications for service. *International Journal of Aging and Human Development, 9,* 1–18.

Ankus, M., & Quarrington, S. (1972). Operant behavior in the memory-disordered. *Journal of Gerontology, 27,* 500–510.

Baer, D. (1970). An age-irrelevant concept of development. *Merrill-Palmer Quarterly, 16,* 238–246.

Baltes, M. M., & Baltes, P. B. (1982). Microanalytical research on environmental factors and plasticity in psychological aging. In T. M. Field, A. Huston, H. C. Quay, L. Troll, & G. E. Finley (Eds.), *Review of human development* (pp. 524–539). New York: Wiley.

Baltes, P. B., & Baltes, M. M. (1979). Plasticity and variability in psychological aging: Methodological and theoretical implications. In *Methodological considerations in determining the effects of aging in the CNS.* Symposium presented at the Department of Gerontology and Institute of Neuropsychopharmacology, Free University of Berlin, Berlin.

Baron, A., & Perone, M. (1982). The place of the human subject in the operant laboratory. *Behavior Analyst, 5,* 143–158.

Barton, E. M., Baltes, M. M., & Orzech, M. J. (1980). Etiology of dependence in older nursing home residents during morning care: The role of staff behavior. *Journal of Personality and Social Psychology, 38,* 423–431.

Bellucci, G., & Hoyer, W. J. (1975). Feedback effects on the performance and self-reinforcing behavior of elderly and young adult women. *Journal of Gerontology, 30,* 456–460.

Beres, C. A., & Baron, A. (1981). Improved digit symbol substitution by older women as a result of extended practice. *Journal of Gerontology, 36,* 591–597.

Birren, J. E., & Woodruff, D. S. (1973). Human development over the life-span through education. In P. B. Baltes & K. W. Schaie (Eds.), *Life span developmental psychology: Personality and socialization* (pp. 305–337). New York: Academic Press.

Cautela, J. R. (1966). Behavior therapy and geriatrics. *Journal of Genetic Psychology, 108,* 9–17.

Cautela, J. R. (1969). A classical conditioning approach to the development and modification of behavior in the aged. *The Gerontologist, 9,* 109–113.

Day, W. F. (1969). Radical behaviorism in reconciliation with phenomenology. *Journal of the Experimental Analysis of Behavior, 12,* 315–328.

Day, W. F. (1975). Contemporary behaviorism and the concept of intention. In W. J. Arnold (Ed.), *Nebraska Symposium on Motivation,* Vol. 23 (pp. 65–131).

DeVries, H. A. (1975). Physiology of exercise and aging. In D. S. Woodruff & J. E. Birren (Eds.), *Aging: Scientific perspectives and social issues* (pp. 257–276). New York: Van Nostrand Reinhold.

Engel, B. T., Nickomanesh, P., & Schuster, M. M. (1974). Operant conditioning of rectosphincteric responses in the treatment of fecal incontinence. *New England Journal of Medicine, 290,* 646–649.

Gallagher, D., & Thompson, L. W. (1981). *Depression in the elderly: A behavioral treatment manual.* Los Angeles: University of Southern California Press.

Garrison, J. E. (1978). Stress management training for the elderly: A psychoeducational approach. *Journal of the American Geriatrics Society, 26,* 397–403.

Haley, W. E. (1983). A family-behavioral approach to the treatment of the cognitive impaired elderly. *The Gerontologist, 23,* 18–20.

Hofland, B., Willis, S. L., & Baltes, P. B. (1981). Fluid intelligence performance in the elderly: Intra-individual variability and conditions of assessment. *Journal of Educational Psychology, 73*, 573–586.

Hoyer, W. J. (1973). Application of operant techniques to the modification of elderly behavior. *The Gerontologist, 13*, 18–22.

Hoyer, W. J., Labouvie, G. V., & Baltes, P. B. (1973). Modification of response speed deficits and intellectual performance in the elderly. *Human Development, 16*, 233–242.

Hussian, R. A. (1981). *Geriatric psychology: A behavioral perspective*. New York: Van Nostrand Reinhold.

Hussian, R. A. (1982). Stimulus control in the modification of problematic behavior in elderly institutionalized patients. *International Journal of Behavioral Geriatrics, 1*, 33–42.

Hutchison, W., Carstensen, L., & Silberman, D. (1983). Generalized effects of increasing personal control of residents in a nursing facility. *International Journal of Behavioral Geriatrics, 1*, 21–32.

Kastenbaum, R. (1968). Perspectives on the development and modification of behavior in the aged: A developmental-field perspective. *The Gerontologist, 8*, 280–282.

Kramer, M., Taube, C. A., & Redick, R. W. (1973). Patterns of use of psychiatric facilities by the aged: Past, present and future. In C. Eisdorfer & M. P. Lawton (Eds.), *The psychology of adult development and aging* (pp. 428–528). Washington, DC: American Psychological Association.

Labouvie-Vief, G., Hoyer, W. J., Baltes, M. M., & Baltes, P. B. (1974). Operant analysis of intellectual behavior in old age. *Human Development, 17*, 259–272.

Langer, E. J., & Rodin, J. (1976). The effects of choice and enhanced personal responsibility for the aged: A field experiment in an institutional setting. *Journal of Personality and Social Psychology, 34*, 191–198.

Libb, J. W., & Clements, C. B. (1969). Token reinforcement in an exercise program for hospitalized geriatric patients. *Perceptual and Motor Skills, 28*, 957–958.

Lindsley, O. (1964). Geriatric behavioral prosthetics. In R. Kastenbaum (Ed.), *New thoughts on old age* (pp. 41–60). New York: Springer.

Linsk, N., Howe, M. W., & Pinkston, E. M. (1975). Behavioral group work in a home for the aged. *Social Work, 20*, 454–463.

MacDonald, M. L., & Kerr, B. B. (1982). Behavior therapy with the aging. In A. M. Horton, Jr. (Ed.), *Mental health interventions for the aging* (pp. 139–154). New York: J. F. Bergin.

MacDonald, M. L., Davidowitz, J. J., Gimbel, B., & Foley, L. M. (1982). Physical and social environmental reprogramming as treatment for psychogeriatric patients. *International Journal of Behavioral Geriatrics, 1*, 15–32.

Mace, N. L., & Rabins, P. V. (1981). *The 36-hour day*. Baltimore: Johns Hopkins.

Magaro, P. A., Gripp, R., McDowell, D. J., & Miller, J. W. (1978). *The mental health industry: A cultural phenomenon*. New York: Wiley.

Marmol, L. M. (1973). An exploratory application of operant conditioning in geriatric nursing (Doctoral dissertation, California School of Professional Psychology). *Dissertation Abstracts International, 34*, 2942B–2943B. (University Microfilms No. 73–27, 567)

Marsh, G. R. (1980). Perceptual changes with aging. In E. W. Busse & D. G. Blazer (Eds.), *Handbook of geriatric psychiatry* (pp. 147–168). New York: Van Nostrand Reinhold.

McClannahan, L. E., & Risley, T. R. (1975). Design of living environments for nursing home residents: Increasing participation in recreation activities. *Journal of Applied Behavior Analysis, 8*, 261–268.

Meichenbaum, D. (1974). Self-instructional strategy training: A cognitive prosthesis for the aged. *Human Development, 17*, 273–280.

Morgan, J. N. (1981). Behavioral and social science research and the future elderly. In S. B. Kresler, J. N. Morgan, & V. K. Oppenheimer (Eds.), *Aging: Social change* (pp. 587–611). New York: Academic Press.

Niederehe, G., & Fruge, E. (1983). *Discussion: Analysis of videotaped interactions in families of senile dementia patients.* Paper presented at the 36th Annual Meeting of the American Gerontological Society, San Francisco.

Neugarten, B. L. (1972). Personality and the aging process. *The Gerontologist, 12,* 9–15.

Nigl, A. J., & Jackson, B. (1981). A behavior management program to increase social responses in psychogeriatric patients. *Journal of the American Geriatrics Society, 29,* 92–95.

Patterson, R. L., Eberly, D. A., & Harrell, T. L. (1983). Behavioral assessment of intellectual competence, communication skills, and personal hygiene skills of elderly persons. *Behavioral Assessment, 5,* 207–218.

Patterson, R. L., & Jackson, G. M. (1980). Behavior modification with the elderly. In M. Hersen, R. M. Eisler, & P. M. Miller (Eds.), *Progress in behavior modification* (pp. 205–239). New York: Academic Press.

Perone, M., & Baron, A. (1982). Age-related effects of pacing on acquisition and performance of response sequences: An operant analysis. *Journal of Gerontology, 37,* 443–449.

Peterson, R. F., Knapp, T. J., Rosen, J. C., & Pither, B. F. (1977). The effects of furniture arrangement on the behavior of geriatric patients. *Behavior Therapy, 8,* 464–467.

Powell, R. R. (1974). Psychological effects of exercise therapy upon institutionalized geriatric mental patients. *Journal of Gerontology, 29,* 157–161.

Rankin, E., Linsk, N. L., Pinkston, E. M., Nelson-Young, R., & Kean-Hagerty, E. (1983). *Caregiver attitudes toward disabled elderly family members in a home-based behavioral treatment program.* Paper presented at the 36th Annual Meeting of the American Gerontological Society, San Francisco.

Rebok, G. W., & Hoyer, W. J. (1977). The functional context of elderly behavior. *Gerontologist, 17,* 27–32.

Reese, H. W. (1973). Life-span models of memory. *The Gerontologist, 13,* 472–478.

Rodin, J., & Langer, E. J. (1977). Long term effects of a control-relevant intervention with the institutionalized aged. *Journal of Personality and Social Psychology, 35,* 897–902.

Rosberger, Z., & MacLean, J. (1983). Behavioral assessment and treatment of "organic" behaviors in an institutionalized geriatric patient. *International Journal of Behavioral Geriatrics, 1,* 33–46.

Sarbin, T. R., & Mancuso, J. C. (1980). *Schizophrenia: Medical diagnosis or moral verdict?* New York: Pergamon.

Schnelle, J. F., & Traughber, B. (1983). A behavioral assessment system applicable to geriatric nursing facility residents. *Behavioral Assessment, 5,* 231–242.

Schnelle, J. F., Traughber, B., Morgan, D. B., Embry, J. E., Binion, A. F., & Coleman, A. (1983). Management of geriatric incontinence in nursing homes. *Journal of Applied Behavior Analysis, 16,* 235–242.

Seimen, J. R. (1976). Programmed material as a training tool for older persons. *Industrial Gerontology, 3,* 183–190.

Shanas, E. (1979). Social myth or hypothesis: The case of the family relations of old people. *The Gerontologist, 19,* 3–9.

Skinner, B. F. (1957). *Verbal behavior.* Englewood Cliffs, NJ: Prentice-Hall.

Skinner, B. F. (1983). Intellectual self-management in old age. *American Psychologist, 38,* 239–244.

Sperbek, O. J., & Whitbourne, S. K. (1981). Dependency in the institutional setting: A behavioral training program for geriatric staff. *The Gerontologist, 21,* 268–275.

U.S. Department of Commerce Bureau of the Census (1979). *Estimates of the population of the United States by age, sex, and race, 1976–1978.* Washington, DC: U.S. Government Printing Office.

Whaley, D. L., & Malott, R. W. (1971). *Elementary principles of behavior.* New York: Appleton-Century-Crofts.

Williamson, P. N., & Ascione, F. R. (1983). Behavioral treatment of the elderly: Implications for theory and therapy. *Behavior Modification, 7*, 583–610.

Williamson, P. N., Clark, C. D., & Wynne, L. (1984, May). *The assessment of verbal behavior in dementia.* S. Leigland (Chair), Indications of Skinner's *Verbal Behavior* for clinical assessment. Presented at the meeting of the Association for Behavior Analysis, Nashville.

Willis, S. L., Blieszner, R., & Baltes, P. B. (1981). Training research in aging: Modification of performance on the fluid ability of figural relations. *Journal of Educational Psychology, 73*, 41–50.

Wisocki, P. A. (1982). Actual and predicted responses of institutionalized elderly to the psychiatric reinforcement survey schedule. *International Journal of Behavioral Geriatrics, 1*, 57–55.

Wisocki, P. A., & Mosher, P. A. (1982). The elderly: An understudied population in behavioral research. *International Journal of Behavioral Geriatrcs, 1*, 5–14.

Wolfensberger, W. (1972). *The principle of normalization in human services.* New York: National Institute of Mental Retardation.

Wynne, L. (1971). Behavior analysis and behavior synthesis. *The Psychological Record, 21*, 171–179.

Wynne, L., Brey, P., Clark, C. D., & Williamson, P. N. (1983, May). *A radical behavioral approach to intervention with psychotic individuals.* Paper presented at the meeting of the Association for Behavior Analysis, Milwaukee.

8 Self-Management, Rule-Governed Behavior, and Everyday Life

Richard W. Malott
Western Michigan University

APOLOGIA

For several reasons, I feel a little out of place writing this chapter for a book with the title *Behavioral Science: Philosophical, Methodological, and Empirical Advances*. In this chapter I make extensive use of case studies, or more accurately, autobiographical retrospections; it is much more like pre-science than experimental science. The technology I describe is not sufficiently reliable or powerful that it should be considered a major advance, and I frequently infer that private events have a causal status; some methodological behaviorists have suggested such inferences are more mentalistic than behavioral.

For several reasons, however, I also feel pleased to offer this chapter. First, preexperimental observations are an important part of our intellectual heritage; for example, Darwin's Theory of Evolution was based merely on field observations, not on experimental methodology with control groups, multiple-baseline and reversal designs, interobserver reliability, and statistical inference; and Freud's valuable observations about human nature were weakened not so much by his use of autobiographical data as by the obscuration resulting from his mentalistic metaphors in which he presented those observations. Second, in general our field contains, at best, very few techniques of behavior management that are both reliable and powerful; we are more like medical technology of 100 or 200 years ago. And third, the philosophical position known as "radical behaviorism" now provides the rationale for the inference that private psychological events are controlled by the same behavioral processes as are public or overt events (Skinner, 1969, pp. 226–230).

I am pleased to have the opportunity to offer this chapter because it is an effort at a congruent integration of theory and practice, with a variety of applications to the normal behavior of normal human beings, in their normal environment, a configuration that has received little attention from behavior analysis. It is a report from the front lines of what I call "thorough-going behaviorism," that is, an attempt to be a behavior analyst 24 hours a day, in all features of life, not just on the job working with special populations. It is a report of an attempt to live up to Roger Ulrich's dictum that we should apply to others only those techniques we are willing to apply to ourselves.

THEORY

Our lives are filled with occasions where the behavioral contingencies and the rules specifying those contingencies often fail to control our behavior; this concerns us when this failure of control causes us to act in ways that do not support our well-being. A behavioral contingency consists of a stimulus, a response, and an outcome the response produces in the presence of that stimulus (Skinner, 1969, p. 7); and for our purposes, a rule is a statement that describes a contingency; it specifies the outcome a given response will produce in the presence of a particular stimulus (Skinner, 1969, p. 160). For instance, if you floss your teeth every day, they will be more healthy. But because such contingencies and rules often fail to control those actions as they should, we often fail to maximize our success or even our survival. For example, we all know rules indicating that we must drastically change our diet and our exercise regime; and we must also floss our teeth and buckle our seat belts if we are to attain the best of health and a long life. And we must stop daydreaming and start writing if we are to get this chapter written. But unfortunately such rules often fail to control our actions. Therefore we often do not deal nearly as well with our world as we might; we do not maximize our successes or minimize our failures. In the next three sections we look at features of those behavioral contingencies and their associated rules that affect their ability to control our actions. (For more details see Malott, 1984.)

Small, Cumulating Outcomes

Dental flossing provides an interesting problem. Most people know the rule that you should floss your teeth once or twice each day, in order to keep them healthy. But most people fail to follow that rule, perhaps because there is no effective behavioral consequence reinforcing their flossing, at least not routine flossing; in other words, we are not talking about the occasional removal of an aversive piece of food lodged between the teeth. In fact, the outcome of a single flossing is minuscule, becoming significant only when the person continues to floss regularly for several weeks or even months. This illustrates the proposition that outcomes of responses do not reinforce or punish the causal response class if the individual outcomes are insignificant and if only the cumulation of many such small outcomes attains any significance for the organism.

Low-Probability Contingency Relationship

But appropriate rules sometimes fail to control our behavior, even when they specify large and significant outcomes. For example, most people know the rule that they should fasten their seat belts; but they usually fail to do so, even though the fastened belts might save their lives, a significant outcome. However, if we had an accident nearly every time we went out in our car, then we would usually fasten our seat belts. This illustrates the proposition that rules often fail to control our behavior when they specify an improbable contingency relationship between our behavior and its outcome, that is when the outcome is only rarely contingent upon the behavior. Such rules often fail to control behavior even though that outcome might be very significant when it does occur.

Delayed Contingency Relationship

There is another kind of contingency relationship between the response and its outcome that prevents the outcome from directly reinforcing or punishing the causal response; that is, the contingency relationship in which the outcome is too greatly delayed from the response. For instance, it would probably be impossible to condition a response in a nonverbal organism using a behavioral consequence (reinforcing or punishing event) that occurred 24 hours after the response. That delay would probably be too great for the reinforcement or punishment process to work.

We often state rules specifying contingency relationships between the response and such delayed outcomes. And such rules often seem to effectively control the behavior of most people in our culture, so this control must involve different mechanisms than the direct reinforcement or punishment of the causal response by such outcomes (as we discuss later). Following are two common examples of the control by such rules: Most cooks are able to prepare meals, even though those meals might require a fair amount of time to cook before they are edible; most people are able to purchase goods through a mail-order catalogue even though it might be days or even weeks before they receive their purchase.

Now professional psychologists and laypersons often warn against expecting delayed outcomes to influence human behavior. But they may not be responding to the crucial dimensions of the contingency relationship. In fact, the relevant examples they offer usually involve more than a delayed contingency relationship. They also involve a low-probability outcome or an outcome that is small and of only cumulative significance. For instance, the outcomes of cancer and other health problems resulting from smoking are not only delayed, but they are not certain, and the impact of a single cigarette is small and of only cumulative significance. The same is true of excess consumption of most unhealthy foods, of exercise, and generally of working for future goals. Therefore, the low probability of the delayed outcome and the smallness of the immediate outcomes may be what make such contingencies so ineffective in controlling our actions, not the delay of the terminal outcome.

Rules Describing Direct- and Indirect-Acting Contingencies

Thus our behavioral problems often involve an outcome each individual instance of which is too small to effectively reinforce or punish the causal response. This usually becomes a problem when those small outcomes have a cumulative significance. Or the behavioral problems may involve a contingency relationship between the response and its outcome that is too improbable for the outcome to either reinforce or punish the causal response class.

Sometimes some people do respond properly in those situations, however: they do floss their teeth, or they do buckle up their seat belts, and most people do put the turkey in the oven 6 hours before dinner. So the question is, how can this be, if the contingencies specified by the rules do not effectively reinforce or punish the behavior? And the answer may be that the behavior is controlled by a second set of contingencies, contingencies involving rule-governed behavior.

Rules can describe either direct-acting or indirect-acting contingencies. For instance, "Don't touch the stove when it's hot or it will burn you" describes a direct-acting contingency, a contingency involving an outcome that will directly reinforce or punish the causal response class; in other words, the outcome is sizable, immediate, and probable. However, the teeth-flossing rule does not describe a direct-acting contingency because the outcome for any single instance of flossing is small and only the cumulation of many such outcomes is significant. Therefore, such significant outcomes are also delayed from any individual act of flossing, so if the teeth-flossing rule controls our behavior it will be through indirect action.

We must find the behavioral consequence that exerts the desired control over the response in question because the outcome specified in the rule does not function as a behavioral consequence (that is, a rewarding or aversive stimulus) for that response. The controlling outcome must be a direct-acting outcome, one that is immediate, fairly certain, and of sufficient magnitude (not of only cumulative significance).

Unfollowed Rules as Motivating Stimuli

One interesting possibility is that the unfollowed rule itself is an aversive condition, and the act of following that rule will be reinforced by the termination of that aversive condition. For instance, the cook might say to himself, "If I don't put the turkey in the oven, then dinner won't be ready on time; and that would make my guests a little unhappy with me." Not following that rule might constitute a mild aversive condition, one the cook could escape by following the implicit instructions in the rule, that is, by putting the turkey in the oven.

The unfollowed rule would function in essentially the same manner as a "warning" stimulus in a traditional cued-avoidance experiment. In the cued-avoidance experiment, the "warning" stimulus, and the electric shock itself, function as aversive conditions; their occurrence causes the termination of that current state of affairs to be reinforcing, often described as negatively reinforcing.

This analysis suggests that the terms "warning" in *warning stimulus* and "cued" in *cued avoidance* are misleading because they imply that the pre-shock stimulus functions as a discriminative stimulus in the absence of which an avoidance response would be unsuccessful. But in fact, in the absence of that pre-shock stimulus, the avoidance response would not be unsuccessful; it would be irrelevant, just like a food-producing response for a satiated organism. In other words, when there is no pre-shock stimulus, there will be no shock; so the avoidance response would be irrelevant.

This may be clearer if you consider the occasions when the warning stimulus is turned off in a typical cued-avoidance procedure. During the warning-stimulus-off condition, a response would have no effect because the shock *would not* occur, regardless of the occurrence of the response. This is not an S-delta condition because, in an S-delta condition, a response would have no effect because the shock *would* occur regardless of the occurrence of the response. Therefore, because the typical warning-stimulus-off condition does not function as an S-delta, the warning stimulus itself does not function as a discriminative stimulus.

Instead, the warning stimulus and the electric shock both function in a manner roughly analogous to food deprivation in a food reinforcement procedure. In other words, food deprivation, the pre-shock stimulus, the shock, and the unfollowed rule all function as motivating conditions. The pre-shock stimulus and the unfollowed rule also both function as conditioned motivating stimuli related to Michael's Type 2 conditioned establishing operation (Michael, 1982, 1985) because neither is inherently aversive.

Note that this statement of an unfollowed rule is not a motivating operation that increases the reinforcing value of the ultimate outcome, the cooked turkey. It does not function like the motivating operation of deprivation of the turkey, an operation that would enhance the reinforcing value of the turkey.

How would unfollowed rules come to function as aversive stimuli in the first place? Presumably by being paired with other aversive stimuli, though the pairing would have to be fairly immediate; and the outcome specified in the rule would often be too delayed to cause the unfollowed rule to become an aversive condition. A more likely candidate might be the earlier intervention by the cook's parents, during his childhood. The parents would state a rule or give instructions and then perhaps mildly punish noncompliance by continuing to prompt, nag, or scold, until the child did comply. Thus the unfollowed rule would become a conditioned aversive stimulus that could be escaped by following the rule; therefore, unfollowed rules (including self-stated rules) would function as motivating stimuli, as conditioned-aversive states to be escaped by the following of those rules.

However, it is not clear what conditions would cause unfollowed rules of this sort to continue to be aversive during the cook's adulthood, when he is out from under the critical eyes of his parents. Surely there must be some continued pairing of unfollowed rules with immediate aversive conditions, and those conditions would need to be more immediate than the social embarrassment awaiting the negligent cook several hours after he should have started cooking.

Behavior Management (Behavior Modification)

Generally behavior management or behavior modification consists of three steps: specification of the desired performance, measurement of the performance, and the arrangement of appropriate contingencies. We can first specify the desired performance by giving the person the appropriate rule; for example, floss your teeth daily and you will greatly improve your dental health. At times, simply stating the rule is all we need do; the person's behavior will immediately comply with that rule. But often, we need more. The next step is to add feedback from the results of the measurement of the performance. This could be in terms of the number of days per week the person complies and it could also be in terms of the amount of plaque buildup on the teeth and the health of the gums. The feedback is actually part of a behavioral contingency; that is, the feedback is an outcome of the response. But often rule compliance will improve even more if we add additional contingencies with additional outcomes. For instance, we might require the person to pay a fine every day he or she fails to floss and apply lavish praise every day the person does floss.

Substituting Easy-to-Follow Rules for Hard-to-Follow Rules

Even the contingencies of behavior modification are often indirect-acting. For example, the feedback, the praise, and the penalties might all occur hours or even days after the proper flossing. So the relevant rules would describe indirect-acting contingencies, because the delays would be too great to directly reinforce flossing. However, such rules are easier to follow than those describing the natural contingencies involving dental health, because the outcome of each individual response or lack of a response would be highly probable and, it is hoped, significant. Thus, much, if not most, behavior modification or behavior management with verbal clients consists of supplementing rules that are difficult to follow with rules that are more easy to follow, rules that specify outcomes that are highly probable and significant, though often delayed.

Behavior Contracts

These rules are often presented in "Behavior Contract," an agreement between a behavior manager and the contractee that the manager will make outcomes contingent on the contractee's performance of agreed-upon behaviors. Sometimes the contract will specify behaviors and outcomes for both parties. Usually the expression "Behavior Contract" is used only when working with individuals, rather than when an identical set of contingency-specifying rules is used for all of the members of a group, such as a grade-school classroom. And usually the contingencies specified result from negotiation between the manager and the contractee.

Self-Management versus Management by Others

It is difficult to distinguish between self-management and management by others. Those two procedures are probably on a continuum. For example, it is clearly management by others when we work with a nonverbal organism, including nonverbal humans, and when we directly reinforce or punish a particular response class, as Fuller (1949) did when he put a drop of milk in the mouth of a vegetative idiot each time the subject raised his arm. And it is clearly self-management when we state a rule to ourselves, record our behavior, and perhaps add some reinforcing and punishing contingencies for compliance with that rule.

But what about when we involve others in our contingencies. For example, most of my own efforts at self-management involve a behavioral contractor to whom I report on a daily basis and to whom I pay a penalty when I fail to comply with my own rules. However, we should note that the daily reports and penalties are too delayed to directly reinforce or punish the acts of rule compliance. And because no one is around most of the time when I comply or fail to comply with those rules, either I must self-deliver the behavioral consequences that reinforce compliance and punish noncompliance, or those behavioral consequences must somehow occur automatically. So I am self-managing, to the extent that I deliver my own behavioral consequences, state the rules to myself, and monitor my own performance. This is self-management, even if someone else originally told me the rules and will eventually monitor my performance in terms of some sort of permanent product that performance produces, even if that person will eventually deliver some sort of rewarding or aversive stimulus contingent on that performance, and even if that person's role is crucial to my compliance with the rule. In that case, my performance is a product of the combined procedures of self-management and management by others. This help from an external manager does not do away with the need for self-management; it simply converts rules that are hard to follow into rules that are somewhat easier to follow; however, those rules still describe indirect-acting contingencies. (Incidentally, it may be difficult to study our own self-management skills, because they may be so subtle that we are not always aware of our use of them.)

Behavior Management and Everyday Life

Many behavior analysts and especially behavior modifiers have attempted to use behavior modification in their everyday lives, but most of those attempts are short-lived and not too successful. The problem is not that the technology does not work but rather that it is so difficult to apply consistently. Behavior modification prescribes a set of rules involving the extinction of inappropriate behavior and the use of rewards to reinforce appropriate behavior. However, those rules are difficult to follow, because the reinforcement with rewards or the extinction of any one instance of a response class usually has only a negligible effect on that response class. (Many instances are usually required before any effect is discernable.) On the other hand, any single use of the reinforcement procedure based on rewards usually has at least two negative effects on the behavior modifier: the implementation requires effort and it interferes with the behavior modifier's other on-going and probably more reinforcing activities. For example, the behavior-modifying parent must interrupt reading the newspaper to occasionally reinforce the child's appropriate play or study behavior. Any one instance of the implementation of the extinction procedure also has a negative effect on the behavior modifier: Extinction is incompatible with more immediate interventions such as asking the person to stop the undesirable behavior, an intervention that often produces prompt compliance but that unfortunately also serves to reinforce that class of undesirable behaviors. Thus the immediate contingencies normally work against a behavior manager using behavior modification in the form of extinction or in the form of reinforcement with rewards.

However, that person will often find it easier to follow those same rules of behavior modification, when working as a professional behavior modifier, possibly for two reasons: First, in the professional setting, the behavior modifier is more likely to state the rules of behavior modification to himself or herself. Also in that professional setting, where the behavior modifer is being paid to follow the rules of behavior modification, an unfollowed professional rule is more likely to act as an effective motivating condition, in which noncompliance is aversive and compliance is thereby immediately reinforced by the termination of that aversive state. It may be more aversive not to comply with rules of our profession, rules we are getting paid to follow, than not to comply with rules of good parenting, when we have so many other concurrent responsibilities in the home setting. Second, in the professional setting, the behavior modifier may have fewer competing activities that are more reinforcing than the behavior modification task at hand, especially if the sole responsibility is to properly shape and maintain a client's behavior as in a therapeutic or training session.

APPLICATIONS

I have personally adopted the following overriding rule: Find the rules for leading the good life, both professionally and personally; and then do your best to follow them. In addition, my behavioral history seems to have set up inconsistency as a powerful aversive condition. Thus, I find myself compulsively arranging and rearranging my environment so it will program my behavior to be consistent with those rules for the good life so I can escape the aversive condition of being inconsistent with those rules. I also find myself being somewhat dogged in my attempts to apply behavior analysis to all features of my life. What follows is a report of an attempt to be a thorough-going behavior analyst, in essentially all features of life. I hope the importance of this topic will compensate for its informality.

I have not looked for everyday problems to which I could apply behavior-management techniques. Instead, the problems seem to look for me. When they find me, I simply try to solve them, using those behavior-management techniques. I have found my approach to life also conforms to another rule, though I am not sure I have consciously or otherwise tried to follow this rule. The rule is "Deal with it. If there is something in your life you do not like, then deal with it. Either try to change it or your values." I have not had much success in changing my values. Many of the problems in my life seem to involve either my behavior or the behavior of others. So I have found behavior-management techniques to be of great value in attempting to "deal with it." In the remainder of this chapter, I discuss efforts to deal with my own behavior. Lack of space prevents reporting on applications to the behavior of friends and family, staff management, higher education, research supervision, and minority participation in education, all of which are attempts to deal with problems that have arisen in my everyday personal and professional life; however, these applications have been or will be reported elsewhere (Dillon & Malott, 1981; Malott, 1984). Furthermore, no attempt is made to review the general experimental literature on self-management, as this has been done elsewhere (Karoly & Kanfer, 1982).

Health-Related and Other Personal Behaviors

Weight and Sugar.   As with so many of us in our low-exercise, high-calorie culture, I have had a running battle with my weight for a long time, at least 16 years. During that time I have tried many self-management procedures and have finally gotten the problem under control. Most of my efforts at weight control originally dealt with sugar-laden desserts and snacks.

By way of baseline data, the maximum number of desserts I have eaten at one meal was ten. And I usually ate at least two or three. For several years I used behavior contracts. For instance, when I was at a gathering with tempting desserts, I would contract with someone there to pay them $1 if I ate any of the desserts; and this always worked, as a temporary solution. For a more long-range solution, I would contract with someone to pay them $1 for each dessert I ate during the week, and we would settle accounts once a week. Often that person would have the same contract with me. This worked somewhat, but on the weekends we often failed; and eventually we would stop using the contracts, only to revive them a few months later.

In January, 1977, I stopped using behavior contracts for this problem and started with a year-at-a-glance form of graphic recording. The year-at-a-glance graph paper contains an abscissa with 52 divisions, corresponding to the 52 weeks of the year, and an ordinate marked off in tens. Data are recorded daily and cumulated throughout the week on a single vertical line corresponding to that week. At the end of the week, the cumulative graph is reset to zero and started on the next week's line. This allows for the recording of an entire year's worth of daily data on a single sheet of graph paper. It also constitutes a small but sometimes significant outcome, making it slightly easier to follow some difficult-to-follow rules. In the present case, I added one unit to the week's cumulative record for each day I avoided eating any processed sugar. The goal for the week was for my graph to reach the seven-unit mark on the ordinate. The longer-range goal was to reach as many successive seven-unit goals as possible. So any violation of my non-sugar rule would have a clearcut, high-probability, and hopefully significant outcome—it would make my graph look less than perfect. In fact, that outcome proved to be very effective; no single violation of the rule was worth destroying my perfect record as presented on the graph. And the value of a perfect graph seemed to increase as a function of successively perfect weeks.

I chose in advance to set aside my contract for two trips out of town, and backslid on one other trip, but otherwise I was able to stay on my sugar-free diet. So that year, I consumed less refined sugar than I ever had in any previous year of my life.

In 1978, I tried to incorporate my no-processed-sugar diet within the context of a more general diet, the Pritikin diet; so I did not chart the sugar-free days separately. But when I found myself violating some other component of the Pritikin diet, on a given day, I had nothing else to lose in terms of damaging my diet graph, so I would often eat some sugar-laden junk food as well.

Therefore, in 1979, I returned to recording my sugar-free days on a graph separate from the rest of my Pritikin diet data. During that year I indulged in only four one-evening sugar binges, two of which were when I was on trips but were not planned for in advance. It seems especially difficult to maintain a self-managed repertoire on trips.

In 1980, I attained my first year completely free of processed sugar. From 1981 until the present (April 15, 1984) I have been able to stay free of processed sugar without the use of the graphs. Since that time I have felt no strong tendency to eat processed sugar, though I do occasionally have nightmares about inadvertently eating a candy bar or some ice cream, and I do consume quite a bit of fruit and fruit juices; however, I have at times restricted my diet to one piece of fruit per day with little difficulty. One result has been that my triglyceride level is usually below 100, an indicator of a low risk of cardiac problems. (On December 23, 1984, at my wedding reception, they insisted that the bride and groom pose for the cameras, feeding each other a piece of the traditional, sugar-laden wedding cake. During the rest of that day, I ate one half of the remaining three-tiered cake. However, I have eaten no more refined sugar in the following 3 months. Incidentally, that illustrates the problem of all-or-nothing rules: after one little sin, you are a sinner, so you might as well go the rest of the way because such rules do not distinguish between little sinners and big sinners.)

Pritikin Diet.   Controlling my consumption of processed sugar was one of the most difficult accomplishments of my life. I have used similar procedures with other health-related areas; one of them is the overall quality of my diet. In 1976, I made my first systematic attempt at eating a nutritious and healthy diet. This attempt consisted of reading a book about nutrition, Jacobson's *Nutrition Scoreboard* (1973), and placing on the refrigerator door a poster indicating the nutrition value, both positive and negative, of the various foods I might encounter, as well as a rating system and recommended daily allotments. Although this had some transient effect on my behavior, it was far from sufficient.

Then in 1978, I read *Live Longer Now* (Leonard, Hofer, & Pritikin, 1974) and began what has come to be known as the Pritikin diet. For me, this consisted of no sugar, salt, cholesterol, and no more than 10% fat, either animal or vegetable. I used a scoring method described in that book. According to the method, you assigned various numbers of points for perfect meals, and I plotted the number of daily points on a year-at-a-glance graph. I no longer have the data for that year; but in 1979, the next year, using their point system, 92% of my meals were Pritikin; in 1980, 99.9% were. Then I stopped using the chart, and I ate one non-Pritikin meal each year in 1980 and 1981. In 1982, I relaxed my standards slightly on two trips to Peru, where it was a little more difficult to stay strictly Pritikin. As a result of that relaxation of requirements, I now find I will occasionally eat something that may have a little excess salt in it such as bread at a restaurant; however, well over 95% of the food I eat is within the Pritikin guidelines, and the remainder is not too far off; so I have felt no need to re-implement my charting.

As far as weight control is concerned, when I was running 60 miles per week and following the Pritikin diet, I could eat as much as I wanted and maintain an appropriate body weight, about 15% body fat. However, when I reduced my running to about 20 miles per week, I needed to restrict the amount of moderate-calorie food I ate, for example Grape Nuts and pita bread. During 1983, I did this using a behavioral contract. I was able to discontinue the behavioral contract in 1984 with little increase in consumption of those foods, to date.

Dental Care.   In addition to daily charting, it is often helpful to add a penalty for failure to comply. I usually use a $1 penalty, enough that I will notice it, for its symbolic value, if nothing more, but not enough that losing it will be a major aversive event, not enough that I will cheat or use aversive counter control with my contractor, not enough that I will spend my life in fear of losing it. And dental care is one area where I find daily charting helps, but the $1 penalty considerably increases the likelihood that I will floss, even if I am on a trip, and even if it is time to go to bed and I am very tired. I have data for the last 126 days of 1981, where I missed 3 days of flossing (98% hit rate), 97% in 1982 (not including 12 days in Peru where I could not find any floss), and 97% in 1983 (not including 9 weeks when I contracted to floss twice a day for a hit rate of 76%). The result has been that following periodontal surgery in 1978, my gums have stayed in excellent condition, whereas they had been in very bad condition for the previous 20 years.

Aerobic Exercise.   I started jogging in 1976, following some 20 years of lethargy. I have used charting most of the time and contracting with a $1 penalty some of the time. Again the contracting seems to help me bring my number of days of jogging per week and number of miles jogged per day much closer to my goals, especially at times when I am having difficulty in approximating those goals. Such goals may make it more aversive to violate rules specifying the running of high mileage. I also find that having extrinsic goals, such as running a marathon or other races, is almost essential for me to set and achieve high weekly standards of mileage. It also seems to help to work out with a group when doing especially arduous runs, such as 20-mile distance runs and speed workouts. And it may also improve reliability to have a routine running partner as well. These group activities may help because the aversiveness of violating a social commitment to participate in such runs may improve the reliability of participation somewhat. The disbanding of such groups often seems correlated with a decrease in running.

Over the last 5 years, my annual mileage has varied between 2,585 miles in 1980 and 1,362 miles in 1983 (low because of illness). And my fitness has improved from being able to run less than a half mile to being able to run a 26-mile marathon and has regressed to something midway between those two extremes. I am not sure whether I will try to increase my mileage to the marathon level again; perhaps.

However, being a distance runner does not always require exceptional skill in self-management; there seem to be mild physiological rewards maintaining distance running, and I have known several outstanding distance runners who have not demonstrated strong self-management skills in other areas of their lives—yet the drop-out rate from aerobic exercise is very high, and self-management procedures do seem to help.

Back Exercises.   Although there may be some immediate physiological rewards that help maintain running, I have not been able to discern any for back exercises; and unfortunately many adult Americans suffer from chronic back pain. In 1960, I encountered my first of several episodes of acute attacks of debilitating lower back pain, and by 1970, I was experiencing chronic pain so that I could not immediately stand up straight after sitting for 2 hours or lying in bed for 8 hours, a problem attributed to a fused disc. In 1975, I started muscle-strengthening exercises to alleviate the problem, with considerable success, but with insufficient reliability. Charting helped, but I've needed contracting to achieve the kind of reliability I wanted with a goal of four sets of sit-ups, chin-ups, push-ups, and leg lifts, 3 to 5 days per week. The result is that for the last 3 years I have been virtually free of all back pain. And charting and contracting seem essential for me to attain this goal.

Self-Pity and Other Self-Defeating Thoughts.   My attempts at self-management of covert behavior have been more equivocal. I have been mainly concerned with eliminating thoughts of self-pity of the ''They won't have Richard Malott to kick around anymore'' sort. I have tried two types of interventions, first simply charting the results as recorded on a wrist-worn mechanical response counter (golf counter) and then the added punishing stimulus of the snap of a rubber band worn loosely about the wrist (at the suggestion of Donald Whaley). I have used these techniques mainly in times of personal stress, and they may have some beneficial effect, though that effect is not so dramatic as to completely convince me that it exists.

But here is what I think happens: The use of both the response counter and the rubber band serve to make an overt response contingent on the covert thought. Thus I start to monitor my thoughts more closely and become more verbally aware of my negative thoughts. Being aware of them allows me to attempt to program some incompatible behavior. For example, I might count backwards from 10. Sometimes that seems to disrupt the chain of negative thoughts. At other times, the negative thoughts begin again, as soon as I reach zero; and so I have to resume my counting. I think the monitoring also allows me to begin to detect negative thoughts and to intervene earlier and earlier in the behavioral chain, until eventually, I get to the point where I can detect them just as they are starting.

At times the negative thoughts occur at a high rate, and I am not able to control them by covertly programming incompatible behavior. At those times, it is often possible to overtly program activities that are incompatible with such thoughts, for example watching a movie or talking to friends with whom it would not be appropriate to discuss the negative topic.

This raises the question "Why do negative thoughts occur in the first place?" Thinking largely seems to be simply covert verbal behavior and therefore to be operant behavior controlled by its consequences. So the question is "What are the reinforcing consequences that maintain negative thoughts?" A large part of those reinforcing consequences might be the emotional reaction, the activation syndrome, the same sort of consequences that may reinforce watching sad or pessimistic movies. However, if these negative thoughts are so reinforcing, why do we want to stop them? Because the immediate effect of each momentary thought is the reinforcing emotional reaction, but the cumulative effect of such thoughts is quite aversive. It is much like the reinforcing effect of the sweet taste of candy, where the cumulative effect of excessive weight gains is quite aversive.

Another question is whether programming incompatible behavior is simply postponing the inevitable confrontation with the negative thoughts. I think not. As time passes without those thoughts, I believe we are much less likely to indulge ourselves in them; the aversive events in our lives that originally evoked such thoughts are less likely to do so or those aversive events become less effective as motivating operations in generating the emotional reactions to such thoughts, the reactions that would reinforce their occurrence.

I suspect the snap of the rubber band, though aversive, may function mainly to cue our monitoring of our negative thoughts rather than to directly punish such thoughts. However, the loud, conspicuous snap of the rubber band makes it somewhat impractical for use in many social settings.

Hobbies. I have had considerable success in using charting and behavior contracting with penalties to program my participation in recreational activities such as playing my drums 15 minutes daily; soaking, relaxing, and reading in the bathtub 15 minutes every day; and writing in my personal journal daily.

There are two interesting issues here: First, many of us seem to have hobbies or recreational activities from which we used to gain a great deal of pleasure but that we no longer seem able to take the time to do. Therefore, we are confronted with the apparent paradox of needing to use aversive control such as the threat of a $1 penalty to get ourselves to take the time to have a little fun. The problem is that we can always put off practicing our guitar for just one more day, because we really do have much more immediately pressing issues to take care of, with the result that we never get around to taking our guitar out of its case. Such examples are of particular relevance to people who raise the traditional objection to behavior modification, the objection that we should not have to use special contingencies to get people to do the studying or work they should want to do anyway. That argument has less force when we realize we may need to use special contingencies to get ourselves to have a good time; so the fact that we need added contingencies does not necessarily mean we do not want to study or work.

The other issue is that a mere 15 minutes of recreation per day can greatly improve the quality of our lives, even though normally practicing a musical instrument for less than an hour might seem hardly worth the effort. This makes less tenable the objection that we do not really have enough time to do it.

Profession-Related Behaviors

Positive Social Interactions.   My high rate of negative or critical overt remarks competes with my high rate of sugar consumption as being my problem of most long-standing concern. It also competes for being originally the most intractable and also, more recently, the problem repertoire I have had the most success with using self-recording and behavioral contracting.

It seems fairly common for people to be unaware of the correctness of the following rule: "Avoid frequent negative remarks, even of a humorous nature, and you will more readily win friends and influence people, in the long run." And even if they do know this rule, it is still difficult to follow, because those beneficial outcomes are not only delayed but also small and cumulative. On the other hand, negative remarks often produce strong, immediate, and highly probable rewards, such as attention, sometimes immediate compliance, and an appreciative smile, when humorous. In addition, the negative remark often has a component of aggression that can be very reinforcing as a reaction to aversive stimulation that may result from a displeasing circumstance. Therefore this rule describing an indirect-acting contingency often fails to control behavior.

It was not until 1965, 2 years after I had received my PhD degree in experimental psychology with an emphasis on behavior analysis, that I learned that my efforts at providing corrective feedback and my asking thought-provoking questions were usually, in fact, extremely aversive to the person under scrutiny. It was not until 1966 that I recognized the potential of several of my colleagues to serve as role models for a more positive, pleasing, and rewarding form of interaction. Although those role models may have served as inspirational motivating operations, their presence did not alter my repertoire noticeably.

In 1969, I started my first systematic efforts to decrease the frequency of my aversive comments. One of those efforts consisted of counting negative remarks to friends. If a criterion number of remarks occurred, I would have to do some extra chore as a penalty. This seemed to decrease the frequency of such remarks. Another effort consisted of wearing a portable electric shocker connected to two electrodes, so that I could self-punish aversive comments. The final procedure simply consisted of using the wrist response counter and charting the frequency of such remarks, occasionally combined with a $1 penalty for any single occurrence of a negative remark.

Generally, I told those with whom I interacted what I was trying to do and asked them to call to my attention any instances of negativity they detected. Many colleagues seemed more than willing to oblige. I followed the policy that the listeners were always correct, even if I did not interpret what I had said as being negative, because it was the effect on them that was most important. Occasionally some of my more astute colleagues would point out subtle instances of sarcasm that I could recognize only after considerable examination.

By 1972, the frequency of my negative remarks had greatly reduced, to the point where most people seemed to feel there was no longer a problem. In fact, on various occasions people have cited me as an exemplar of non-negative verbal behavior. My graduate students often claim to have never seen an instance of my negative verbal behavior, though about 5 years ago one or two suggested I might consider putting my response counter back on again; and I did. People who knew me before and after claim the transformation was considerable. My major efforts took place at home and at work; however, much to my surprise, people in other social settings, not knowing of these efforts, have commented on the great and positive change in my personality, even though I had not been aware of a problem before and was not aware of any change afterward. My own impression is that my rate may still be too high, but it is definitely much lower than before and usually does seem to be well within the range of social acceptability.

One setting that has been more difficult than most has been our departmental faculty meetings; I still have difficulty containing my sarcasm and general negativity in that setting, even though I spent one year recording the number of positive, negative, and neutral comments in that context. The main problem there is the difficulty I have in monitoring and editing my own comments before they occur.

One interesting side effect of this decrease in negative remarks has been that I now find it much more aversive to be around others who have a high rate of negativity. Here is another interesting side effect: I think the frequency of my critical thoughts about others has also decreased. It may be that, before, much of my critical thoughts were in the form of covert rehearsals of critical observation to share with someone else. Once I no longer had the opportunity to speak about these negative topics, the occasions for such rehearsal may have decreased or at least allowed for less reinforcement.

In summary of my work on negative remarks, self-recording and penalties have facilitated my self-monitoring to the point where I was able to greatly reduce my rate of negativity. Initially, this was a form of rule-governed behavior. But eventually, this negativity came under some form of contingency control, so that now I rarely need to monitor my performance in order to keep the rate of negativity acceptably low.

For one year, I also contracted to send out one piece of written positive feedback every day to either one of my students or colleagues or others. I found this feedback to be greatly appreciated by the recipients, many of whom had rarely received such feedback. The only problem occurred when I would send some feedback to only one of several assistants on a particular project; the others would then wonder why they had not gotten any. Under the press of time, I dropped this technique but plan to adopt it again, at least on a weekly basis.

It is my strong impression that smiling greatly increases the reward value of a person's presence, and therefore I have attempted to increase my rate of smiling. But it is necessary to be very covert in the recording of your own smiles, to avoid detracting from their reward value for others. Thus I found it impossible to monitor my own behavior and state the instructions to myself frequently enough. Therefore I have abandoned this project.

Long-Range Projects—Writing.   Casual observation of myself, my students, and my colleagues suggests that sitting down to write is one of the most difficult professional behaviors we ever try to control. This is true whether we are trying to write a book or a post card. The problem is that the immediate rewards for writing are not great enough to get it to occur reliably, and normally there is no aversive outcome if we simply postpone writing for one more minute, or hour, or day. The aversive outcome accumulates only as our procrastination accumulates from days to weeks, to months, and sometimes to years. But even then, there is still no aversive outcome for one more day's procrastination.

Since 1967, I have been using behavioral self-management techniques to increase my writing time and output. I made my weekly salary contingent on the number of hours I spent writing, when I was working full-time writing a book. But more typically I have contracted to write 4 hours per day, 5 days per week and pay $1 for every hour below criterion. During the preceding 4 years, I have also set up an additional contingency—a commitment to write 20 to 30 weekly newsletters per year. Each newsletter required about 10 hours of writing. This commitment was only supplemental, however, being far from an ironclad behavioral-control technique, as it did not prevent me from sometimes falling behind schedule.

Over the last 5 years, my total hours of writing per year have varied from 269 to 705; and my number of perfect weeks per year (20 hours of writing in a week) has varied from 2 to 33. During the first 18 weeks of 1979, I did not use a contract and only wrote an average of 2.17 hours per week; however, during the next 30 weeks, I used a contract and wrote an average of 21.1 hours per week.

My theoretical goal was 20 hours per week for 52 weeks or 1,040 hours per year; however I never actually contract for this much, as I make exceptions for days out of town and days when other responsibilities will clearly prevent following my ideal writing schedule. This latter loophole causes problems, as my judgment may vary quite a bit as to the criterion for what will clearly prevent me from following my ideal schedule, and thus I may often fail to require as much of myself as I might. This seems to be somewhat less of a problem when I prepare an entire week's contract in advance, rather than one day at a time. I seem to be especially inclined to lower my standards when I am contracting for writing to be done during the next few hours. I sometimes discontinue contracting altogether, until my cumulative lack of productivity becomes so aversive that I escape that condition by reinstating the contracting procedure.

The other problem is that I may fail to meet my contracted obligations. This occurs at times because I fail to monitor the number of hours available before leaving my writing table at home to go to the university, I do not calculate the amount of time needed for other tasks before leaving, and I do not notice the number of hours of writing remaining to be done. Although this monitoring requires a very simple repertoire, its failure is a common source of problems. In addition, I sometimes put off some of my writing until I return from the university, but then I am too tired to write, so I say to myself that it is worth the $1 penalty not to have to write. In the past, I have dealt with this problem by contracting to have all of my writing done before leaving my home at noon. This year, I reduced my required hours to 2 per day and raised the penalty for noncompliance from $1 to $5 per hour. This has worked well over a 10-week period, where I have only had to pay one $5 penalty; this penalty occurred because my monitoring was so faulty I did not realize, until the next day, that I was an hour behind in my writing. However, for most behavioral contracts, it usually seems to work better and be less aversive to break the tasks into smaller subgoals and to add more deadlines than to increase the size of the penalty.

Also, I sometimes can spend an hour at my typewriter daydreaming about irrelevant issues and produce no written words. When I was working in an office near a secretary, I would contract to write 100 words every hour or pay the $1 penalty. Then every hour I would bring the new words in to the secretary to monitor. She also initialed them so I would not resubmit the same paper. When I was doing multiple edits of the same page, I would contract for a few pages of editing using a new color of ink for the editing marks on each new editing.

At times writing requires a period of thinking and shuffling pages with no permanent product for proof of productivity. To deal with this, as well as the above productivity problems, I have used a recycling timer set to beep every 5 minutes. When it beeped, I recorded on a cumulative graph whether or not I was on task. The result is that I was on task 94% of the time, whereas my subjective impression is that I might otherwise have been on task only 50% of the time, especially during times when I was having difficulty thinking through an issue or was distracted by thoughts about some other problem in my life. The timer seems to achieve its effectiveness by increasing my monitoring of my own performance so that I will be more likely to detect that I am daydreaming and thus will be more likely to get myself back on task. It also provides a high probability aversive outcome for being off task—my cumulative graph will not look as good if I am not on task when the timer sounds next. Incidentally, I do not detect much of a tendency to be off task during the first part of the 5-minute interval and then start to work as the timer's beep approaches.

For one semester, I found it necessary to do my daily writing after I had finished a full day's work, and I was not getting many words written. A solution I used for several weeks was to feed myself a bite of pizza after every sentence written. This seemed to help, and I did not have much problem with bootleg reinforcement, with eating unearned pizza, though others have reported this problem. On the other hand, now that I write in my home, I often find myself eating a bowl of popcorn while I am writing. I notice that eating popcorn and thinking about my writing seem to be incompatible activities, so the popcorn inevitably wins out. Perhaps I should revert to the work-eat contingency.

What about quality? Do I tend to generate low-quality writing, simply to comply with my contract? I do not think so. I see no difference between my writing when I have a contingency on quantity and when I do not. I believe that the reinforcers for generating reasonable writing and the aversive stimuli resulting from doing otherwise suffice to control the quality of the writing, once I actually start putting the words on paper.

Obviously I have not demonstrated experimental control over my writing and productivity; however, subjectively it is quite clear to me that these techniques work. When I do not have the contracts in effect, I am much less productive. I also find myself often needing to state the following rule to myself: If I do not get my quota in for the day, I will have to pay a penalty. I have little question about the immediate contingencies that control my writing behavior.

But this raises another interesting issue: If I have to go to such extreme measures to force myself to write, why do I do it? Because I love to write! Because I find it very rewarding to find out what I have to say. Because it is very rewarding to have completed my writing. Because I feel guilty when I am not living up to my potential as a professional. And probably least of all, because there are some long-range professional benefits for writing. But as with many hobbies that fall by the wayside, the immediate rewards for this professional activity are not sufficient to compete with the immediate rewards for other activities, like watching television; and they are not sufficient to compete with the avoidance and escape contingencies that cause us to spend so much time putting out brush fires rather than working on long-range projects like writing.

We might also consider another factor—psychological effort, a critical issue (though I know of no work on this topic). Psychologically, it is more of an effort to write than to read, though the difference in the physical effort is negligible. Thus, many would-be thesis and dissertation writers fall into the library trap— the tendency to spend all of their time doing library research rather than dealing with the psychologically more effortful tasks of thinking and writing. Thus, though writing may produce more rewards for me than the much less effortful activity of browsing through a magazine, I usually need supplemental contingencies to cause my writing behavior to dominate over the browsing behavior. In fact, I sometimes cheat a bit by claiming that my reading is really important for my writing and therefore appropriately counted as part of my writing time.

However, when I become aware that this is a problem, I define more explicitly, in a written contract, just what will and will not count as writing behavior.

Will I ever be able to eliminate the explicit self-management procedures and still maintain acceptable writing performance, as with the diet and negative remarks? I doubt it. First of all, I have been using these self-management procedures off and on for quite a few years, with no apparent decrease in my need for them. In addition, many, if not most, productive professional writers also use self-management procedures throughout all of their careers (Pear, 1977). The major difference between my approach and that of such professional writers is in my use of added behavioral consequences. They all set daily quotas, count and record their productivity, and sometimes even use charts.

Non-Recurring Tasks.   Another constant problem involves the routine paper work confronting us all, for example, writing letters of recommendation, reading thesis proposals, and reviewing articles submitted to journals. I call these "non-recurring tasks." I can often measure the amount of nonrecurring tasks in terms of the height of the pile of papers I need to process. And the age of the tasks can often be measured in months. My most successful effort with these consisted of a one-semester contract that I would buy junk food for a class I was teaching if the age of any incoming nonrecurring task ever exceeded 1 week. There was a qualification that I could prorate over weeks those tasks that required more than 1 hour to complete. I implemented a similar contract to dispose of the $1\frac{1}{2}$ feet of backlog I had accumulated.

The method I have been using for the last year and a half consists of a contract to complete at least one nonrecurring task each day. This works fairly well, though I probably should contract for specific tasks, as I sometimes select the easiest rather than the most important task to complete.

In addition, if a student gives me a proposal or a manuscript to read, I usually suggest that we make a specific appointment to discuss it, because I need a clear-cut deadline to prevent infinite procrastination.

Professional Reading.   For 1 year, I contracted to do 15 minutes of professional reading 5 days a week. This allowed me to at least stay current with the abstracts of a few journals, which was considerably more than I have typically done.

Hours Worked.   I have sometimes contracted to work a specific number of hours per day, regardless of the particular tasks. But I have found that one of the main reasons I fail to spend as many hours working as I would like is because I do not start working early enough in the morning, because I do not get out of bed early enough. So for $4\frac{1}{2}$ years, I contracted to be in bed by 9:00 P.M., out of bed by 4:00 A.M., and at my desk by 5:00 A.M., 5 days per week, with a fair amount of variation in the contracted details as the circumstances warranted, for example vacations. As an illustration, in 1980, I charted but did not contract for the first 23 weeks, during which I was scheduled to be at work by 5:00 A.M. 68 times and succeeded 69% of the time. However, when I started contracting during the remainder of the year, I was successful 89% of the 112 scheduled days. Generally I have found this procedure to be quite satisfactory, though at the present it is more convenient to contract to work on the weekends instead.

Other Behaviors.   With varying degrees of success and for varying durations, I have contracted to deal with the following behaviors: preparing courses, gardening, not using profanity, not pulling hairs out of my beard, speaking fluently, studying Spanish, studying systems-analysis flash cards, doing various auxiliary dental care routines, keeping house, and spending a few minutes in quiet appreciation of my environment.

CONCLUSIONS

Many important contingencies in our daily lives fail to control our actions, because those contingencies involve outcomes that are not only delayed but also improbable and of only cumulative significance. Furthermore, rules describing these contingencies also often fail to control our actions. We can supplement those rules that are difficult to follow with rules that are easier to follow, rules that specify additional outcomes that are sufficiently probable and sizable that they can control our behavior, at least indirectly. These supplemental rules often involve self-recording and behavioral contracting. However, the behavior of following these easier-to-follow rules often needs additional behavioral consequences, perhaps in the form of self-given aversive stimulation, such as guilt or anxiety, when we are not complying with those rules. In addition, we must often repeat the rules to ourselves, and monitor our own compliance. In this sense we are self-managing our behavior.

In most areas, self-recording and behavioral contracting have helped me come much nearer to achieving my objective than I might have otherwise, and in a few cases, I have essentially achieved those objectives. These procedures have greatly enhanced the quality of my life and have generated the rewarding condition of feeling in control of my own destiny. Furthermore, this vast amount of programming of my life does not become aversive—in fact quite the opposite; it is very rewarding to have the sort of productive day such programming produces. Perhaps a well-programmed day is not aversive because the penalties are small, usually only $1, and the probability of success is high; and I always have the possibility of voiding my contracts in advance, when that seems necessary.

Presently, I contract for the following daily behaviors: reporting to my contractor, writing for 2 hours, doing one nonrecurring task, studying Spanish for 2 hours, doing four sets of exercises, running three miles, and flossing. I am now using my computer and an electronic spread sheet to record and summarize my data; and thus far it takes me about 1½ hours per week to do that work, whereas before it took about 15 minutes.

REFERENCES

Dillon, M. J., & Malott, R. W. (1981). Supervising masters theses and doctoral dissertations. *Teaching of Psychology, 8*, 195–202.

Fuller, P. R. (1949). Operant conditioning of a vegetative human organism. *American Journal of Psychology, 62*, 587–590.

Jacobson, M. (1973). *Nutrition scoreboard: Your guide to better eating*. Washington: Center for Science in the Public Interest.

Karoly, P., & Kanfer, F. H. (1982). *Self-management and behavior change: From theory to practice*. New York: Pergamon.

Leonard, J. N., Hofer, J. L., & Pritikin, N. (1974). *Live longer now: The first one hundred years of your life: the 2100 program*. New York: Grosset & Dunlap.

Malott, R. W. (1984). In search of human perfectibility: A behavioral approach to higher education. In W. L. Heward, T. E. Heron, D. S. Hill, & J. Trap-Porter (Eds.), *Focus on behavior analysis in education*. Columbus: Charles E. Merrill.

Malott, R. W. (1984). Rule-governed behavior, self-management, and the developmentally disabled: A theoretical analysis. *Analysis and Intervention in Developmental Disabilities, 4*, 199–209.

Michael, J. (1982). Distinguishing between discriminative and motivational functions of stimuli. *Journal of the Experimental Analysis of Beavior, 37*, 149–155.

Michael, J. (1985). *Motivative relations or the establishing operation (EO)*. Unpublished manuscript, Western Michigan University, Department of Psychology, Kalamazoo.

Pear, J. (1977). Irving Wallace's self-control techniques of famous novelists. *Journal of Applied Behavior Analysis, 10*, 515–525.

Skinner, B. F. (1969). *Contingencies of reinforcement*. Englewood Cliffs, NJ: Prentice Hall.

9

The Utility of Continuous Programmed Environments in the Experimental Analysis of Human Behavior

Daniel J. Bernstein
University of Nebraska

Joseph V. Brady
Johns Hopkins University

There is an inherent conflict in research between ecological richness in a behavioral repertoire and precision of experimental control. This conflict is never more apparent than in the experimental analysis of human behavior. Although applied behavior analysts have convincingly demonstrated the utility of an experimental analysis of naturally occurring human behavior, fewer basic research programs have brought behavior analysis to bear on human behavior. Though basic operant research with human subjects is increasing in frequency each year, much of it is derived from procedures developed for use with animals. Analysis of discrete manual responses such as button pressing in 1-hour sessions (cf. Lowe, 1979, 1983) is certainly useful, but that approach is limited to the extent that it does not take advantage of a full repertoire of human behavior.

One line of human research involving "programmed environments" has been dedicated to an experimental analysis of more complete repertoires of human behavior. These studies have combined the conceptual framework of experimental analysis with the naturalistic goals of an ethological approach to continuous observation. This chapter first identifies the origin of this approach in experimental analysis and then outlines three research programs of this type. The descriptions include the rationale for development of the methods, typical procedures employed, and conceptual contributions of these studies. There is also a description of the essential characteristics of programmed research environments for humans, and a discussion of how they compare with other methods in the experimental analysis of behavior. Finally, there is discussion of ways that such environments could be useful in the development of new research programs.

EARLY CONCEPTION AND DEVELOPMENT

Animal Research.   The earliest experimental use of continuous research and living environments is found in a monograph by Findley (1962) on multiple response analysis. The rationale for these studies was the exploration of behavioral phenomena in the context of a broader repertoire of response alternatives. Findley argued that limitations in operant theory resulted in part from studying limited behavioral repertoires, and he reported several experiments with combinations of concurrent and chain schedules that attempted to identify functional units of behavior more complex than a key peck or lever press. The first several experiments with rats and pigeons were run in short sessions with food-deprived animals, but these studies did not provide clear examples of the extended operant class Findley proposed. He then did two studies in which monkeys lived continuously 24 hr per day in an experimental chamber and obtained all of their food, water, and stimulation as scheduled parts of the experiment. He presented the subjects with a programmed sequence of concurrent choices between different reinforcement schedules operating independently on a variety of response manipulanda. Completion of one schedule presented the subject with a new choice between schedules. Contingencies placed on a complex sequence of choices produced changes in the rate of completion of the sequence, suggesting that the entire sequence functioned as a single operant class. Findley also studied a pigeon using a similar 24 hr per day procedure, and the complex sequence functioned as a unit of behavior in that setting as well.

Findley (1962) concluded that performance on complex units could be best maintained by explicit stimulus control and that series of sequential concurrent choices were more stable units of behavior than long chains of individually scheduled responses. He also observed that the continuous environment was a useful approach to the conduct of such research. Most of his discussion of the value of the new procedure focused on practical details such as increased session time and convenience of animal maintenance, but he also noted that continuous environments provided better experimental control over the subjects' behavior.

Human Research.   Findley later used this procedural approach with a human research subject who lived continuously in a residential laboratory setting for $5\frac{1}{2}$ months (Findley, 1966; Findley, Migler, & Brady, 1963). The single subject worked through a sequence of choices between activities that followed the branching pattern used with monkeys in the first continuous experiments. The first part of the sequence was a fixed set of activities that maintained the subject's health during the extended duration of the experiment. Next came a series of concurrent choices among different classes of activities. First the subject engaged in one of several psychomotor work activities, followed by the availability of a range of intellectual activities such as reading. The subject could engage in one activity from that class, and on its completion a range of leisure activities such as games became available. Completion of one selected leisure activity completed a cycle, and the subject was again required to go through the health check sequence. A complete cycle lasted about 2 hours, and sleep could be chosen as an alternative to the work activities. No constraints were put on the subject's distribution of activity cycles and sleep periods during each 24-hr day. The laboratory was fully automated for both recording and programming of choices.

The main conclusions from this initial study focused on the feasibility of maintaining human performance over extended time periods by scheduling consequences for complex sequences of individual activities. The number and pattern of cycles were sensitive to reinforcement in the same way that discrete operants are. Over the entire experimental period there were several changes in the subject's overall pattern of activities. Sleep periods, for example, became shorter and more frequent. Time spent in the toilet doubled, and there was a matching decrease in time on intellectual activities. A similar indirect effect occurred when the number of lever pulls for a cigarette was gradually raised from 25 to 500. Apparently because of the time devoted to obtaining cigarettes, there was less time devoted to maintenance of the laboratory. Findley (1966) noted the value of automatic operation for both measurement and control of behavior, and he again commented on the convenience of continuous environmental control for carrying out research. He also claimed that the use of naturalistic activities and extended application of the controlling variables represented a major advance in the experimental analysis of human behavior and in the generalizability of research results.

Methodological Summary.   There is a clear continuity between the original procedures used with animals and those in the single-human study. The cycles of activities for humans were modeled after the programmed sequences used with monkeys, and Findley attributed much of the success of the environment to the structure it provided for the daily lives of its subjects. The procedures represent Findley's resolution of the conflict between ethological validity and experimental requirements in research. Complex behavior is routinely broken down into its components for purposes of experimental analysis, but Findley (1962) argued that such experiments (and the theories they generated) lacked the richness and complexity of the behavior to which the results were to be generalized. His strategy was to synthesize a complex repertoire by placing contingencies on long sequences of laboratory tasks, rather than to work on existing molar behavior transplanted into a naturalistic laboratory setting.

GENERAL CHARACTERISTICS OF A PROGRAMMED ENVIRONMENT

Findley's laboratory was called a programmed environment because subjects worked through a structured sequence of choices between activities while living

continuously for extended periods in the experimental space. The response repertoire was created on conceptual grounds to approximate behavior outside of the
laboratory, and performance on the full range of responses was automatically
recorded. A broad behavioral record allowed for assessment of subtle or indirect
effects on responses not directly involved in a contingency. Continuous long-
term residence in the laboratory provided additional control over extraneous
influences not related to the experimental variables and extended the duration of
assessment for both baseline performance and the effects of interventions. In
addition to the enhancement of experimental control, Findley noted that a programmed environment was easier for the experimenter to manage and that structured routine helped subjects deal with long periods of experimental participation.

Over the last decade several new research programs have used Findley's
programmed environment as a point of departure for research on human operant
behavior. In each case subjects have lived continuously in a laboratory for weeks
at a time, engaging in a variety of ordinary human activities under the control of
contingencies programmed by the experimenter. Detailed records are made of all
of the subjects' responses, and the effects of each intervention are analyzed in
relationship to the entire response repertoire. Although these research programs
share a common methodological base, they have pursued substantive issues
ranging from group cooperation to reinforcement theory to gender mix in work
crews. The following descriptions of these programs illustrate the utility of a
programmed environment for the study of a wide range of human operant
behavior.

RESEARCH ON COOPERATION AND GROUP
COMPOSITION

Brady, Bigelow, Emurian, and Williams (1975) developed a residential laboratory at the Johns Hopkins University School of Medicine using a programmed
sequence of activities like Findley's, but the experimental space was expanded to
include three subjects in individual living chambers. Each subject had a required
cycle of activities selected from health maintenance, work tasks, intellectual
tasks, and leisure activities. Contingencies were placed on entire cycles as the
basic unit of operant behavior. The laboratory had two additional rooms for
social and work activities, and subjects talked with each other through an inter-
com when they were in individual rooms. The operation of laboratory procedures
and recording of data were fully automated.

Cooperation Studies.   Emurian, Emurian, Bigelow, and Brady (1976) used
this programmed sequence format to investigate the effects of contingencies on
cooperation in three-person groups. Following the usual required sequence of

activities was a final choice between two social activity options—a group meal or a group workshop for maintenance chores. Each subject followed the program in his or her individual room, and access to the social area and to social activities came only in the final choice period of each cycle. Subjects' pay for participation was a flat daily rate independent of performance on the program.

Subjects in this experiment lived under two experimental conditions. During the noncooperation condition each subject could pick a social activity without regard to the other subjects' choices. During the cooperation condition subjects could select either social activity only if all three subjects were at the same choice point and selected the same activity. The contingency requiring cooperation produced greater synchronization of performance of the subjects' program cycles.

In a related study by Emurian, Emurian, and Brady (1978) the cooperation requirement was varied within groups so that in *triadic* conditions all three subjects had to select the same social activity and in *dyadic* conditions only two subjects could select a social activity together. There was greater synchronization of program performance, more time in social activities, and greater use of the communication system under triadic conditions. There was no difference between dyadic and triadic conditions in the amount of task effort required for access to the social choices. Emurian et al. (1978) concluded that a dyadic arrangement was inferior at maintaining social interaction and could lead to isolation of an individual group member.

In the same laboratory, Brady and Emurian (1979) explored the contrasting effects of positive (appetitive) and negative (aversive) reinforcement procedures on group cooperation. Unlike previous research that provided a constant daily rate of pay for participation, this experiment used subjects' performance to determine pay. Subjects worked through the same program used in previous cooperation studies, but at each choice point there was the additional option of completing a separate 1–2 hr sequence of lever pulling, problem solving, exercise, and health maintenance. During the positive reinforcement (appetitive) condition $10 was added to a common bank account to be divided equally at the end of the experiment. During the negative reinforcement (aversive) condition, the group was required to match its collective work output from the appetitive condition. If group performance was below its previous level, the common account lost $10 for each work unit below the required amount.

This procedure produced a marked difference in subjects' attitudes and social behavior, but little change in the number of work units produced by the groups. Subjects knew the total work output and the individual contributions to the total, but failure to contribute equally was a source of irritation only in the avoidance conditions. The hostility was expressed both toward group members performing less than average work and toward the experimenters. In general the number of work units performed during aversive conditions was the same as the number in the appetitive conditions surrounding them, although there was an increase in work units under appetitive conditions in the two groups for which the experiment ended with a return to appetitive conditions. The aversive conditions produced more formal cooperation as evidenced by an even distribution of work units across subjects.

Emurian, Emurian, and Brady (1982) used a similar procedure in which a video monitoring task replaced the work sequence for earning credit to the joint payment account, and access to the video station could be selected at any choice point in the program. Only one subject could be earning money (or avoiding losses) at any given time, and there was a marked deterioration in the attitudes and cohesiveness of the group under the aversive condition. During the aversive schedule, performance on the video monitoring task was quite variable, being initially 10%–15% higher than during the first appetitive condition and later being reduced nearly 50%. When the appetitive schedule was restored for the last day of the experiment, there was a burst of responding above previous levels by all three subjects.

The combined studies suggest that control by negative reinforcement (avoidance) schedules has undesirable effects on group performance and cooperation. Even when task performance did not deteriorate, group morale and cohesion did. Emurian et al. (1982) drew close parallels between their laboratory results and behavior observed during one of the Skylab missions, suggesting that some of the problems were created by the procedures used to control the astronauts' performance.

Changes in Group Composition. The most recent experiments using the programmed activity sequence examined the effects of adding a group member to an established laboratory crew or replacing a group member with a new person. Emurian, Brady, Meyerhoff, and Mougey (1981) began with two subjects engaging in similar programmed sequences under the appetitive payment conditions from earlier research, and after 3 or 4 days a third subject was added to the experiment. The new subject sometimes had a fixed daily pay rate and sometimes was on an individual appetitive pay schedule based on video task performance. In one group the new subject was a female, the only one included as a subject in this study. There were no losses in productivity attributable to the changes in personnel, and adjustments in work time and schedule were made with minimal disruptions in the social climate. The program conditions even maintained performance on the video task by new subjects who were not required to work for payment.

In a second study, Emurian, Brady, Meyerhoff, and Mougey (1983) used the same experimental conditions but a different strategy for changing personnel. Each group began with three people, and after 5 days the one performing the video task at the lowest level was replaced by a new subject. Despite differences in experience with the video task, the behavioral program maintained task performance without major disruptions of the social climate. Although transitory negative attitudes were noted at replacement times, overall productivity on the work task remained high. The combined studies suggest that the behavioral program maintained very robust performance despite changes in membership of the group.

Throughout the experiments on changes in group membership, urinary testosterone levels were determined for all subjects to assess possible effects on selected aspects of endocrine regulation. The sensitivity of testosterone levels to changes in group size was most evident in those groups in which work routines and/or wake-sleep schedules were disrupted for some members but remained stable for others. More specifically, work schedules least disruptive of established wake-sleep routines were sometimes accompanied by elevations in testosterone levels when changes in the group composition occurred. Conversely, decreases in testosterone levels were associated with changes in group composition that produced less than optimal work and/or sleep schedules. These studies also revealed interactions between broadly defined ''dominance-submission'' and ''success-failure'' relationships and testosterone levels that are similar to observations reported on changes in group composition and organization in lower primates. The presence of some relationships between environmental events and the endocrine system suggest that programmed environments may be useful for investigating the continuity across species of fundamental interactions between behavior and biology.

Methodological Summary.   This series of studies represents continued development of Findley's programmed behavioral laboratory. The core of the procedure is a sequence of activities and concurrent choice points through which subjects repeatedly work during extended periods of residence. The rationale for using the behavioral program is both practical and conceptual. On the practical side, the program maintains stable behavior in people confined to a laboratory for periods of up to 15 days. Given an interest in evaluating the effects of variables over periods of several weeks, it is important that a reasonably constant baseline be available for purposes of comparison. On the conceptual side both the entire program and the different work routines used for payment are complex operant classes, and the rates of completion of each operant provides a dependent variable to assess the effects of interventions.

RESEARCH ON REINFORCEMENT THEORY

During the same period that the Hopkins group developed their lab, a separate line of research used a long-term residential laboratory to explore the nature of reinforcement. Following Findley's (1966) demonstration that a human subject could thrive in a controlled laboratory for extended periods, Bernstein and Ebbesen (1978) had individual human subjects live for 3 to 6 weeks in a self-contained laboratory apartment. Subjects distributed their time among ordinary activities such as reading, art work, and sewing without following any fixed sequence determined by the experimental procedures. The unstructured research setting was modeled after continuous envirnoment research with animals by Kavanau (1969) and by Collier, Hirsch, and Hamlin (1972) in an effort to examine the effects of reinforcement operations on responses other than those directly involved in the contingency.

Reinforcement and Substitution.   Bernstein and Ebbesen (1978) extended Premack's (1965) formulation of reinforcement value to human behavior in a naturalistic setting. Based on the baseline percentages of time devoted to activities such as reading, exercise, and learning Russian, contingencies were established in which time devoted to one activity was required for access to another activity. Consistent with the findings of previous work with humans and animals, there were large increases in the time devoted to a designated low-probability activity. By conducting the experiment in a naturalistic multiple-response environment, Bernstein and Ebbesen (1978) observed changes in the time devoted to all activities, not just those involved in the contingency.

Following the contingency, a response independent restriction on the contingent response reduced the amount of time available for that activity to the level produced by instrumental performance during the contingency period. If response substitution contributed to the reinforcement effect, the former instrumental response should increase during the restriction even without a contingency between the two responses. In general, there was selective redistribution of the time formerly devoted to the restricted activity, but the increase due to the full contingency was substantially larger than the increases due to substitution alone. Bernstein and Ebbesen concluded that the substitution structure of a repertoire should be considered in evaluating the effects of contingency procedures and in creating category boundaries within the stream of behavior.

Momentary Probability as a Measure of Value.   The human reinforcement work initially used fixed-ratio schedules identical to those used with animal subjects. Once the procedure demonstrated successful control of human instrumental performance, a new schedule was instituted that was more equivalent to human behavior in natural conditions. Subjects could obtain any amount of access to the restricted activity, and credit could be accumulated across bouts of instrumental performance. The schedule was called "proportional" because the access produced was not fixed but an amount proportional to the time devoted to the work activity. The proportional schedule was different from the reciprocal fixed ratio schedules typically used with animal subjects (cf. Timberlake & Allison, 1974) in that it included no constraints on when the instrumental responding occurred or on the duration of work periods. Bernstein and Dearborn (1980) used proportional contingencies to reinforce low-probability responses with high-probability responses, and they also used low-probability responses as reinforcers for high-probability instrumental responses, as predicted by Timberlake and Allison's (1974) response deprivation formulation. The results supported the response deprivation contention that deviation from baseline level is the fundamental determinant of reinforcement value, not rank order as suggested by Premack (1965).

Premack (1971) responded to response deprivation accounts of reinforcement by asserting that the procedures used to restrict and deliver a consequence may alter its true probability, rendering the original baseline an inappropriate estimate of the reinforcement value of a response during the time it is actually used in a contingency. The combined facts of restriction and limited periodic access could increase the momentary value of the restricted activity to a level higher than the baseline value of the instrumental response, thus preserving Premack's original rank order formulation.

The proportional schedule has neither a limited hold procedure nor a reciprocal contingency that would require the prompt use of access to the contingent response, so the momentary probability could be assessed during the contingency periods. Despite clear increases in instrumental performance when low-probability contingent responses were used, the overall conditional probability never exceeded the baseline level of the instrumental response. The results supported Timberlake and Allison's (1974) response deprivation formulation rather than Premack's (1965) probability differential rule. The major implication of this finding is that virutally any activity can be an effective reinforcer, regardless of its relative standing in the current hierarchy of activities. If the interaction of baseline level and the exact schedule values results in a net deprivation of the contingent response, there will be an increase in instrumental performance, regardless of the relative rank order of the two activities.

Verbal Measures of Value.   The necessity of an extended free-access baseline for prediction seriously limits this approach to an employment setting, for most managers do not have the time needed for behavioral assessment. Self-report assessment of the hierarchy would be an attractive alternative to an observed baseline, but there are limited conditions that produce correspondence between verbal and observed estimates of response probability (reinforcement value). Bernstein (1983, in press) included both verbal and observed measures in a programmed environment study to estimate the utility of verbal measures for prediction of the effect of reinforcement contingencies. Guided by previous judgment research, Bernstein developed a psychophysical technique for estimating the distribution of time to all responses in a hierarchy, and subjects in the live-in laboratory periodically estimated how their time was distributed across the activities available.

There were very high overall correlations between verbal estimates and the observed distributions of time, so predictive utility was generally very good.

There were a few discrepancies between verbal estimates and the observations of time actually devoted to an activity, and the two estimates were compared by constructing contingency values so that one ratio predicted an instrumental increase and the ratio derived from the other assessment method did not. In seven of eight cases, the ratio based on observation made a better prediction than the ratio based on self-reported value. Bernstein (in press) concluded that verbal reports of the time devoted to individual activities in combination with Premack's response probability approach can be a very useful tool in the analysis of reinforcement value in human behavior. Given the amount of effort needed to make long-term observations of baseline values, use of verbal measures as a first attempt at prediction seems worthwhile.

Patterns and Constraints.   Initially the programmed environment was used to study a model of reinforcement based on the time devoted to a set of activities as a measure of their value. Dunham (1977) proposed that the pattern of behavior was a component of performance that subjects would also work to preserve or restore. Dunham suggested that subjects would generate instrumental output to maintain typical bout lengths and interresponse times (IRTs). Bernstein (1982) used the programmed environment to study the effects of constraints on patterns. Complete ethological records were obtained from the ordinary behavior of human subjects, and several potential measures of pattern were derived from the raw data. In addition to percentage time, the daily record during free-access baseline provided the number of bouts for each activity (rate), a distribution of bout lengths for each activity, and a separate percentage of time for each of the 15 hr per day of observation (daily pattern).

Based on those baseline patterns, constraints forced individual activities out of their typical patterns. For example, the length of any individual occurrence of reading might be limited to the median length of the baseline distribution, with a pause required before starting the next bout. That constraint would mean that half of the occurrences of reading would be terminated by the experimenter before their natural conclusion. Alternatively, if baseline reading occurred mostly in the evening and rarely during the day, a constraint procedure would restrict reading completely in the evening and leave it available during day hours. After the effect of the constraint by itself was assessed, contingencies were implemented in which increased time on a designated instrumental activity produced time without the constraint on pattern. The results indicated that contingent removal of constraints on pattern can produce an instrumental increase, but the effect was neither as strong nor as consistent as the effects of reduction in the total amount of time available for an activity. Bernstein concluded that reinforcement value is inherent in the pattern or structure of a repertoire of responses. If a contingency procedure includes a disruption of the pattern of the restricted response, constraint per se will contribute to the total reinforcement value of the contingency.

Methodological Summary.   The research in a programmed environment done by Bernstein developed from the joint goals of adding human ethological richness to theoretical questions about reinforcement value and of bringing maximum precision to research on human behavior. The primary characteristics of those studies were the use of ordinary human behavior observed during continuous residence, the use of free-access baseline for assessment of value, and the use of a set point or homeostatic model of reinforcement value. Use of a programmed environment for this research provided isolation from the influence of extraneous events, leaving the experimental variables as the main source of variance. The facility allowed for continuous measurement of many observable features of behavior and control over subjects' access to all activities, and everything the subject did was part of the experiment. The main independent variable was a program (in the form of contingencies) through which subjects worked to obtain control over how they spent their time.

RESEARCH ON GENDER MIX, MEANINGFUL WORK, AND CREW PERFORMANCE

During the same period that the first two laboratories were developing lines of basic research, other researchers were working closely with the National Aeronautics and Space Administration on questions immediately relevant to the space program. Jon Rogers and Walter Sullins at the University of Alabama in Huntsville operated a programmed environment in which people lived alone and in groups for up to 10 days. Because the space program necessarily includes confinement, limited availability of activities, continuous measurement of activity, and control over access to activities, a programmed environment is ideal for simulation of the working and living conditions of space crews.

Gender Mix in Crews.   With the addition of women to the astronaut corps, concern arose about the nature of interactions among the crew in the confined conditions of spacecraft. Sullins and Rogers' (1977) earliest research on mixed crews was conducted in a 40 square meter living area divided into four rooms and a bathroom. Crew size varied from three to six people and the gender mix varied from three females and one male to two females and four males. There were many convenient leisure activities along with a core of meaningful work to be done for 7 to 10 hr each day. After 279 person-days of mixed-crew observation, there were no dramatic differences between mixed- and single-gender crews in either the quality of social interaction or work performance.

In a second study of mixed crews, Rogers and Sullins (1978) examined the effect of having meaningful work on crew performance. The laboratory was programmed so that most choices of activity or materials were bought with laboratory economic credit. For example, subjects used lab credit to control the temperature, to rent extra space or a bed for sleeping, and to buy privacy, food, or access to TV. Some groups earned credit by working on a college course, whereas other crews had no work available and were given yoked amounts of credit. The earning and use of economic credit were recorded as measures of performance. Both types of crews performed equally well on all parts of the exerpimental routine. The mixed crews purchased less privacy than all-male crews, but crews without meaningful work (mixed and all-male) purchased more material for decorating the laboratory, more extra space, more furniture, and more carpet than the working groups. Differences due to lack of work were much larger than the differences between all-male and mixed crews, and Rogers and Sullins concluded that gender mix should not be a major consideration in environmental or program design.

Stability of Reinforcement Hierarchy.   Rogers and Sullins (1979) also used a programmed environment to see if the use of economic credit was sensitive to variables of ecological richness, personal characteristics, and work conditions. When the environment was bare of furnishings for the first several days of the experiment, subjects did not use credit to purchase decorations when they later became available. When the environment was well decorated for the first several days, however, subjects used their economic credit to keep the furnishings when a rental charge was instituted later. This experiment also included two mixed-gender crews (out of six group studies), and those groups used more credit for decoration than the all-male crews. The presence or absence of meaningful work also influenced the use of credit, with those groups without work spending more credit on extra space, decorations, and access to entertainment. Use of credit for the remaining items such as temperature and light control, hygiene, and meals did not vary systematically with regard to the variables studied.

Methodological Summary.   The Rogers and Sullins research program was developed to simulate conditions of confinement and automation expected to be part of space missions. Because space missions run according to fixed schedules and preplanned sequences of activities, the laboratory simulation appropriately included some programmed patterning of the time crews spent on various activities. The lab program also included some contingencies to assess the relative value of the consequences delivered by those contingencies, and access to every feature of the laboratory was available only through participation in the economic credit system. In this research, the programming of the subjects' activities was derived partially from the external situation to which the results are to be generalized and partially from methodological interest in assessing the value and use of various features of the environment.

CONCEPTUAL ANALYSIS OF CURRENT
PROGRAMMED ENVIRONMENTS

There are several features of the current programmed human environments that demonstrate their common origin and focus. All laboratories have human subjects living continuously in the experimental space for extended periods. Because the experimenters control access to all materials and activities, it is possible to construct very precise independent variables. Measurement of subjects' performance is also very precise because the experimenter can define the range of responses to fit either automatic recording or highly reliable observational categories. Because there are usually many different dependent variables being simultaneously recorded, these procedures produce a wide range of results that can potentially show the effects of the manipulated variables.

Having subjects participate in the experiment 24 hr each day also means that the experimental designs are very sensitive to the effects being studied. The independent variables are strong, and extraneous influences are kept to a minimum by continuous maintenance of the experimental setting, so programmed environment experiments are very well suited to the within-subject replication designs suggested by Sidman (1960). The amount of time in the experiment is also unusually long for human research, so steady-state performance can be systematically studied. As a result, it is less likely that a transitional phenomenon will be mistakenly identified as an important effect of the variables under study.

There are also ways in which current human programmed environments differ from each other in both methodology and substance. An environment cannot be simply characterized as programmed or not programmed; there is a continuum of structure, and some laboratories will include more of the subjects' activities and choices in the program. In addition, the programming or structure on a macrobehavioral level can be independent of the amount of structure at a microbehavioral level. The exact sequences of subjects' activities could be tightly controlled whereas the total amount of time devoted to each activity could be left to vary. Alternatively, there could be strict programming of the amount of overall access to each response category without any control over the exact time, duration, or pattern of each occurrence. The behavioral repertoire provided for the subjects can also vary from ordinary activities that subjects frequently engage in outside the laboratory to sequences of responses on laboratory manipulanda borrowed from animal research. Often the laboratory includes activities that are human in character but not necessarily typical of the subjects' natural response repertoire.

The research currently being done covers a wide range of substantive questions. There are problem-oriented studies that simulate specific human interaction settings and explore various strategies for change or maintenance of performance. There are programs that study group processes in a more abstract vein with the goal of providing general strategies for human engineering in a variety of specific contexts. There are also programs that pursue theory-driven basic research questions that are not specific to human behavior. A programmed environment is sometimes used as a simulation of a specific situation and sometimes only as a standard experimental space for maximizing the systematic variance due to a particular variable.

One application of the experimental analysis of behavior closely approximates programmed environment technology. Token economies have been employed in full institutional settings such as psychiatric hospitals (e.g., Ayllon & Azrin, 1968; Winkler, 1980) and prisons (e.g., Cohen & Filipczak, 1971). In general, these programs have demonstrated the therapeutic relevance of institutional contingencies, but there has been little systematic exploration of broader principles of behavior in those settings. One exception is Winkler's (1980) work on economic models of choice that was done as part of a therapeutic program. There are close parallels between Winkler's procedures and analysis and those used by Rogers and Sullins.

Another operant research area that is closely related to the programmed environment research described here is the work on open and closed economies. The procedures used by Collier (e.g., Collier et al., 1972) and Hursh (1978) closely resemble those typical of a programmed environment. The major difference is that those researchers have used animal subjects and studied the kind of schedule and feeding questions typical of animal behavior analysis. Comparison of this research with human programmed environments reveals greater similarity of methodology than of substantive interest.

FUTURE RESEARCH DIRECTIONS

There is great potential for further research using human subjects in a programmed environment. In the area of human operant behavior, there is a need for extension of basic phenomena from short-term laboratory experiments to long-term maintenance of performance. It is very rare to find an experimental analysis of human behavior that even approximates the extended stability and replicability of the data routinely provided by researchers using animal subjects. It would also be important to use more naturalistic response classes to replicate results found with laboratory operant responses. A programmed environment that provides an ethologically relevant response repertoire has the potential to produce results that can be more readily generalized. Research under way in programmed environments continues to elaborate the necessary conditions for reinforcement in human behavior, including analysis of the role of constraint and the limits of the response deprivation formulation in handling low-valued activities.

There are also many areas of application of experimental analysis that would benefit greatly from research in a programmed environment. The simulation of working conditions under extended confinement and isolation has been of great interest to NASA, and that agency has supported programmed environment research. More generally, the conditions of any employment situation can be readily simulated in a programmed environment, and there exists an ideal opportunity for research on management and performance maintenance. The systematic scheduling of consequences for varying kinds of work is the heart of effective management, and this kind of laboratory provides a very close approximation of the workplace.

Recently, work has begun to assess the effects of drug self-administration by looking at changes in performance over extended periods in a programmed environment. Because some chemicals have accumulating effects, the extended duration of the research is essential to studying the results of continued drug use. It is also convenient to have continuous supervision of the subject population so that accurate control of drug dose can be maintained and drug contamination can be avoided. There is also some work on feeding being done in a programmed environment, providing a unique opportunity to monitor and influence all food intake as an integral part of the subject's behavioral repertoire. The programmed environment combines the extended, continuous sample and behavioral richness typical of field research with the sensitivity and control associated with laboratory research. As such it can provide an ideal research preparation for studying a wide range of questions concerning human behavior.

SUMMARY

Findley (1962, 1966) developed a rationale for the experimental analysis of the behavior of subjects living in a multiple-response laboratory, and he demonstrated that the procedure was both feasible and useful with animal and human subjects. Following his lead, several research groups have undertaken extensive experimental analysis of human behavior in continuous residential laboratories. These programmed environments have studied a wide range of questions, taking advantage of the increased power and precision of both measurement and experimental intervention. The procedures allow for tight control of extraneous influences, so experiments are very sensitive in identifying the effects of research variables. Although these laboratories share some properties with other approaches to the experimental analysis of human behavior, the opportunity for long-term, continuous application of contingencies of reinforcement provides a unique contribution to the analysis of basic processes that affect human behavior. The potential general utility of programmed environments is now being addressed with problem-oriented research that uses research environments to study many of the controlling conditions of ordinary human life.

ACKNOWLEDGMENTS

The authors are grateful to Dan Leger and Julie Horney for comments on an earlier draft. Preparation of this chapter was supported by National Aeronautics and Space Administration grant NAG2-139 and by National Institute of Drug Abuse grant DA03476.

REFERENCES

Ayllon, T., & Azrin, N. H. (1968). *The token-economy: A motivational system for therapy and rehabilitation.* New York: Appleton-Century-Crofts.

Bernstein, D. (1982, May). *Freedom from constraint as a determinant of reinforcement value in human behavior.* Paper presented at the meeting of the Association for Behavioral Analysis, Milwaukee.

Bernstein, D. (1983). *A comparison of cognitive and behavioral assessments of value in human behavior.* Unpublished manuscript.

Bernstein, D. (in press). Correspondence between verbal and observed estimates of reinforcement value. In L. J. Parrott & P. N. Chase (Eds.), *Psychological aspects of language: The West Virginia lectures.* New York: Charles C. Thomas.

Bernstein, D. & Dearborn, M. (1980). *The utility of time-based theories of reinforcement.* Unpublished manuscript.

Bernstein, D. & Ebbesen, E. (1978). Reinforcement and substitution in humans: A multiple-response analysis. *Journal of the Experimental Analysis of Behavior. 30,* 243–253.

Brady, J. V., Bigelow, G. E., Emurian, H. H., & Williams, D. M. (1975). Design of a programmed environment for the experimental analysis of social behavior. In D. H. Carson (Ed.), *Man-environment interactions: Evaluations and applications. 7: Social Ecology* (pp. 187–208). Milwaukee: Environmental Design Research Association.

Brady, J. V., & Emurian, H. H. (1979). Behavior analysis of motivational and emotional interactions in a programmed environment. In R. Dienstbier & H. E. Howe (Eds.), *Nebraska Symposium on Motivation* (Vol. 26, pp. 81–122). Lincoln: University of Nebraska.

Cohen, H. L., & Filipczak, J. (1971). *A new learning environment.* San Francisco: Jossey-Bass.

Collier, G. H., Hirsch, E., & Hamlin, P. H. (1972). The ecological determinants of reinforcement in the rat. *Physiology and Behavior, 9,* 705–716.

Dunham, P. (1977). The nature of reinforcing stimuli. In W. Honig & J. E. R. Staddon (Eds.), *Handbook of operant behavior* (pp. 98–124). New York: Prentice-Hall.

Emurian, H. H., Brady, J. V., Meyerhoff, J. L., & Mougey, E. H. (1981). Behavioral and biological interactions with confined microsocieties in a programmed environment. In J. Grey & L. Hamden (Eds.), *Space Manufacturing 4* (pp. 407–421). New York: American Institute of Aeronautics and Astronautics.

Emurian, H. H., Brady, J. V., Meyerhoff, J. L., & Mougey, E. H. (1983). Small groups in programmed environments: Behavioral and biological interactions. *Pavlovian Journal of Biological Science, 18,* 199–210.

Emurian, H. H., Emurian, C. S., Bigelow, G. E., & Brady, J. V. (1976). The effects of a cooperation contingency on behavior in a continuous three-person environment. *Journal of the Experimental Analysis of Behavior, 25,* 293–302.

Emurian, H. H., Emurian, C. S., & Brady, J. V. (1978). Effects of a pairing contingency on behavior in a three-person programmed environment. *Journal of the Experimental Analysis of Behavior, 29,* 319–329.

Emurian, H. H., Emurian, C. S., & Brady, J. V. (1982). Appetitive and aversive reinforcement schedule effects on behavior: A systematic replication. *Basic and Applied Social Psychology, 3,* 39–52.

Findley, J. D. (1962). An experimental outline for building and exploring multi-operant behavior repertoires. *Journal of the Experimental Analysis of Behavior, 5,* 113–166.

Findley, J. D. (1966). Programmed environments for the experimental analysis of human behavior. In W. Honig (Ed.), *Operant behavior: Areas of research and application* (pp. 827–848). New York: Appleton-Century-Crofts.

Findley, J. D., Migler, B. M., & Brady, J. V. (1963). *A long-term study of human performance in a continuously programmed experimental environnment.* Technical Report to the National Aeronautics and Space Administration, University of Maryland, College Park.

Hursh, S. R. (1978). The economics of daily consumption controlling food- and water-reinforced responding. *Journal of the Experimental Analysis of Behavior, 29,* 475–491.

Kavanau, J. (1969). The behavior of captive white-footed mice. In E. Willems & H. Rausch (Eds.), *Naturalistic viewpoints in psychological research* (pp. 221–270). New York: Wiley.

Lowe, C. F. (1979). Determinants of human operant behaviour. In M. D. Zeiler & P. Harzem (Eds.), *Advances in analysis of behavior: Reinforcement and the organization of behavior* (pp. 159–192). Chichester: Wiley.

Lowe, C. F. (1983). Radical behaviourism and human psychology. In G. C. L. Davey (Ed.), *Animal models of human behaviour* (pp. 71–93). Chichester: Wiley.

Premack, D. (1965). Reinforcement theory. In D. Levine (Ed.), *Nebraska Symposium on Motivation* (Vol. 13, pp. 123–180). Lincoln: University of Nebraska.

Premack, D. (1971). Catching up with common sense or two sides of a generalization: Reinforcement and punishment. In R. Glaser (Ed.), *The nature of reinforcement* (pp. 121–150). New York: Academic Press.

Rogers, J. G., & Sullins, W. R. (1978). *Environmental preference of mixed gender crews in isolation.* Paper presented at the meeting of the American Psychological Association, Toronto.

Rogers, J. G., & Sullins, W. R. (1979). *Stability of reinforcers in a contingent economic system.* Paper presented at the meeting of the American Psychological Association, New York.

Sidman, M. (1960). *Tactics of scientific research.* New York: Basic Books.

Sullins, W. R., & Rogers, J. G. (1977). *Crewmembers vs. crewmen in isolated duty station simulations.* Paper presented at the meeting of the Human Factors Society, San Francisco.

Timberlake, W., & Allison, J. (1974). Response deprivation: An empirical approach to instrumental performance. *Psychological Review, 81,* 146–164.

Winkler, R. C. (1980). Behavioral economics, token economies, and applied behavior analysis. In J. E. R. Staddon (Ed.), *Limits to action: The allocation of individual behavior* (pp. 269–297). New York: Academic Press.

Author Index

Subject Index